International Regulation of Multinational Corporations

Don Wallace, Jr.

The Praeger Special Studies program—utilizing the most modern and efficient book production techniques and a selective worldwide distribution network—makes available to the academic, government, and business communities significant, timely research in U.S. and international economic, social, and political development.

International Regulation of Multinational Corporations

PRAEGER SPECIAL STUDIES IN INTERNATIONAL BUSINESS, FINANCE, AND TRADE

Praeger Publishers New York Washington London

Library of Congress Cataloging in Publication Data

Wallace, Don, 1932-

International regulation of multinational corporations.

(Praeger special studies in international business, finance, and trade)

Includes bibliographical references.

1. International business enterprises. 2. Industry and state. 3. Financial institutions, International. 4. International economic relations. I. Title.

HD2755.5.W34 338.8'8 75-8411

ISBN 0-275-05880-8

PRAEGER PUBLISHERS
111 Fourth Avenue, New York, N.Y. 10003, U.S.A.

Published in the United States of America in 1976
by Praeger Publishers, Inc.

Printed in the United States of America

PREFACE

International investment, and more specifically foreign direct investment in productive enterprises and services, has flourished since the end of World War II. Large corporations, many of them American, that engage in international activity, which are often called multinational corporations, have risen to prominence. In many countries, economic and other problems have been attributed to these corporations, and national legislation and other responses have been suggested.

This book is not concerned mainly with the rise or the phenomenon of the multinational corporation; nor is it, generally, concerned with what U.S. policies should be toward inward or outward foreign direct investment or multinational corporations, whether or not they are based in the United States. It is concerned with a specific set of proposals for dealing with multinational corporations; this set of proposals calls for the creation of an international organization that would regulate multinational corporations and foreign direct investment. I take up the question of whether it is realistic to propose an international investment organization and what in fact the prospects for such an organization are.

Although the crisis brought about by the large increase in the price of oil may have diverted attention from multinational corporations other than oil companies, they again seem to have become controversial. There has been a flurry in the United States about bribes paid to foreign officials. There have been discussions about the propriety of selling various drugs and baby foods in developing countries. Congress continues to threaten a stiffer tax treatment for the foreign operations of U.S. companies. Many labor unions remain hostile to the multinationals.

At the same time there seems to be no enthusiasm for international organizations, although they seem necessary in light of various problems of resources, of food, and of the sea. The division between developed and developing countries in the United Nations, a division that is extremely relevant to the possible regulation of multinational corporations, may explain this current mood.

The Group of Eminent Persons has reported to the United Nations, and the United Nations Commission on Transnational Corporations has been established; nonetheless, national controls, whether in host or home country, seem to be more in fashion. Weak international guidelines, either for the behavior of multinational corporations or as a restraint on national controls, seem to be all that is in the offing at present.

There have been enough proposals for the regulation of multinational corporations at the international level to suggest that the subject is worth exploring, if only in a tentative and modest manner. The subject of the prospective regulation of multinational corporations is still undefined, but the pressures for scrutiny, regulation, and taxation within countries, even home countries such as the United States, and the inevitable pressures from outside and from host countries, suggest that the option of an international organization should at least be kept in view. However, I believe it is now too early to seriously contemplate an effective international investment organization, which may indeed be impossible under the present nation-state system. The oil crisis and the associated petrodollar recycling problem have, if anything, made free investment flows of many kinds, if not foreign direct investment from the oil-producing countries, so desirable that any suggestion to regulate international investment is not likely to be encouraged.

I first became interested in the subject of this book at a conference at the U.S. Department of State in 1969 on the subject of investment in developing countries. As I recall, almost all of the participants were interested in exploring the ways in which such investment might be promoted, but one participant, Charles Kindleberger, a professor at the Massachusetts Institute of Technology, raised the question of whether such investment should not be regulated. Later Kindleberger wrote an article entitled "A GATT for Investment" in <u>Law and Policy in International Business</u>, a journal I had helped to establish at the Georgetown University law school; this article was followed by one or two other articles in the journal on the same subject. In 1973 the Institute for International and Foreign Trade Law at Georgetown, which I direct, and its sister institute of the same name in Frankfurt, Germany, held a conference in Dusseldorf on the prospects for an international investment organization. The results of this conference were published by Praeger Publishers in February 1974 as <u>International Control of Investment: The Dusseldorf Conference on Multinational Corporations</u>.

I began work on this book during the 1973-74 academic year when I was a visiting fellow at St. Antony's College, Oxford, while on sabbatical leave from Georgetown. The substance of the final draft was prepared during the winter, spring, and summer of 1975. The book does not deal with developments occurring after September 30, 1975, such as the various U.S. investigations into overseas bribery, the adoption by the OECD of a Declaration on Guidelines for Multinational Enterprises, and various legislative proposals in the United States and elsewhere.

CONTENTS

Chapter Page

Chapter | Page

LIST OF TABLES

LIST OF ACRONYMS

ANCOM	Andean Common Market
COMSAT	Communications Satellite Corporation
ECOSOC	Economic and Social Council, of UN
EEC	European Economic Community
GATT	General Agreement on Tariffs and Trade
IBRD	International Bank of Reconstruction and Development (also known as the World Bank)
ICSID	International Center for the Settlement of Investment Disputes
IMF	International Monetary Fund
OAS	Organization of American States
OECD	Organization for Economic Cooperation and Development
OPIC	Overseas Private Investment Corporation
UNCTAD	United Nations Conference on Trade and Development

PART I

PROPOSALS FOR THE INTERNATIONAL REGULATION OF MULTINATIONAL CORPORATIONS AND FOREIGN DIRECT INVESTMENT

CHAPTER 1

INTERNATIONAL ECONOMIC DEVELOPMENTS SINCE WORLD WAR II AND THE RISE OF THE MULTINATIONAL CORPORATION

There has been considerable worry about the impact of the increase in oil prices since 1973, and there has also been some fear about the problem of recycling petrodollars, although concern about the latter appears to be receding, whether rightly or wrongly. Some see the oil crisis as the beginning of chaos; a few see symptoms of the new international economic order that some developing countries seek. In the early 1970s more attention was paid to the emergence of "multipolarity" in the international economy: not only the United States, but also Europe and Japan and to a lesser and different degree the Soviet Union and the People's Republic of China were then seen as important components of the international economy, whereas previously the United States had been seen as uniquely dominant. The poorer and developing countries were, and still are, seen as less central to the fate of the international economy.

In the 1970s at least, the multinational corporation, its significance to particular countries and to the international economy in general, have been one of the strands in the consciousness of international economic matters. Associated with this have been questions about the magnitude of these corporations and about the investment activities with which they are often connected, questions about the benefits and disadvantages of such corporations and investments, and even questions about the proper theoretical framework for the consideration of all these other questions. Countries have developed policies and enacted laws, regulations, and rules to control and/or to attract these companies and this investment. There has been much debate about such national policies and about similar regional policies. Official and unofficial proposals have been made for controlling the companies and their investment or for providing guidance to the governments seeking this control, but the exact purpose of international regulation and organization has not always been made clear.

Against this background it would be possible to sketch out a rough scenario of the way an international investment organization with given purposes and powers might come into existence in the foreseeable future, although no such organization of any real strength seems likely in the next few years. Nonetheless, the following scenario is at least possible:

1. a continued increase in restrictions and burdens of various kinds on foreign direct investment by multinational companies in the major foreign markets, whether in developed or developing countries, with the feeling that these would continue to increase;

2. a rise in pressures in the United States, both on U.S. multinational companies and also on direct investment by foreign multinational companies in the United States, and similar pressures in other countries;

3. a fear that in some cases the restrictions in the United States might lead to retaliation against U.S. investment in the home countries of the foreign multinational companies. This mixture might conceivably lead U.S. corporate executives and sympathetic policy makers in the U.S. government to believe that an international investment organization with power over national governments, including our own, might be the lesser risk.

We have not come anywhere near this point. For one thing, risks rise and fall and there is no continuous progression; for another, the oil and petrodollar problems and similar problems affecting other commodities continue to distract attention from the problem of multinational companies.

THE RISE (AND FALL?) OF PAX AMERICANA ECONOMICA

It is quite possible to maintain that the international economic policy of the United States since World War II has been an even more resounding success than its political policy of containment of the Soviet Union. Of course the two are not unrelated, and both are subject at the present time to a certain fluidity. It may not be an exaggeration to say that after the war a pax Americana economica reigned and to a large extent still continues to do so.

The policy of the United States and its allies that created this condition is probably most formally called the Bretton Woods system, after the 1944 discussions at Bretton Woods, New Hampshire, that led to the creation of the International Monetary Fund and the World Bank. Because some of the formal rules of the International Monetary

Fund have been suspended over the past few years--especially par values for foreign exchange rates--it is sometimes said that the Bretton Woods system has ended; but in fact these obituaries are premature.

The growth in exchange of money and capital, trade and investment that was stimulated by the Bretton Woods system, a growth that took place largely among the more developed or industrial countries, but also among the developing countries, has been enormous, and so has the growth of gross national product in the developed countries. The stimulus to development in the poorer countries has also been large.[1]

Although the exact relationship between the growth and development of domestic economies and the degree of international economic exchange is of course debatable, it seems reasonably clear that the amount of international economic exchange, or economic interdependence, among most countries has grown substantially in the period since World War II. To a large degree this has been made possible and indeed dictated by the Bretton Woods system, that is, by the operation of the International Monetary Fund (IMF), of the General Agreement on Tariffs and Trade, and of other related institutions and by enormous technological progress in such fields as communications, transportation, and computers.* This growth is shown by the great amount of trade; the frequency of international payments and indeed of capital movements; and the growth in telephone calls, telex messages, satellites, and travel. One need only add the Eurocurrency markets and the near universality of the impact of the increased oil prices to suggest that the proposition of interdependence is fairly self-evident.[2]

Some writers have suggested that these economic changes have been so substantial as to, in effect, transform the international political system from one dominated by nation-states, to one in which power is shared by independent economic actors such as the multinational corporations,[3] although I do not myself share this "transnational" view.

Although the extent of economic interdependence is debated, people in many countries seem to be unhappy with at least some of its manifestations. The transmission of inflation or recession from abroad is disliked. Domestic pressures are generated, for example wage demands by workers, which in turn can create other international consequences. These external and domestic pressures have created problems for the nation-states. These are examined in Chapter 6.

---

*Although GATT was not actually created at Bretton Woods, it certainly has been a strong part of the system that was created there.

Even as nation-states adjust to current international economic conditions, suggestions are made for further reform of international organizations, including the International Monetary Fund and the General Agreement on Tariffs and Trade (GATT). The reform of the GATT would deal with the right of access to raw materials. There are suggestions for an international organization to assure access to food, and an international authority to regulate the economic exploitation of the sea bed.

THE RISE OF THE MULTINATIONAL CORPORATION

Interestingly, the Bretton Woods system, or at least its formal institutions as they have evolved, has not concerned itself to any great degree with international investment or capital movements. The IMF has been exclusively concerned with the promotion of free payments for trade on current account, and the articles of agreement of the IMF provide that its resources shall not be used to stimulate capital payments and, contrariwise, governments are explicitly stated to be free to impose capital controls.[4]

The GATT deals with trade, that is, the export and import of goods, and not capital movements. The World Bank, although initially conceived to facilitate private capital movements, has in fact developed principally into an agency to finance social infrastructure in the developing countries. The World Bank's affiliate, the International Finance Corporation, seeks to promote private investment in developing countries; it is not a regulatory body.[5] The Organization for Economic Cooperation and Development (OECD), as we shall see, has sought to deal with capital movements, but it is not a universal body.

Although the Bretton Woods institutions, principally the IMF and the GATT, were concerned with current trade transactions, and although the IMF articles did not bar national capital controls, the generally open economy that was promoted by the Bretton Woods system, by changes in technology, and by the political influence of the United States and its allies resulted in an enormous growth in capital movements after World War II. This increased volume included short- and long-term movements and increased portfolio and direct investment. Thus the percentage increase in the outstanding stock of U.S. foreign direct investment between 1950 and 1970 exceeded the increase between the same years of the total gross national product of industrialized countries outside the Communist bloc and of the annual trade flows among these countries, as is shown in Table 1.1.

TABLE 1.1

Growth in Trade, Gross National Product, and Foreign Investment of Industrial Countries, 1950-70
(in billions of dollars)

Economic Indicator	1950	1960	1970[a]	Average Annual Growth (in percentage)	
				1950-60	1960-70
World exports	60	128	310	7.8	9.3
U.S. exports (f.o.b., merchandise)	10.3	20.6	43.2	7.2	7.6
U.S. imports (c.i.f., merchandise)[b]	9.6	16.4	42.5	5.5	10.0
Exports of other industrial countries[c]	26.5	54.4	156.2	7.7	11.1
Imports of other industrial countries[c]	29.9	58.1	157.2	6.8	10.5
U.S. foreign direct investment (book value)	11.8	32.0	78.1	10.5	9.4
U.S. direct investment in industrial countries[c]	5.2	17.7	46.4	13.2	10.2
Foreign direct investment in the United States (book value)	3.4	6.9	13.2	7.4	6.8
GNP of industrial countries[b] (including the United States	449	873	1,923	6.8	8.2

[a]Preliminary.

[b]U.S. imports are reported c.i.f. to facilitate comparison with foreign import figures. The difference between f.o.b. and c.i.f. valuation is roughly 9 or 10 percent of f.o.b. values.

[c]The United Kingdom, Canada, Japan, France, Germany, Belgium, the Netherlands, Italy, Sweden, and Switzerland.

Source: Staff of the Senate Comm. on Finance, Implications of Multinational Firms for World Labor and Investment and for U.S. Trade and Labor: Report to the Committee on Finance of the United States Senate and Its Subcommittee on International Trade on Investigation No. 332-69, under Section 332 of the Tariff Act of 1930, 93rd Cong., 1st Sess. (Comm. Print 1973).

This increase has been accompanied by the development of the Euro-capital markets, the growth of the U.S. capital market, and the increased linkage of the several capital markets. At different times many countries have seen inward foreign direct investment as important to their domestic economic plans, and incentives to such investment have been given by many developing and developed countries.[6]

The consequence of these developments has been the rise of the multinational corporation. As business, trade, and exchange have assumed an increasingly international scope, large corporations have increasingly conducted their productive and service activities on an international scale. Investment in productive enterprise, whether foreign or domestic, private or public, is of central importance to the development of each national economy. When investments in different countries are linked through a common investor, this development achieves an international dimension; it may be this fact that gives the multinational corporations their greatest global significance.

A word or two is in order about the relationship of foreign direct investment to multinational corporations as such.

Direct investment refers to investment accompanied by significant ownership or management control. This has been defined as 10 percent ownership, or 25 percent ownership or significant management control. Direct investment is to be distinguished from portfolio investment, as in securities traded on the market and purchased for their yield, and from investment in bank instruments such as certificates of deposit, or government notes.

To a degree the relationship is circular. As companies invest in many countries, the consequence of their investment in local productive facilities is to make them increasingly multinational in their operations. Contractual arrangements, short of formal equity investment, can also provide this multinational dimension, as in certain arrangements in Eastern Europe or in the increasing use of work contracts in the petroleum industry. Herbert Gray, former Canadian Minister of National Revenue, has in fact referred to the multinational corporation as the "institutionalization" of foreign direct investment.[7]

The circle is completed by the fact that the multinational companies are now the principal foreign direct investors in many developed and developing countries, and it is with them that investment arrangements must increasingly be negotiated. Some idea of the scope of multinational corporate activity is suggested by the estimate that 15 percent of the 1975 gross world product of about $3 trillion will be produced by multinationals.[8]

I will not attempt a precise, quantitative definition of the multinational corporation or a sophisticated economic explanation of the form these corporations have taken or the timing of their rise. Although any political, economic, or legal definition of the multinational corporation would generate a good deal of debate, what most people have in mind is a large business enterprise, usually but not inevitably in corporate form, that conducts business in a fair number of countries on a reasonably large scale, generally with some coordinated business strategies and policies.

The enterprise may be engaged in manufacture or assembly, whether of automobiles, of electronics, or of chemicals or petrochemicals; or in the extraction of oil or minerals or their processing or downstream fabrication; or to a lesser extent in such service sectors as banking, tourism, or retail trade. The multinational corporation is often associated with high technology, but this is certainly not an essential element of its definition.

Multinational companies are often very large in terms of assets or sales, especially in relation to most local industrial concerns; again, however, this is not an inevitable element of the definition. R. Vernon defines the multinational corporation in terms of size, activities, and "geographical spread." Most of the companies so considered are very large in terms of the Fortune 500 group.[9] M. Watkins, on the other hand, considers any company with operations in more than one country as a multinational corporation.[10] In effect this would mean that U.S. companies with operations in Canada are multinational corporations. There are many other definitions that distinguish international companies from multinational companies, from multimarket companies, from transnational companies, and so on. A distinction is made between enterprises and corporations, but possibly a more useful distinction might be between the activity in different sectors of the economy, whether manufacturing, raw materials, banking, hotels, or agri-business. These sectors are often subject to different regulations and legislation in individual host countries, although of course some companies straddle several sectors. For the purposes of this book, these several distinctions will not be emphasized.

Detailed theories abound that attempt to explain why multinational companies have emerged or more specifically why U.S. companies have invested abroad. Some of these are associated with theories of the product cycle, while others are related to the behavior of companies in an oligopoly and still others are related to tax calculations or to the necessity of protecting previous export markets in the face of the establishment of local tariff walls. There are other explanations.[11]

The Gray Report refers to the United States as the "largest capital exporter and bastion of the multinational enterprise."[12] However, not all multinational corporations are U.S. corporations, although a great many are. To the extent that the problems of the multinational corporation are political, its geographic origin or home base may be important. Thus for Canadians the problem is largely of U.S. multinational companies, while for Southeast Asian nations it is Japanese companies and for certain African countries it is British companies. Politically it is the "neocolonial" economic relationship that causes trouble. The problem has not been limited to developing countries: the French resistance to U.S. multinational companies in the 1950s and early 1960s was certainly a reflection of the feeling of the French about their political and general economic relations with the United States and about their position in the world. Much has now been written about the benefits and detriments of the multinational company to host countries, both developing and developed, and about the phenomenon of the global economy with which it is believed to be associated. To the extent that the multinational corporation is essentially a political problem to host countries, as it is to a degree to home countries, there is a certain fascination in its ambiguity. As a gifted minister of one Southeast Asian country once said to me, thinking no doubt of the technological and economic benefit and the political sensitivity, "The only thing worse than having multinationals, is not having them."

There have been repeated suggestions that the host countries try to seek to break up the foreign direct investment package offered by multinational companies, which is to say the technology, management, capital, and access to markets, and take only the elements they wish. For instance, they may make use of the technology while seeking to obtain the other elements elsewhere. Although this has certainly happened to some extent, the mixture of management; technology; and at least finance, if not equity, continues to flourish even in projects in Eastern Europe.[13] What the companies often have is not some isolable and patentable or licensable technique, but rather such technique plus knowledge and methods of operation, inextricably tied up with the personnel of the company. The personnel shifts, however, and the technology continues to evolve and change.[14]

The mixture of that which is attractive in the multinational corporation and that which is not is reflected in the ambivalence many nation-states feel about their relationship with and dependence upon all international economic activity. (See Chapter 6.)

Unquestionably there are those who believe that the multinationals either individually or collectively threaten to overwhelm economic arrangements of the world and most importantly the political sovereignty and independence of its nations. This view of things is often dramatized by charts that list the gross national product of nations next to the gross revenues or sales of the largest corporations, with the latter often bunched near the top of the chart.[15]

A number of people, Charles Kindleberger among them, have pointed out how misleading this comparison can be.[16] For one thing, gross sales do not represent disposable income or even added value. More to the point is the profound question of the political power of the nation-state. Recent developments in the oil industry suggest that the multinational companies, no matter how large or resourceful, need not have the last say.

Multinational companies are a large, important, and probably lasting phenomenon. However, those nation-states that feel threatened have it within themselves to "fight back." Although the bulk of U.S. direct foreign investment is in developed countries, it is the developing countries that most tend to have grievances against it. Among others, Argentina, Mexico, and the Andean group of nations as well as Canada and Australia have taken legislative and other political steps to strengthen themselves in their dealings with the multinational company and the foreign investor. Even the United States, as a home country, has faced this problem.

NOTES

1. See, for example, Economist Intelligence Unit, The Growth and Spread of Multinational Companies (1971); I. Litvack and C. Maule, Foreign Investment: The Experience of Host Countries (1970); S. Rolfe and W. Damm, The Multinational Corporation in the World Economy (1970). See also Staff of the Senate Comm. on Finance, Implications of Multinational Firms for World Labor and Investment and for U.S. Trade and Labor: Report to the Committee on Finance of the United States Senate and Its Subcommittee on International Trade on Investigation No. 332-69, under Section 332 of the Tariff Act of 1930, 93d Cong., 1st Sess. (Comm. Print 1973). [Hereinafter cited as Tariff Study.]

2. R. Cooper, The Economics of Interdependence: Economic Policy in the Atlantic Community 49-110 (1968).

3. R. Keohane and J. Nye, "Transgovernmental Relations and International Organizations," 27 World Pol. 39 (Oct. 1974). Keohane and Nye first expounded their "transnational" view in Transnational Relations and World Politics (1972).

4. Articles of Agreement of the International Monetary Fund, Washington, Dec. 27, 1945, as amended, July 28, 1969, art. XIX (i).

5. This text was prepared before the delivery of Secretary Kissinger's speech to the special session of the General Assembly of

the United Nations on September 1, 1975, with his request, among other things, for various new programs of the IMF and the World Bank. Even if these programs were adopted they would not change the general conclusions of this text. See 73 Dept. State Bull. 425 (1975).

6. See, for example, S. Dixon-Fyle, "Economic Inducements to Private Foreign Investment in Africa," 4 J. Development Studies 109 (1967); A. Fatouros, Government Guarantees to Foreign Investors (1962); Gillespie, "The Policies of England, France and Germany as Recipients of Foreign Direct Investment," Machlup et al. International Mobility and Movements of Capital 397 (1972).

7. Canadian Government, Foreign Direct Investment in Canada (1972), also known as the Gray Report.

8. A. Said and L. Simmons, "The Politics of Transition," The New Sovereigns, Multinational Corporations as World Powers 1-9 (Said and Simmons, eds., 1975).

9. R. Vernon, Sovereignty at Bay: The Multinational Spread of U.S. Enterprises 3-11 (1971).

10. M. Watkins, Foreign Ownership and the Structure of Canadian Industry (1968).

11. See, for example, Y. Aharoni, The Foreign Investment Decision Process (1966) and R. Vernon, op. cit.

12. Canadian Government, op. cit.

13. See, for example, "Dow to Launch Largest Western Joint Venture in EE," Bus. Int'l/Eastern Europe Report 34 (Feb. 7, 1975); "A Hungarian Interpretation of Joint-Venture Questions," Bus. Int'l/ Eastern Europe Report 65-66 (March 7, 1975); G. Lauter and P. Dickie, Multinational Corporations and East European Socialist Economies 18-19 (1975).

14. This point has been made in Richard Caves, "International Corporations: The Industrial Economics of Foreign Investment," in International Investment 265, 267 (J. Dunning, ed., 1972).

15. See L. Brown, World Without Borders 214 (1972).

16. C. Kindleberger, Power and Money 180 (1970).

CHAPTER 2 THE PROBLEM DEFINED

A great deal has been written about the definition of the multinational corporation, yet far more important to any systematic study is a definition of the problem, that is, what it is about the multinational corporation that bothers the writer, the legislator, the country. The aspect of the multinational corporation that is focused on in this book is the question of the degree to which, if any, it can be regulated or controlled at the international level and whether or not a strong international organization can be created to perform this function.

To some extent the task has been made easier by the report of the Group of Eminent Persons of the United Nations and the establishment of the United Nations Commission on Transnational Corporations. Furthermore, the Organization for Economic Cooperation and Development (OECD) is also examining the question of the multinational corporation and international investment and the degree to which these phenomena can be regulated or guided, as well as the degree to which the reactions of national governments to this kind of investment can be made the subject of international agreement.[1]

To say that the focus of this book is on an international organization to deal with the problem of the multinational corporation is not definite enough; the ultimate purpose that such an organization should serve must also be considered. Of course, like any public agency, whether national or international, it should serve the "public interest," although at the international level it is not at all clear that it is possible to define the public interest.

The open economic system created at Bretton Woods, of which the United States has been a principal supporter and beneficiary, is fundamental to U.S. foreign and economic policy. Therefore, the purpose of an international investment organization should be to preserve one particular, and indeed important, aspect of this open economic system, that is the international investment and multinational corporation powers from the stresses to which it is subject. At the same time, the emergence of international business has raised the question of whether it should, or can, be subjected to a degree of social control at the international level, especially with respect to its most characteristic and largest part, the multinational corporation.

The vast array of products and activities of the large international companies and the variety of these companies gives us a very large subject. It is not merely the activities of the multinational corporations, or transnational enterprises, no matter how these are defined, that are the problem, although they are a crucial part of it. Unquestionably the associated capital flows and monetary phenomena, trade activities, and governmental reactions must be taken into account. On the other hand, it would be too extreme to say that all international economic activities are at issue, unless from the viewpoint of some sort of Marxist "monopoly capital" explanation of the international economy.

Foreign direct investment is a key economic factor, especially in productive enterprise in developing countries but also in developed countries, many of whose principal sectors are also in process of development. This is increasingly revealed by the figures. In 1970 multinationals based in the United States alone accounted for 13 percent of all capital spending in the United Kingdom, France, West Germany, Belgium-Luxembourg, Canada, Mexico, and Brazil.* They accounted for 22 percent of the total capital spending in the key industrial sectors of metal, machinery, and capital equipment in these countries.[2]

It should be realized that foreign direct investment, which is at the core of the process we are going to discuss and the regulation of which is at issue, cannot be separated from other short-term and long-term capital movements associated with foreign direct investment, such as working capital, suppliers' credits, and long-term lending in support of foreign direct investments, not to mention some portfolio investment, which is inevitably associated with certain kinds of foreign direct investment.

It is this foreign investment that gives rise to the totality of the international business activities of multinational corporations; but surely this is too broad to be thought of as a problem in need of regulation. Any multinational corporation is involved in an endless variety of everyday activities in many countries through its many subsidiaries,

---

*This percentage presumably excludes capital spending for public services.

including the purchase of an infinite variety of components and raw materials, the employment of many classes of personnel, the sale of many kinds of goods through wholesale and retail channels, day-to-day labor relations, plant maintenance, relations with banks, tax payments, and subjection to local regulation.

We will have to impose parameters and carve out relevant aspects of international business activity. Moreover, this activity is engaged in not only by multinational corporations, but also by many others, including small companies with some international activity, whether in exports or finance; local companies; individuals; partnerships; state trading organizations; state banks and holding companies; or shipping carriers. Many of these entities do not fall into the core definition of the multinational corporation mentioned above. Another related phenomenon that does not fall within the activities of the core corporations we are dealing with is the investment flow from oil-producing countries in the Middle East.

THE SCOPE OF ACTIVITIES SUBJECT TO REGULATION

I propose to focus on those activities of the multinational corporation that may lend themselves to regulation. Needless to say this will be arbitrary, but the criteria will be given by which certain activities are included and others not. Activities are excluded if they will inevitably be dealt with by national governments or if they involve more than one country and will be dealt with through bilateral or similar diplomatic means. Activities are excluded if regulating them is clearly unfeasible: an example of this, to pick one out of the air, might be the daily management-labor relations in every country in the world.

Also excluded will be activities that are already subject to other international organizations such as the IMF or the GATT or to more specialized agencies such as the Intergovernmental Maritimes Consultative Organization (IMCO), the International Civil Aviation Organization (ICAO), or the International Telecommunications Union. Moreover, I will exclude certain areas that seem related but that constitute their own systems, such as the operations of local capital market, of the Euro-currency market, and of the "international security market." It has been suggested that such a market as this last is already emerging, but the evidence is not conclusive.[3]

The scope of the relevant business activities of the multinational corporation would impose limits on any prospective international organization. Limits are also imposed by the international political system. I assume that it is wholly unrealistic to expect any sort of international welfare state in the foreseeable future. Indeed, the far narrower proposals that have been made by George Ball and others who call for an international organization to charter corporations are unrealistic. There will be no global budget in the foreseeable future, and the various aid programs do not add up to a welfare state or anything like it. There is no global taxing authority; indeed, the various attempts of international aid bodies and consortia to investigate the total budgets and economies of aid recipient nations and their economic plans, have not been well received.[4] The hopes of Jan Tinbergen for an international welfare state have certainly not come to pass.[5]

This book will consider the possibility of establishing, at this time or in the foreseeable future, an international investment organization to regulate and thereby preserve the essential integrity of multinational corporations and their related foreign direct investment activities. The emphasis of such an organization would not be on the defense and protection of individual companies and their investments, but rather on the preservation of the process and on regulation of the aggregate activities of these companies. This would be done only to the extent that it was necessary in order to preserve the open economic system. To some degree entrepreneurial and indeed corporate dynamism requires an underlying business confidence and morale, even in the large corporate setting. This dynamism is a central quality of the large international company as well as the small entrepreneur; it may be generated and sustained by market forces, but it is not to be confused with them. Certainly there are abusive practices that do not fit into the process we seek to preserve; indeed, some state enterprises will fit into this process more closely, although they too can be guilty of abuses.

The range of activities relevant to this book commences with the entry of a company into a particular nation, the expansion of a company's activities there, or the acquisition of a company there. The associated financing of these activities is relevant, as are the central ongoing operations of the company and the financing associated with that, as well as, possibly, the retention of the necessary professional assistance. The financial returns derived by the parent multinational company, as through dividends, interest, or royalties, are of course relevant, since they affect the expectation of profits, without which the process of foreign investment or multinational business activity would not take place. Finally, the long-term stability or security of foreign investments by multinational companies in the aggregate is highly relevant. I am not thinking here of the way a prospective investor assesses all the intangibles of the investment climate or of the way a particular investor protects himself from expropriation or seeks compensation; rather, I am referring to that perception of basic stability without which investment would not take place or at least would not take place without an extremely rapid payout to compensate for the perceived high risk.

The process to be protected is one side of the coin. On the other side are those national and regional laws and regulations that governmental authorities impose on the investment process. A related problem, which has received a probably disproportionate amount of attention, is the clash of competing national jurisdictions that sometimes affects the operations of multinational companies.[6] For instance, past assertions by the United States, in the face of Canadian government resistance, of U.S. jurisdiction over Canadian subsidiaries of U.S. companies in such areas as export control, securities regulation, and antitrust has probably exacerbated the problems of U.S. companies in Canada.

MULTINATIONAL CORPORATION DEFINED: THE CORE CORPORATION AND THE RELEVANT PARAMETERS

The "atmospheric" definition of a multinational corporation as a big company, frequently based in the United States, that does business in a number of, or indeed many countries and has a central policy, can be carried somewhat further. The economic sector or sectors in which the company is active in the various countries in which it invests and operates is often thought to be a relevant factor. A distinction has often been made between manufacturing companies and foreign investors active in the extraction of raw materials, but a more helpful distinction might be based on history, since investment in petroleum and minerals, as well as in other raw materials such as timber or bananas, was often the earliest or indeed the only investment in some of the poorest developing countries; indeed, only the availability of such raw materials brought the investment in the first place.

As a result, such investment has become associated with notions of the enclave; of the concession agreement; of the consequent expropriation of property and the resultant legal controversies; of exploitation; and because exhaustable resources were often though not always involved, of a feeling that the national patrimony had to be protected. Nevertheless, as economies develop, other areas such as utilities or even retail trade or manufacture may also become more sensitive; I have heard a citizen of the Philippines speak of the need of protecting the "domestic market" from foreigners. Furthermore, companies in the extractive industries are increasingly involved in processes that take place within the host countries, such as smelting and other processing, refining, and petrochemicals.

A distinction is also made between heavy industrial investments on the one hand and operations in such areas as banking, hotels, tourism, and other service sectors. However, if these operations are permanent, as distinguished from short-term operations such as construction or consulting engineering or other professional service contracts, the distinction may be overdone; many of the problems of running a banking operation or a hotel chain may be similar to those of certain activities in the manufacturing area.

Another way of distinguishing among types of operation suggests that high technology, possibly with respect to investments in more developed countries, is the key; this will usually be found in certain areas of manufacturing such as electronics or computers or airplanes, and it suggests a sensitivity that is different from that in the raw materials area.

Canadians have become sensitive about the penetration of U.S. businesses into the "cultural" sector, as in the Canadian editions of _Time_ and _Readers Digest_.

Behind some of these definitions may be the Leninist notion of the commanding heights of the economy. Almost all countries have historically excluded foreign investors from certain sectors; this includes the United States, which has excluded foreign investment from coastal shipping, federal mineral properties, telecommunications, and one or two other areas.[7] However, the sectors from which foreign investors are excluded vary rather widely from country to country and do not necessarily coincide with those areas in which the bulk of multinational operations are concentrated. I do not propose to draw the line at this point to include steel, for example, but to exclude insurance, or to include airplanes but exclude shipping.

The typical multinational corporation might engage in some line of petroleum or mineral extraction, any industrial or manufacturing activity, possibly retailing, tourism, banking, finance, and some other sectors. We should not artificially limit the core corporation to certain sectors or give it too precise a legal definition. A simple core definition might be that it is a corporation based in one country with subsidiaries in four or five other countries, each of which the parent controls either by the requisite share ownership, such as 50 percent or more, or by comparable arrangements. Its principal production, sales, and financial policies and activities are coordinated to a degree, and the volume of its business is substantial, whether in the respective domestic markets of the parent and subsidiaries or through export to other markets.

There can be many variations on this. Two of the largest multinational corporations are Royal Dutch Shell and Unilever, which operate through parent holding companies in Holland and Britain and have corporate structures that are therefore somewhat more complicated than the simple one I have suggested. Moreover, a multinational operation could be limited to subsidiaries in fewer than four or five countries.

A majority of voting shares is not necessary for control over or substantial influence in a company. For example, if it is publicly held, a much smaller percentage of shares will do, although many countries do not have large enough capital markets to permit wide public holding.

There has been much writing on the definition of a multinational corporation. I have already suggested R. Vernon's book, which finds 25 percent ownership of the voting shares of the subsidiary sufficient and suggests a minimum of four or five subsidiaries.[8] The Gray report uses a 50 percent test.[9] The U.S. foreign direct investment controls, now terminated, used a 10 percent beneficial ownership test, and the U.S. Internal Revenue Code, for purposes of Sub-part F, has both percentage and "effective control" tests.

At the level of potential international organization it seems to me that no refined test is appropriate at this time. As mentioned previously, M. Watkins found one foreign subsidiary sufficient and suggested a rather low minimum for the volume of business test. A minimum asset or sales test, on the large side, might be appropriate.[10]

To a Canadian, Frenchman, Nigerian, or American, the fact that a company or investor is foreign may be the key, especially when linked with largeness, but local economic planners and politicians may be more troubled by the business consequences that seem to flow from the legal structure. More specifically, it is the common strategy of the multinational enterprise, coordinated across national borders and having an impact within them, that seems significant. This aspect of the business administration of multinational corporations has also been the subject of a great deal of writing that deals with structure, strategy, and operations.[11] The multinational corporations in which we are interested do reveal some of this common policy, although the degree of centralization varies from company to company and may vary from product to product and country to country within the company as well.[12]

It is useful to define to some extent the parameters of the activities that would be subject to regulation; of course, not every single thing that these large companies do in many parts of the world can be regulated. It is difficult to decide just what the parameters should be. To some extent the range of activities included within the essential investment and multinational company activity process, which it would be the purpose of any international investment organization to preserve, has already been indicated: it runs the gamut from entry through operations to long-term stability.

This is both a very broad and very narrow focus. It is narrow in the sense that it concentrates on the operations of individual subsidiaries in individual countries; in this sense the approach is rather legal. Others like to think of the multinational corporation on a global basis, although this latter approach is rather abstract and even unrealistic. In fact the world is still divided into nation-states, and they are the source of legal authority. Therefore it is still correct to think of these corporate enterprises as functioning within the jurisdiction of nation-states even as they do business across and within their borders, sometimes fairly indiscriminately.

We shall see that entry, whether by new investment or by acquisition of an existing company, can give rise to many problems. The financing associated with such entry can also be critical; indeed, since a subsidiary may be established largely with local capital, the expansion of a multinational corporation can take place without the international capital flows it is sometimes thought to be part of.

The reinvestment of earnings and the expansion of an original operation would certainly be within the parameters, although this brings in the operations of the company with its infinity of day-to-day activity, an aspect of the problem that may be more intelligently considered from the point of view of those government measures that might affect operations, whether through taxation, antitrust laws, or various regulations. Certainly the effects of some or the principal possible government measures and operations would fall within the parameters.

We have already seen that the repatriation of capital and earnings through dividends and interest and the long-term stability of the corporation in each country fall within the parameters. This aspect must be included within the parameters of the problem if the international investment organization is to serve its purpose of preserving the process of international production and the associated finance and innovation.

Do the parameters relate exclusively to foreign direct investment, especially the traditional form of operation through wholly owned subsidiaries, manufacturing in local plants, and exporting from there? What of export from the parent and/or licensing by the parent to otherwise independent local companies? What of construction and turnkey projects, whether linked with management or not? Obviously it is difficult to know where to draw the line; I would not include the traditional national companies that merely export to foreign markets or companies that merely have certain limited licensing arrangements with otherwise wholly independent companies and merely receive royalties. On the other hand, these devices are used increasingly by what are otherwise multinational enterprises, and where they are, they would fall within the relevant parameters.

What of the purchase of supplies and raw materials as such? For example, are the current contractual arrangements between the oil companies and the producing countries within the parameters? This is a difficult question; writers have described some of the traditional concessions, as well as later joint-venture and production-sharing arrangements, as glorified supply contracts, although many of them are much more and involve substantial, even vast, industrial, commercial, and other operations abroad.

The local acquisition of raw materials is not at the core of the activities with which we are concerned, which are rather the ongoing operation of global enterprises, but this aspect can not be separated out completely. Any international arrangements with respect to access to commodities would represent an independent regulatory system, as would the regulation of the international securities market or the regulation of insurance companies or banks. Although services, including banking, might be included within the activity of multinational corporations, any detailed regulation of banking would be a specialized and separate operation.

Access to finance at various points in the operations of a company, whether it be for entry into a new economy, for expansion, or for working capital, comes within the parameters of the activities that are essential to the preservation of the process with which we are concerned. At the same time, the regulation of such operations as the Euro-currency markets would not be within the scope of the international investment organization.

More precisely, I would not include the problem of the regulation of the movement of short-term capital, which has sometimes been associated with multinational corporations, since these movements result from characteristics of the exchange rate adjustment system, which is associated with the International Monetary Fund, whether the fixed or floating system. They are engaged in by multinational corporations to a degree, probably defensively, but more actively by banks, governments, central banks, and others. The regulation of this activity would presumably be the responsibility of a reformed International Monetary Fund.[13]

I have already adverted to the question of whether the multinational corporation is a U.S. phenomenon. It has in fact been suggested that the distribution of multinational corporations and of foreign direct investment follows fairly closely the distribution of gross national product.[14] Table 2.1 shows the stock for foreign direct investments held by companies or other nationals of the larger capital-exporting countries.

I think it is fair to say that U.S. companies are dominant, much as the U.S. economy is dominant. U.S. multinational companies are active not only in developing countries but in other

TABLE 2.1

Market Economies: Stock of Foreign Direct Investment (Book Value), 1967 and 1971

Country[a]	1967 In Millions of Dollars	1967 In Percentage	1971[b] In Millions of Dollars	1971[b] In Percentage
United States	59,486	55.0	86,001	52.0
United Kingdom	17,521	16.2	24,019	14.5
France	6,000	5.5	9,540	5.8
Federal Republic of Germany	3,015	2.8	7,276	4.4
Switzerland	4,250	3.9	6,760	4.1
Canada	3,728	3.4	5,930	3.6
Japan	1,458	1.3	4,480	2.7
Netherlands	2,250	2.1	3,580	2.2
Sweden[c]	1,514	1.4	3,450	2.1
Italy	2,110[d]	1.9	3,350	2.0
Belgium	2,040[d]	0.4	3,250	2.0
Australia	380[d]	1.9	610	0.4
Portugal	200[d]	0.2	320	0.2
Denmark	190[d]	0.2	310	0.2
Norway	60[d]	0.0	90	0.0
Austria	30[d]	0.0	40	0.0
Other	4,000[e]	3.7	6,000	3.6
Total	108,200	100.0	165,000	100.00

[a]Estimate (except United States, United Kingdom, Germany, Japan, and Sweden).

[b]Relatively accurate.

[c]1965 and 1970.

[d]Only investment in developing countries is available, but distribution correlations permit estimates.

[e]Estimate including developing countries.

Source: United Nations, Multinational Corporations in World Development (ST/ECA/190/Corr. 1), at 139 (1974).

developed markets, especially in Europe, although they are much less active in Japan because of the Japanese resistance to foreign direct investment. Indeed, as noted in Chapter 1, the bulk of U.S. foreign direct investment is in developed countries.

From the U.S. point of view it is of course the attitude of other countries and their peoples to U.S. companies that is of first importance, although the companies of other countries are active in many parts of the world including the United States and often have similar problems. Moreover, developing countries such as Mexico and Brazil are becoming bases of multinational enterprises, and it is not unlikely that countries in Eastern Europe will also. In terms of foreign direct investment that is possibly not linked with multinational enterprises, the Chinese of Singapore and Taiwan are the source of substantial investment in Southeast Asia, and Iranians and Arabs are also making substantial investments in industry abroad. In other words, the problem should not be seen exclusively as a problem for the United States.

THE PROBLEM RECAPITULATED

My interest in multinational companies is that of a public international lawyer interested in exploring the possibility of controlling multinational corporations and related foreign direct investment through international means at the international level, with a view to preserving the open economic system while at the same time imposing certain social controls, defined at the international level, on the multinational company and its related investment activities. It is this concern that leads me to the relevant definition of the core corporation and the parameters of relevant activities.

NOTES

1. The Impact of Multinational Corporations on the Development Process and on International Relations: Report of the Group of Eminent Persons to Study the Role of Multinational Corporations on Development and on International Relations, UN Doc. E/5500/Add. 11, Rev. 1-ST/ESA/6; New York Times, Oct. 27, 1975, sec. C, at 41, col. 8. See also N. T. Wang, "Towards an International Code of Conduct for Transnational Corporations," paper presented to the Conference on the Nation States and the Transnational Corporations in Lesser Developed Countries in Aspen, Colorado, Dec. 13-18, 1974; G. Rueber et al., Private Foreign Investment in Development (1973); and Draft Declaration of the O.E.C.D. Member Countries

on the Guidelines for Multinational Enterprises (reproduced Nov. 3, 1975), materials for the American Bar Association Section of International Law, Subcommittee on Multinational Corporations of the Committee on International Investment and Development.

2. Hearings on Multinational Corporations Before the Subcomm. on International Trade of the Senate Comm. on Finance, 93d Cong., 1st Sess., 401 (1973).

3. See M. Cohen, "Toward an International Securities Market," 5 Law and Pol. Int'l Bus. 357 (1973).

4. See J. Bhagwati, "Fiscal Policies, the Faking of Foreign Trade Declarations and the Balance of Payments," in Trade, Tariffs and Growth 266 (1969).

5. J. Tinbergen, International Economic Integration (1954).

6. P. Goldberg and C. Kindleberger, "Toward a GATT for Investment: A Proposal for Supervision of the International Corporation," 2 Law and Pol. Int'l Bus. 295 (1970).

7. See Legal Environment for Foreign Direct Investment in the United States (R. Rosendahl, ed., 1972).

8. R. Vernon, Sovereignty at Bay: The Multinational Spread of U.S. Enterprises 19, note a (1971).

9. Canadian Government, Foreign Direct Investment in Canada 17 (1972).

10. M. Watkins, Foreign Ownership and the Structure of Canadian Industry (1968).

11. See, for example, J. Stopford and L. Wells, Managing the Multinational Enterprise: Organization of the Firm and Ownership of the Subsidiaries (1973).

12. Ibid.

13. See, for example, Comm. on Reform of the International Monetary System and Related Issues (Comm. of Twenty), International Monetary Reform 13, 78-87 (1974).

14. L. Brown, World Without Borders 212 (1972).

CHAPTER

3

EXISTING PROPOSALS AND INITIATIVES FOR INTERNATIONAL REGULATION

As we have seen, the Bretton Woods system did not explicitly deal with the subject of capital movements or multinational corporations or their regulation by nations or at the international level. Since 1970 there have been a number of proposals to deal with the multinational corporation, and the United Nations, the Organization of Economic Cooperation and Development (OECD), the Organization of American States (OAS), and others have begun to address themselves to the subject.

A GAP IN THE INTERNATIONAL ORDER?

It is clear that consensus has not yet developed on the international treatment of multinational corporations or foreign direct investment. Indeed, until the early 1970s there was not really that much international attention given to the subject. In 1929 the League of Nations considered a proposal for the protection of foreign investment, but this did not make much progress. The ill-fated Havana Charter of 1948, which would have established an International Trade Organization (ITO), contained provisions with respect to restrictive trade practices and the protection of investment. The provisions with respect to restrictive trade practices, interestingly, would at least in early drafts have provided some standing for private parties. The provisions with respect to the protection of investment were considered too weak, which may indeed have been one of the causes for the demise of the Havana Charter in the United States Congress. Later attempts in the antitrust area that were not much more successful involved the U.N. Economic and Social Council (ECOSOC) in 1951, the United Nations proper in 1953, and the General Agreement on Tariffs and Trade (GATT) in 1958. In the late 1920s and the 1930s the League considered certain proposed model bilateral tax treaties that contained an interesting provision for the allocation of taxes between two taxing jurisdictions, based on division of sales, assets, and other factors between the two countries. These treaties did not gain much acceptance.[1]

We have already discussed the "gap" in the IMF with respect to capital movements and multinational corporations. The result of this gap and of the defeat of the ITO was that the Bretton Woods system did not deal with the basic multinational corporate investment process with which we are concerned. From time to time since the second world war, efforts have been made to develop codes to protect foreign investment, including the Abs code*, a proposed OECD Convention, and a proposed code of the International Bank of Reconstruction and Development (World Bank), but these have gotten nowhere. Proposals for a multilateral guarantee fund for foreign investment that would replace, coordinate, or supplement national insurance programs have also not made much progress.[2]

Possibly the closest to filling the gap, and this very little, are the OECD Code for the Liberalization of Capital Movements, reprinted as Appendix C of this book, and Code of Liberalization of Current Invisible Operations, reprinted as Appendix D. A review of these codes indicates that they are not addressed to the multinational company or its related investment processes as such, although they do deal with inward and outward capital movements, including direct investment, and with lending as well as access to capital markets, dividends, and interest. These embrace a large part of the basic process with which we are concerned. The application of the codes is limited to the members of the OECD and is therefore less than universal; on the other hand, the OECD embraces within itself most of the principal investor countries in which multinational corporations are based. However, the tables reveal that countries often invoke reservations and derogations that make the codes inapplicable to them. Although the codes fairly reflect the commitment of the OECD members to the open economic system, as it applies to the processes with which we are concerned, this has not prevented individual countries from taking more restrictive views.

Interestingly, the codes arise not out of the Bretton Woods system of institutions but rather from the Marshall Plan and the gradual freeing of European payments after World War II. Even more specific is the Treaty of Rome, binding on the members of the European

---

*So called after Herman Abs, member of the board of the Deutsche Bank.

Economic Community, which specifically provides for free capital movements as well as the right of entry and hence for investment by member country companies, including the local subsidiaries of foreign, that is, U.S. companies, in other member countries.[3] For example, the European Commission once charged France with a violation of the Treaty of Rome in barring a particular foreign investment, that of FIAT in Citroen. The French charged the restriction to an exchange control, not barred by the Treaty of Rome, rather than an investment control, which would be barred by the relevant provisions of the Treaty of Rome.[4]

The OECD codes are an interesting antecedent; however, the OECD itself does not consider them adequate, even with respect to its limited membership, and the OECD is examining the entire question of multinational corporations and international investment. (See the first section of Chapter 2 of this book.)

The recent OECD efforts are in fact part of a wider development that began about five years ago in an effort to come to terms with the problem of multinational corporations at the international level.[5] This attempt reflects the eruption into the public consciousness of what are thought to be the problems posed by multinational corporations. Not everyone feels that these problems must be handled by international regulation or attention. Many, if not most, will be prepared to respond at the national level, by means of national legislation and regulation. Others would say that effective negotiation with multinational corporations, at the time of initial investment in the country and also with respect to their continuing operations, is sufficient. Others would do nothing. Nonetheless some seek an international regulatory solution. There is some confusion or at least a basic lack of agreement about the purpose to be served.

The most prominent efforts are those centered in the United Nations and the OECD. The United Nations has set up a Commission on Transnational Corporations and will be seeking to develop a code of conduct for multinational corporations and to make treaties in specific areas such as tax and antitrust, develop information, and provide technical assistance, especially to the governments of developing countries, that will enable these countries to deal with multinational corporations.

The OECD is also exploring a code of conduct for multinational corporations, as well as guidelines for nation-states that seek to deal with them. It is studying various tax and antitrust questions and examining the lack of consistency in investment incentives in various countries. The OAS has also decided to develop a code of conduct for multinational corporations operating in Latin America.

A full catalog, let alone a comparison, of the various proposals and suggestions for regulating multinational corporations and foreign direct investment, official and unofficial, is difficult. Their relevance to the focus of this book may be even more so. None indicate clearly that they are concerned only with the activities of the core multinational corporation within the parameters I have outlined; some would appear to be broader, others narrower in their thrust. Some grapple with a definition of the multinational corporation; others do not, or do not relate it to a definition of foreign direct investment. Some deal with the activities of multinational corporations in both developed and developing countries, while some would limit themselves to one or the other.* More basically, not all make clear what their underlying purpose is, and we have already seen that this is crucial to any understanding or evaluation of a proposed international investment organization. Is their purpose to establish a minimum of legal order, or is it to establish something in the nature of an international welfare state? Is their purpose to preserve an open world economy or not? Do they wish to "free" the multinational corporation of national and regional restraints, or do they wish to "control" the multinational corporation? Are the proposals, whether official or unofficial, serious? Do they address the question of the actual period of time that would be required to implement international regulation?

What is the provenance of the proposals? Do they come from economists who believe in free trade and almost by unstated analogy in free capital movement, or do they come from spokesmen for developing countries, who are, whether rightly or wrongly, often afraid of multinational corporations? Do the proposals come from people with a sense of political reality or from technicians such as lawyers?

Where would an international organization be located? Should it be part of an existing organization, such as the OECD?

Possibly the most profound difficulty in the existing proposals and suggestions relates to the necessity of combining a political with a technical approach. The reaction of nations and peoples to the growing fact of the multinational corporation is after all a highly political phenomenon, but a technical approach is needed for dealing with questions of tax, antitrust, disclosure of information, entry into

---

*The United Nations Commission on Transnational Corporations plans to develop a definition of the multinational, or transnational, corporation. The OECD deals principally, although not exclusively, with the operations of multinational corporations in developed countries. The United Nations Commission on Transnational Corporations, the United Nations Conference on Trade and Development (UNCTAD), and other UN bodies, focus largely on the operations of the multinationals in developing countries. The text below brings out yet other perspectives.

nations, and the like. This relationship has not been explicitly addressed to the degree necessary. In fact, the principal thrust, as is probably inevitable, behind proposals for the regulation of multinational corporations has been political; one highly placed official once suggested to me that there was a need to do something "symbolic," even if impractical, with respect to the multinational corporations to satisfy the anxieties of the developing countries and others.[6]

A CATALOG OF PROPOSALS

It is impossible to systematically categorize or create a "taxonomy" of the proposals. Some proposals do not deal specifically with multinational corporations as such but rather envision reforms in the international economic order that would inevitably affect the multinational corporation and lead to some regulation of it. However, the proposals can be broken down into a number of groups or schools.

Adjustment of Existing Institutions

Reform of the IMF has been prominent among the suggestions for reforming existing international institutions to cope with the multinational corporation or with the problems thought to be created by it. Specifically, an extension of the jurisdiction of the IMF to short-term capital movements, which were thought to be a problem a few years ago, has sometimes been thought relevant, on the assumption that these capital movements were largely generated by the activities of multinational corporations. In point of fact this has been disputed, and many would suggest that these movements have been a function of the adjustment mechanism, whether of fixed or floating exchange rates, and that the multinational corporations act largely in a defensive way, albeit in considerable volume.[7]

Reform of the GATT may also affect some of the operations of multinational corporations.

Global Economic Reform

From time to time there are proposals to, in effect, give the world a government rather like that of an individual country, at least for dealing with economic problems. These proposals can take a traditional liberal form and call for international taxation and a budget or for some sort of welfare state. The name of Jan Tinbergen is associated with the notion of an international welfare state.[8]

Related to this type of proposal is the call for strong international institutions to deal with problems of food, population, and the environment; some progress is in fact being made in these areas.

More recent themes include global income redistribution and the necessity of imposing limitations on growth in order to conserve our finite resources. The Club of Rome, which has been principally concerned with the necessity of limiting growth, has suggested a "fair trade commission" that would set standards of fairness with respect to terms of trade and other international economic arrangements.[9] Lester Brown has suggested that there is a need for a set of more powerful international organizations dealing with a variety of international issues.[10]

From time to time it is suggested that the economies of the world and their monetary arrangements would be more effectively harnessed by the creation of a world central bank. Again, it is believed that the world can lend itself to this degree of international organization.[11]

The theme of a new international economic order has been insistently pressed by the developing countries, and some writers have suggested that an overall international deal could be struck, which no doubt would have institutional implications.[12] A fundamental part of this deal might be an exchange of raw materials for technology, which the multinational companies are thought to provide.[13]

Another line of approach is political. It includes two schools of thought, one of which suggests that the multinational corporations are now so large that a countervailing force, going beyond trade unions, for example, or even nation-states, is necessary. Related to it is the school that sees the multinational corporations, through their global scope, their activities independent of nation-states, and their ability to deal with and in nation-states, as having transformed the nation-state political system into a new "transnational" system. This view suggests that some international organization is necessary.[14]

Proposals that deal with corporate behavior as such are in some ways more limited and in others more ambitious. One such proposal is that of Jack Behrman, that international productive organizations be created that would themselves engage in industrial activities. Some of the suggestions with respect to the exploitation of the deep sea bed by international agencies are similar. Intelsat, which operates a system of international communication satellites through the U.S. operating agency Comsat and in turn contracts with private U.S. companies, is also similar to Behrman's proposed system in some ways.[15]

A New Legal Order for Corporations

The name most frequently associated with the suggestion that the multinational corporations be given a new international legal order is that of George Ball. The proposals for this new legal order take various forms, but essentially an international body would be created that would charter these corporations, thus freeing them, at least to some extent, from competing national regulations. There are a number of difficulties with this suggestion, which is touched on further in Chapter 9. On first view, the idea that an international organization could be created that could supervise vast numbers of corporations as thoroughly as some national authorities do, with the attendant requirement that an international body of corporation law be created, seems very unrealistic; yet to an extent that is what would be contemplated by some of the deep sea bed proposals now being discussed. Whether the chartering of corporations at the international level carries with it broader economic and social regulation, and if so to what degree, has not always been made clear.[16] Ralph Nader and others have suggested federal incorporation, to replace state incorporation, in the United States, for reasons that may be analogous to those of George Ball.[17]

Ball basically proposes to liberate the multinational corporation, which he considers a powerful force of economic progress, from competing and inadequate national regulations.[18] This idea has also been stated in slightly different form as the suggestion that corporations become "anational," that is, without nationality, possibly headquartered on or incorporated by an island state and thus made free of petty national regulation.[19]

Raymond Vernon has made a somewhat different proposal. He has argued for an extension of the "Clavo" principle, which is normally understood to hold that the home country of a corporation will not espouse the claims of one of its companies against expropriation or similar measures by a host country, leaving the solution of the problem to the law of the host country. Vernon suggests that corporations be freed entirely from the laws, regulations, and constraints of the home country and in each case be subject only to the laws and regulations of the host country, which are presumably applicable only to the relevant subsidiary.

Harmony between the Nation-State and the Multinational Corporation

Many of the numerous suggestions for promoting harmony between the nation-state and the multinational corporation are really unanalytic and appear to seek harmony for its own sake. These proposals probably exaggerate the equality of power of the multinational corporation and the nation-state, ignoring the fact that regulatory power lies exclusively with the nation-state, although I do not mean to deny the economic power wielded by many of the corporations.

These proposals may underestimate the difficulties of countries that while desiring the benefits of international economic exchange, at the same time are trying to control their domestic economies. Domestic control is made difficult by such international exchange, as discussed in Chapter 6. Moreover, harmony must extend to a range of issues that extends from taxation, financing, information, takeovers, and mergers to plant closings and labor issues. Most or all of these issues are considered in a November 1973 resolution of the Commission of the European Community, which has been submitted to the European Council for action. The council has so far given final approval to only a few of these proposals.[20]

Lurking behind the ambiguity of harmony is the question of purpose. Is the essential purpose of harmony to assist the multinational corporations, or is it to reduce frictions or assist nation-states? Some proponents of harmony take gentle forms, suggesting that minimum discussions may serve the purpose. Seymour Rubin is analytic and is among the gentlest of harmonizers.[21]

The International Chamber of Commerce has proposed a set of guidelines for investors that would apply to both companies and countries.[22] These guidelines basically call for good behavior on both sides. Some corporations, most priminently the Caterpillar Tractor Co., have proclaimed a code for their own self-regulation.[23] It is too early to know whether the codes of behavior that the United Nations, the OAS, and the OECD may produce will be essentially harmonizing.

Specific Suggestions

Most of the suggestions already referred to have been neither specific nor detailed; indeed, most, although not all, represent small parts of particular books or sets of ideas. There are a number of approaches that are more developed, although this does not mean that they are necessarily more viable or of greater influence. The bulk of them, however, have official sanction.

The United Nations

The efforts of the United Nations since 1973 are probably the most well known and detailed. They include the report of the Group of Eminent Persons[24] and the resultant Commission on Transnational Corporations. Although the United Nations is more attentive to problems within developing countries and to some extent to the relationship of developing with developed countries, the efforts of the United Nations do represent a move toward creation of an international order, even a legal order, with respect to the activities of multinational corporations. What seems to be lacking is any suggestion about what the normative outline and content of that order will be, although the report and the related statements suggest the desire for specific agreements among nations with respect to particular matters such as tax and antitrust as well as for a general code. A code of behavior for companies would be an interim measure that would be concurrent with an attempt to gather information and to effect surveillance. The effort is still rather indefinite, being subject to the particular difficulties to which the United Nations is prone. Apparently a tight normative prescription will not be formulated until the 1980s or later.[25]

The Organization for Economic Development (OECD)

The OECD also faces the problem of international investment and multinational corporations; the OECD attack on these two problems in tandem is more likely to correspond to the parameters of the problem that I will use. This will be discussed at length in Chapters 9 and 10; at this point it is only necessary to say that the most interesting work seems to be the development of a national treatment standard with respect to the continuing operations of corporations in a country, and possibly also their entry into a country. No doubt this work will increasingly be related to the existing Code of Liberalization of Capital Movements and Code of Liberalization of Current Invisible Operations.

Forums

Seymour Rubin has suggested that any international agreement between nations, certainly if it is to deal with substance, is not readily foreseeable. At the same time Rubin acknowledges the need for action, whether "symbolic" or otherwise and suggests that one way to proceed would be to establish forums to deal with particular problems and disputes and seek to develop a substantive and procedural consensus from them, an approach I tend to favor.[26]

Other Proposals

It is not easy to categorize the numerous other proposals. In 1970, P. Goldberg and C. Kindleberger suggested a "GATT for investment," the principal purpose of which would have been to resolve the competing or overlapping jurisdictions among nations, in which individual companies sometimes get caught.[27] P. Goldberg and C. Kindleberger suggest such areas as the securities and antitrust laws, foreign direct investment controls (now terminated), and export controls, asserted by the United States, as the kinds of areas that might be regulated.

Indeed, it is the United States that often makes these assertions; this has caused concern, particularly in Canada, as well as other countries such as Argentina.[28] Seymour Rubin once wrote a letter to the New York Times that stated that attempts by the United States to impose its foreign economic policy on companies that, though owned by U.S. citizens, are national corporations of other nations, give rise to valid complaints by these nations.[29] Formerly the U.S. Cuban Asset Control Regulations were applied to foreign subsidiaries of U.S. corporations; this policy was not changed until 1975.[30]

Herbert Gray once proposed a code that would include renunciation of extraterritorial regulatory authority by home governments. Gray's code would contain the following elements:

1. recognition by home governments that foreign affiliates of their national firms are not, in principle, to be used as vehicles for the extension of their laws into foreign countries;
2. recognition by host states of their obligation to act in a fair and equitable manner (these terms would require definition) regarding foreign investment;
3. renunciation by any government that itself engaged in foreign direct investment, of any special rights, privileges, or status for that investment by virtue of its being made by or on behalf of a government;
4. provision of Most Favored Nation treatment to foreign investors, rather than national treatment. This would guarantee to investors from any country that signs the code that they would be treated no worse than firms from any other foreign country;
5. recognition of the right of host countries to fix rules that ensure adequate domestic control of their economies.[31]

Some of these elements represent the Calvo Principle. Moreover, on several occasions Canada has announced guidelines relating to the behavior of governments with respect to the competing assertion of jurisdiction. The United States now cooperates with Canada in the enforcement of its antitrust laws where these may affect Canadian interests.

Another approach, which is somewhat more conceptual, sees trade as regulated by the GATT, current monetary affairs regulated by the IMF, and international investment and multinational corporations regulated not at all; this suggests that the gap should be filled by an international organization. To some extent this is the approach implicit in this book.[32]

Yet another approach, to which I have already referred, seeks to deal with different international "systems," the operation of which relates closely to multinational corporations, especially within the parameters of activities in which we are interested. Reform of the IMF would fall into this class, as would suggestions for the further promotion and regulation of an international securities market. (See the second section of Chapter 1.)

ANTIPROPOSALS

There are a number of approaches to the problem that can be thought of as "antiproposals," in that they do not really suggest the creation of an international organization, although they do address themselves to the solution of the same problems as the proposals for an international organization. One approach suggests that since many of the issues associated with multinational corporations are not limited to multinational corporations, they should be handled on an issue by issue basis. Thus the problem of double taxation, with which international organizations have been concerned for over 40 years, should be considered as part of a continuing series of international tax issues. The tax issue has been addressed by the OECD and the UN. The OECD Committee on Fiscal Affairs has had over 20 working groups dealing with international tax problems. Significantly, the aspects that are relevant to the multinational corporation have been consolidated, at least administratively, into the OECD work on international investment and multinational corporations. Other issues would include antitrust, labor relations, and pollution control.

However, because of the political magnetism of the multinational corporation problem, the issues may increasingly be drawn into the multinational corporation field.[33]

Many of the developing countries that wish to do something about multinational corporations would distrust an effective international organization because it would not be fully under their control. They therefore have an interest in working individually or with groups of other developing countries on approaches to the solution of the multinational corporation that might not be called international control. They wish to improve their stance and their ability to conduct negotiations, which would be enhanced by more information about the multinational corporations. An international organization might gather information and also train officials, give advice, and send advisers and experts. Such action may be of even greater interest than some of the "symbolic" efforts at regulation.

THE SILENT MAJORITY

Many, if not most of the interested parties, including governments, international agencies, and academics as well as the companies, have said nothing about this kind of international regulation. Perhaps they believe that the present system is tolerable and should be left alone or that nothing can be done: one is reminded of Winston Churchill's observation that democracy is a bad system but that it is the best attainable.

Notwithstanding changes, this attitude may survive. The oil-producing countries, which have certainly engineered a major change, may feel that they can take care of themselves; conceivably, the members of the Andean group may feel the same way. It is possible that trade unions working through international secretariats may be able to protect their interests without further international governmental intervention, although this is questionable. The European Economic Community (EEC) may feel that it can protect the interests of its members sufficiently.[34]

NOTES

1. The proposed ITO foreign investment protection scheme is discussed in S. Rubin, Private Foreign Investment, Legal and Economic Realities 20-21, 82-83 (1956). The antitrust efforts are discussed in C. Edwards, Control of Cartels and Monopolies: An International Comparison (1967). Tax treaties are discussed in B. Bittker and L. Ebb, United States Taxation of Foreign Income and Foreign Persons 381-486 (1968).

2. With respect to codes for the protection of foreign investment, see Rubin, op. cit. With respect to proposals for multilateral investment guarantees, see H. Steiner and D. Vagts, Transnational Legal Problems 357-58 (1968). Henry Kissinger's Sept. 1, 1975 speech to the special session of the General Assembly of the United Nations suggests the creation of multilateral guarantees.

3. The relevant Treaty of Rome provisions are, Treaty Establishing the European Economic Community, March 25, 1958, 298 U.N.T.S. 11, arts. 52-58 (right of establishment), esp. art. 58, and arts. 67-73 (freedom of capital movements).

4. See C. Torem and W. Craig, "Control of Foreign Investment in France," 66 Mich. L. Rev. 669 (1968).

5. See for example, N. T. Wang, "Towards an International Code of Conduct for Transnational Corporations," paper presented to the Conference on the Nation States and the Transnational Corporations in Lesser Developed Countries in Aspen, Colorado, Dec. 13-18, 1974; G. Rueber et al., Private Foreign Investment in Development (1973).

6. Conversation with Philippe de Seynes, United Nations Under-Secretary-General for Economic and Social Affairs in Dusseldorf, West Germany, Jan. 6, 1973.

7. See Comm. on Reform of the International Monetary System and Related Issues (Comm. of Twenty), International Monetary Reform 13, 78-87 (1974).

8. J. Tinbergen, International Economic Integration (1954).

9. The London Times, Feb. 5, 1974, at 5, col. 4.

10. L. Brown, World Without Borders (1972).

11. See for example, J. Tinbergen, op. cit.

12. Richard Gardner suggests that a "survival bargain" be struck, with developing countries agreeing to assure access to energy and raw materials and to changes in their domestic policies such as population, and the developed countries agreeing to assure access to capital, management, technology, and markets, and agreeing to greater developing country participation in international institution decision making. R. Gardner, "Making a Safe Interdependent World," 177 Current, 15, 20 (1975).

13. See R. Cooper, The Economics of Interdependence: Economic Policy in the Atlantic Community (1968).

14. A. Buchan, Can International Relations Be Professed? 24-26 (1973).

15. J. Behrman, "Sharing International Production through the Multinational Enterprise and Sectoral Integration," 4 Law and Pol. Int'l Bus. 1 (1974).

16. The proposals of George Ball are set out in G. Ball, "Cosmocorp: The Importance of Being Stateless," 2 Colum. J. of World Bus. 25 (Nov.-Dec. 1967).

17. See Corporate Power in America (R. Nader and M. Green, eds., 1973).

18. Seymour J. Rubin has discussed both the Nader and Ball approaches in S. Rubin, "Corporations and Society: The Remedy of Federal International Incorporation," 23 Am. U. L. Rev. 263 (1973).

19. See the similar suggestion in L. Brown, op. cit., at 214.

20. Comm'n of the European Communities, Multinational Undertakings and Community Regulations 6-15 (Comm'n communication to the Council, Nov. 7, 1973).

21. See S. Rubin, "Multinational Enterprise and National Sovereignty: A Sceptic's Analysis," 3 Law and Pol. Int'l Bus. 1 (1971).

22. Int'l Chamber of Commerce, Guidelines for International Investment (1972).

23. See Bus. Int'l, Oct. 18, 1974, at 329.

24. "The Impact of the Multinational Corporations on the Development Process and on International Relations: Report of the Group of Eminent Persons to Study the Role of Multinational Corporations on Development and on International Relations," UN Doc. E/5500/Add. 11, Rev. 1-ST/ESA/6. New York Times, Oct. 27, 1975, sec. C, at 41, col. 8.

25. See N. T. Wang, op. cit.

26. See S. Rubin, "Multinational Enterprise and National Sovereignty," op. cit.

27. P. Goldberg and C. Kindleberger, "Toward a GATT for Investment: A Proposal for Supervision of the International Corporation," 2 Law and Pol. Int'l Bus. 295 (1970).

28. See J. Corcoran, "The Trading with the Enemy Act and the Controlled Canadian Corporation," 14 McGill L. J. 174 (1968); New York Times, Mar. 18, 1974, at 45, col. 8; Business Week, April 13, 1974, at 80-81.

29. S. Rubin, "Of Cuba and Our Foreign Subsidiaries," letter to the editor, New York Times, Mar. 13, 1974, editorial page.

30. 40 Fed. Reg. 47108 (Oct. 8, 1975) revoking 31 C.F.R. secs. 515.412, 515.541 and adding sec. 515, 559; see Wall Street Journal, Aug. 22, 1975, at 1, col. 2.

31. Canadian Government, Foreign Direct Investment in Canada 392 (1972).

32. See P. Goldberg and C. Kindleberger, op. cit.

33. See D. Vagts, "Multinational Enterprise: A New Challenge for International Law," 83 Harv. L. Rev. 739 (1970).

34. See The Conference Board, The Search for Common Ground: A Survey of Efforts to Develop Codes of Behavior in International Investment (1971).

CHAPTER 4 VALUES

There has been a flood of literature about multinational corporations, although to be sure this literature has not been limited to the core corporation or to activities within the parameters we have defined, and the portion of it that is specifically about international organizations is small. Indeed, there is increasing scepticism about the feasibility of an international organization and a growing opinion that nothing should be done or that national controls must suffice. At the same time, suggestions for international control continue to be made, and the literary background is relevant.[1]

The literature seems to reflect a confusion of moods, data, economic theories, political positions, government reports, proposals, investigations, and international agency pronouncements. Probably the sheer size and rapidity of the growth of multinational corporations is part of the explanation. The word "multinational" has not been carefully defined, and a large part of the literature relates to the impact of the multinational company on particular countries and sectors through foreign direct investment. Some of the literature is also related to international capital flow and movement.

As the discussion in Chapter 5 will bring out, there has been a paucity of relevant data and of relevant economic theory. This has underlined the lack of definition and encouraged variant views. In turn, because of its breadth and newness and the resultant controversy, the multinational corporation seems to have attracted every imaginable opinion and political position.

Much of the debate does not relate to the prospects for an international investment organization but rather to the underlying phenomenon of the multinational corporation. The literature about the prospects for an international investment organization is quite inchoate, as we have seen with respect to the proposals in Chapter 3.

Finally, there is no coherent U.S. policy with respect to multinational corporations or to foreign direct investment, whether inward or outward. However, this is also true with respect to other international economic problems, including oil, other raw materials, and the international monetary adjustment mechanism, although there does seem to be a consensus with respect to traditional free trade.

ARE VALUES RELEVANT?

The prospects for an international investment organization can be best understood in terms of the current international economic system and the international political system. The relevance of values in general is extremely difficult to determine, and I do not propose to supply a general theoretical judgment: each reader must provide his or her own.

The nation-state and the system of nation-state relations is the bedrock reality, though there are other relevant realities, such as the growth of population. The volume and direction of economic growth, and the way its product should be distributed represent extremely important questions, the answers to which clearly depend on values and ideas. For most of us the vitality of democratic institutions is extremely important, and social movements and the requirements of justice are relevant to our view of the international economy and the international political system. Our notion of human nature colors and shapes our ideas and our behavior.

How do values relate to the nation-state system? There are some, such as Charles de Gaulle, who have attempted to explain international relations almost entirely in terms of the calculus of nation-states and the promotion of their interests; yet the interests of nation-states often embrace values, as in the American ideals and the ideology of the Soviets. Other nations will view a nation-state in terms of values; thus the United States is seen as the font of much that is modern and much that is technological in the world. This perception reflects the values of those looking at the United States as well as those of U.S. citizens.[2] Values impinge on the resolution of the problems confronting the nation-state, which are discussed in Chapter 6, and on the state of the currently preferred international economy discussed in Chapter 5.

Thus, as the prospects for an international investment organization are measured by the international economic and political realities of the world, the extent to which these realities are conditioned by values will in turn bear on the prospects for the international investment organization, as well as on national and other policy toward multinational corporations in general.

I cannot hold with all of the values reflected in the literature on multinational corporations; for example, the apparent distaste sometimes shown for material achievement is quite beside the point. The world needs to continue to develop economically.

Some of the values expressed are not realizable in the foreseeable future. For instance, it would probably be useful to have a measure of international accountability for multinational corporations, but the world is not organized in a way that would make this possible.

Also, all the values reflected in the literature and proposals are not all equally important. They range from idealism to realism and from revolution to reform, and they vary according to the politics and philosophy of the individual author.

No classification of the values reflected in the literature and in the existing proposals for international investment organization can be provided here; indeed, no logical order is possible. Much of the literature and the values that it reflects are unrealistic in the sense that they do not realistically take into account the directions the world will take. This is probably more important than the question of what directions the world should take, since such preferences and ideas cannot have any effect. More specifically, they are unrealistic with respect to the probable evolution of the multinational corporation. Finally, to the extent that they bear on the prospect for an international investment organization, the values expressed in the literature do not seem to be very realistic at all.

NATIONALISM

What are some of the critical attitudinal factors with respect to both the multinational corporation and the prospect for, or tendency toward, international investment organization and international control? The principal factor probably is nationalism, which may take the form of resistance to multinational corporations and an international investment organization. It may favor national control of the local activities of the multinational corporation. This would mean host country control, which usually would be control by a developing country, although the experience in Canada and to some extent in Australia suggests that this is not always the case. Of course, Canada is a capital importing country, and its gross annual inflow of investment exceeds the outflow.

In this era of pronounced economic interdependence, some of this nationalist reaction may be unrealistic. Some of it is not especially economic or addressed to the multinational corporation but may represent, for example, resentment of U.S. power. As the predominant power, at least outside the communist world, the United

States will inevitably, because of policies pursued or not pursued, be blamed for the unsatisfactory aspects of the current situation. U.S. culture, which is different from many national traditional cultures but which is to some extent communicated by the multinational corporations, is resented in various countries in Latin America and Europe, for instance, as well as in Canada.

Similarly, there is resentment against European countries and their postcolonial policies, and this may be reflected in attitudes toward European-based multinational corporations. Some of the activities of the Organization of Petroleum Exporting Countries (OPEC) and of the Arab countries can be understood in these terms. There are similar feelings about Japan in parts of Asia. Also, as empires recede, former colonies, now often developing countries, assert themselves. The OPEC may be an example of this.

Much of the resistance to multinational corporations is not a resistance to an economic system as such but arises from the conditions of local geography and politics. This is reasonably self-evident to most people, although often exaggerated in the literature. Thus a fair number of Latin American intellectuals have elevated this relationship of international business to local conditions into a theory of "dependencia," in which peripheral societies, including Latin American ones, become dependent on central nations such as the United States and those of Europe in almost inevitable economic servitude. Needless to say, the multinational corporations are seen as instruments for maintaining this servitude.[3]

A now somewhat abated slight variant was offered by Jean-Jacques Servan-Schreiber, who suggested in the middle 1960s that if Europe did not learn from the management techniques of the U.S. multinational corporations, it was doomed to be subordinated to them. Servan-Schreiber made it clear that he believed that the European national cultures could not assert themselves and flourish unless they mastered these techniques.[4]

The outbreak of some resentment in the United States against Japanese investment in Hawaii, California, and the midwestern farm lands and against the threat of investment by the Arabs and Iranians certainly has nationalist elements, in the sense of resentment against foreigners or xenophobia. With respect to the Japanese and also the Arabs and Iranians, there has been no realistic prospect of their dominating any important element of our economy through direct investment in the United States, although the control exercised by Arabs and others over U.S. oil supplies overseas is of course another matter. The fact that Arab bloc investment was not contemplated by multinational corporations neatly separates out the nationalist element.

The problems of the contemporary nation-state, and the attempts by most states to regulate and influence their economies through the application of Keynesian and similar techniques, suggest another sort of nationalism, namely the economic nationalism of the planner or economic policy maker. This can sometimes take an anti-internationalist direction or tone.

This tone can also be shared by those advocates of "private enterprise" who object to any social control, whether national or international.

Those who believe in national control of the economy, particularly of the activities of local subsidiaries and branches of foreign companies, can be divided into at least two schools: the realists, who may believe that international control is unrealistic in the foreseeable future and therefore that if there is to be control it has to be national; and the socialists, who wish to use national control as a means of imposing their socialist values and who suspect that international control would be "capitalist" in its orientation. Watkins and possibly Muller may belong to this category.[5] One is reminded of the opposition since 1973 of the left wing of the British Labour Party to continued membership in the European Economic Community (EEC), which it alleged would hamper the ability of British socialists to impose their values in Britain in the face of the market-oriented and "capitalist" EEC Commission.

The activities of the Andean Common Market (ANCOM), and the OPEC and the EEC--the latter, especially, to the extent that it has responded to French influence--are in some ways analogous and reflect nationalist or regional values.

ANTIMATERIALISM

The second most predominant attitudinal factor in the literature is antimaterialism. This set of values is unrealistic in terms of the economic requirements of the mass of people, who require a materialist approach to world affairs, although some of the means that have been used in order to satisfy the material needs of the people have shown excess. Some of the antimaterialist literature is plainly romantic, reminiscent of the Luddites in the early years of the Industrial Revolution in England, who wished to destroy machinery because it was destroying traditional values.[6] With the increased weight of technological change this must be inevitable; after all, not all technological change is good. The romantic theme can sometimes combine with a Marxist one.

Related to this development is the recent emphasis on the "limits of growth," which reflects a just awareness of the limitations of our resources, which we have been consuming with accelerating rapidity. Much of the concern about the impact of industrialism on the environment is appropriate, as is the general concern about ecological balance; however, environmentalism seems to have attracted to it some of the excess of the zealot. Uncontrolled population growth represents ultimate disaster for our system and our values, but these pressures should not necessarily lead to an attack upon the multinational corporations, since they are productive economic instruments. Rather, environmental considerations should lead one to appreciate the enormous and increased importance of economic efficiency, which the multinational corporations at their best may exemplify.

Another related development is the "technology assessment" movement, which must be accepted to the extent that it advocates that technology should be more efficient and less inimical to the environment. However, where this movement advocates a slowdown in the development of technology that may assist us in the solution of our problems, it is necessary to object.[7]

To some extent, the resentment of U.S. culture, as exemplified by U.S.-based multinational corporations, is resentment of what is believed to be the materialist basis of our culture. Frequently this masks anxiety about the changes in familiar local traditional institutions that are brought about by economic and social change. This is sometimes easy to identify with the United States and its corporations because of their power and their prominence in the world scene. This attitude is highly evident in the literature that attacks or resents multinational corporations.

One could put much of this in a broad, long-term historical perspective. The most basic and abiding human developments are illustrated by the materialist and antimaterialist attitudes, which represent the ambiguity of human nature in society. Since the Renaissance, individual and collective human aspiration for earthly results has been encouraged, especially in the West, but now in most other societies as they have followed in the Western way. Science and the Industrial Revolution, which represent the application of rational and technical developments, have converted this into a massive aspiration for a good life for everyone, which finds its basis, if not its total fulfillment, in material and related social and political arrangements. As this development sweeps the developing countries, which have not previously shared very much in this post-Renaissance movement, the problems become many and acute. Modernization is desired yet resented, and the disturbance of the familiar and traditional is regretted. This dilemma is most acute in the more rapidly evolving developing countries as well as in Europe, where the U.S. presence can be fixed upon as an expression of the problem, and even in the United States, although different countries cope with this problem differently.

MATERIALIST CRITICS

A third school of critics of the multinational corporation is that of the materialists, in the sense that they believe in economic growth and development but object to the forms this growth and development has taken. One line of criticism is that of the labor unions, which believe that the multinational operation of companies gives them an advantage in collective bargaining in individual countries. To some extent this school hopes to develop an international countervailing force in the form of international union secretariats, although this has not made much progress. The movement in Europe for worker participation on boards of directors is somewhat related to this.[8] The union does not attack the basic materialist assumptions of the corporations.

The basic and most pervasive criticism of the multinational corporations may also be considered a materialist critique. This criticism is associated especially with the demands of the developing countries for a new international economic order. Basically what is called for is a redistribution of income and benefits from the developed to the developing countries. This is a cry for social justice or a greater international egalitarianism. It can be joined with a domestic egalitarianism that would redistribute income and other benefits within a given society, while internationally this movement may emphasize the redistribution of income among nations. Whether these two developments are compatible is another matter, since the pressure for redistribution within a nation-state may cause that nation-state to attempt to enlarge its national economy to meet the domestic problem, which may very well run counter to a redistribution from that nation to another. For instance, in the United Kingdom the Conservative Party followed a growth policy as a way to cope with pressures for redistribution within the country. However, a British growth policy is not necessarily compatible with a redistribution of the income and wealth of the United Kingdom to developing countries, unless of course the total economy of the world continues to grow rapidly. This in turn runs into some of the antimaterialst values which we have already mentioned.

The redistribution of income among nations is certainly related to the assertion of the developing countries that we have already called a nationalist phenomenon. Whether this pressure is applied to the multinational corporation appropriately is another question. The ability of the multinational corporation to redistribute wealth among nations, not to mention classes, is limited, and such redistribution will depend on the domestic policy of individual nation-states and the formulation of international policy by nation-states.

Another line of thought in this area is the eternal tension between "order" and "freedom"; the individual asserts himself and yet needs social order. In domestic politics this can take many forms, with individualism, private enterprise, free speech, and other forms of self-expression in opposition to social control, governmental regulation, governmental authority, and governmental legislation. In the international setting the attitudes range from laissez faire, which allows governments and multinational corporations to do whatever they wish, to controls on both.

The best known materialist critique is that of Marxism. In its traditional form this critique postulates the necessity of material achievement to satisfy human want; in this respect it is very different from the romanticism of Charles Reich.[9] It holds that the present arrangements for the production and provision of material, and indeed other, goods is distorted by monopoly capitalism and similar evils.

One could speculate endlessly about why the intellectual class of the world so often seems to be leftist and why it is so conscious of the injustices of the world and of life, although today the intellectuals themselves are generally reasonably prosperous. S. Huntington suggests that the intelligentsia have no interest in the status quo or in fixed arrangements of society, although they have an interest in the intellectual examination and criticism of society.[10]

The last group of materialist critics can be called the "anti-oligopolists." Many of these are economists who are not necessarily leftist. Those who take seriously the notion of Adam Smith that perfect competition with many competitors, preferably small in scale, is possible, inevitably believe that the organization of markets around a small number of large corporations is a distortion, and they tend to think that this has been brought about by corporate malevolence. There is a kind of romance here: although these critics tend to be materialists in the sense that they believe in the inevitability of economic activity, they are nevertheless unrealistic. Some of this line of thinking is evident in U.S. antitrust reasoning, while others believe that oligopolies are not only inevitable but potentially beneficial, bringing innovation through competition supported by large resources, laboratories and the like. The late Steven Hymer was a leftist anti-oligopolist who wrote suggestive analyses of the multinational corporation.[11] Joseph Schumpeter is often associated with the view that oligopolistic competition is more innovative than competition among smaller units.[12]

THE ACCOUNTABILITY MOVEMENT

Accountability is associated with domestic consumerism and similar developments of the late 1960s and early 1970s. It has realist and nonrealist components and is essentially materialist in its orientation. It is a reform movement, although it is not always clear what purpose the reformers seek to serve. In the United States, Ralph Nader and Campaign GM are associated with this movement, as well as attempts to get social issues on proxies or to change the composition of corporate boards. The corporate democracy movement, which would suggest that boards be held responsible by their shareholders, is only partially relevant, since the shareholders of a particular company may not and probably will not reflect the greater social concern.[13]

In his writings on the U.S. corporation and the corporate form in general, Willard Hurst, an excellent legal and economic historian, has stressed the need of a corporation to establish its legitimacy in the eyes of the various groups with which it deals. He finds that legitimacy rests in a combination of utility to those whom the corporation serves and accountability to the domestic society. This is probably the basic strand in the accountability movement, both domestically and internationally. There has been some suggestion that there should be social as well as financial audits and accounting. The frequently repeated suggestion that there should be more information about multinational corporations is generally intended to making a greater accountability possible.[14]

The accountability movement has run into difficulties in particular countries. Unfortunately, at the international level there is a further difficulty because of a lack of suitable international machinery to enforce corporate accountability, not to mention a lack of agreement about the social values that would determine exactly what the purpose and content of that accountability would be. To some extent this problem besets the proposals of George Ball that are mentioned in Chapter 3.[15]

THE STATUS QUO

Support for the status quo may represent an intellectual position or a confluence of practical factors. The basic position that underlies the status quo group would be that the existing system works as well as any other; this is the Churchillian position.

To some extent this is reinforced by the inertia that results from the delicate balance of existing and competing forces, but there is more to it than that. Many liberal economists, seeking the most efficient allocation of resources, believe that the most effective mechanism available is free trade and the associated free movement of capital, which they increasingly think of as part of free trade. They object not only to government barriers to trade but also to private barriers to free trade and capital movement; thus many of them believe in the antitrust law approach to economic regulation and object to discriminatory exchange rates and other artificial payments barriers. For them the right sort of an international investment organization, one promoting an open economic system, might be desirable.

Some economists have sought to document the actual beneficial effect of foreign direct investment on particular economies. For someone with the same beliefs as C. Kindleberger, this does no more than document the rational working of a global economy.

Another line of economic reasoning holds that the system has been successful and that criticism of the multinational corporation represents a "failure of success" that would occasion an even stronger attachment to the present system.

Another group of economists believes that the present situation should be left alone; that legislation or legalistic regulation at the international level is neither wise nor feasible, and that any human intervention should take the form of macroeconomic policies. Here we have a mixture of inertia with a belief in the invisible hand and a definite antibureaucratic bias.[16]

There are those who make almost a virtue of the status quo. Among them are the internationalist romantics who believe that the multinational corporation will break down the nation-state system and contribute to a genuinely international world. Again, there are those who believe in economic interdependence as such, possibly because of political and other benefits they expect from it. There is a group that believes not only that the multinational corporation will change the world but that it already has, and that we now have a more "transnational" form of international politics.

A related group, which one might almost call the "apologists" for international corporate activity, believes that the multinational corporation contributes to an international economic prosperity and efficiency which would otherwise be unavailable. There are those who feel that, in order to assist the developing countries by the provision of technology and even a redistribution of income benefits, the multinational company must be left untrammeled. George Ball sometimes reads like an apologist.[17] Lester Brown has written about the advantages for the developing countries.[18]

It is difficult to determine whether the status quo position represents a realistic position. It is probably more realistic than promotion of a comprehensive and strong international organization. On the other hand, the status quo changes daily, and there have been movements toward national control and away from a pure laissez faire system, in both the domestic and international economy, for a very long time.

ORDER OF PRIORITY OF VALUES

I have suggested a few of the values evident in the literature and in the proposals that have been made with respect to multinational corporations and their regulation. I believe that the nation-state, and nationalism in various forms, will remain preeminent in the future. The next in preeminence will be the push for economic growth, materialism, and modernization. Internalism or "UNism" seems at present to be in a rather precarious state in some of the western countries, especially in the United States. This precarious situation combines with an antibureaucratic feeling, all of which tends to indicate that it will not be possible to institute a strong international investment organization, although at the same time there is pressure against the concentration of private economic power and a desire for accountability, which is not inconsistent with private economic activity or economic efficiency. Unfortunately, international accountability is unlikely in the late 1970s. Therefore, in terms of these widespread values and ideas, I do not see a real possibility for a strong international investment organization in the foreseeable future. This will be brought out by a more detailed discussion of the present international economic and political systems as well as by a further consideration of the demands of the nation-states. Most nations do not have a coherent foreign investment policy, not to mention a policy directed toward formation of an international investment organization.

The antirational antitechnological values cannot survive, although the demand for greater social justice must continue. Untrammeled laissez faire cannot survive, yet there will be a preference for openness in the world, both as a value and as an operating procedure. The crunch will come if economic growth slows down while egalitarian pressures continue, although these latter pressures need not be inimical to the efficiency or the basic integrity of multinational corporations and international investment.

NOTES

1. See, for example, D. Burtis et al., _Multinational Corporation--Nation State Interaction: An Annotated Bibliography_ (1971); L. Nehrt et al., _International Business Research, Past, Present and Future_ (1968); OECD, _Foreign Investment and its Impact in Developing Countries: A Special Annotated Bibliography_ (1968); S. Lall, _Foreign Private Manufacturing Investment and Multinational Corporations: An Annotated Bibliography_ (1975).

2. C. Bohlen, _Witness to History, 1929-69_ (1973).

3. See, for example, O. Sunkel, "Big Business and 'Dependencia': A Latin American View," 50 For. Affairs 517 (1972).

4. J. J. Servan-Schreiber, *Le Defi Americain* (1967).

5. M. Watkins, *Foreign Ownership and the Structure of Canadian Industry* (1968); R. Muller, "The Political Economy of Global Corporations and National Stabilization Policies," Paper presented to the Assoc. for Evolutionary Economics, Annual Meeting of the Allied Social Sciences Association, in San Francisco, California, Dec. 28, 1974.

6. See, for example, M. Thomis, *The Luddites; Machine-breaking in Regency England* (1970).

7. I. Kristol, "The Environmentalist Crusade," Wall Street Journal, Dec. 16, 1974, at 14, col. 4.

8. See, for example, C. Levinson, *International Trade Unionism* (1972); C. Levinson, *Industry's Democratic Revolution* (1974).

9. C. Reich, *The Greening of America* (1972).

10. S. Huntington, *Political Order in Changing Societies* (1968).

11. S. Hymer, "The Efficiency (Contradiction) of Multinational Corporations," 59 Amer. Econ. Rev. Papers and Proc. 441 (1970).

12. J. Schumpeter, *Capitalism, Socialism, and Democracy* (1950). For an example of an author who does not share this view, see J. Galbraith, *The New Industrial State* (1971).

13. See, for example, B. Manning, "Shareholder's Appraisal Remedy: An Essay for Frank Coker," 72 Yale L. J. 223 (1962).

14. See J. Hurst, *The Legitimacy of the Business Corporation in the Law of the United States, 1890-1970* (1970). For a discussion of social responsibility see E. Dodd, "For Whom are Corporate Managers Trustees?" 45 Harv. L. Rev. 1145 (1932); E. Rostow, "To Whom and For What is Corporate Management Responsible," in *The Corporation in Modern Society* (Mason, ed., 1959). Compare S. Rubin, "Multinational Enterprise and National Sovereignty: A Skeptic's Analysis," 3 Law and Pol. Int'l Bus. (1971).

15. See also S. Rubin, "Corporations and Society: The Remedy of Federal International Incorporation," 23 Am. U. L. Rev. (1973).

16. See, for example, J. Dunning, *The Role of American Investment in the British Economy* (1969); M. Steuer et al., *The Impact of Foreign Direct Investment on the United Kingdom* (1973); D. Brash, "United States Investment in Australia, Canada, and New Zealand," in P. Drysdale, *Direct Foreign Investment in Asia and the Pacific* 95 (1972); A. Safarian, "Perspectives on Foreign Direct Investment from the Viewpoint of a Capital Receiving Country," J. Finance, Papers and Proceedings 419 (1973). Outward investment studies are also plentiful. See, for example, W. Reddaway, with S. Potter and C. Taylor, *Effects of U.K. Direct Investment*

Overseas, Interim Report (1967) and Final Report (1968). C. Kindleberger, American Business Abroad: Six Lectures on Direct Investment (1969). Compare R. Vernon, Sovereignty at Bay: The Multinational Spread of U.S. Enterprises (1971).

17. See G. Ball, "Cosmocorp: The Importance of Being Stateless," 2 Colum J. of World Bus. (Nov.-Dec. 1967).

18. See L. Brown, World Without Borders (1972).

PART II

RELEVANT NATIONAL AND INTERNATIONAL REALITIES

CHAPTER

5

THE CURRENTLY PREFERRED INTERNATIONAL ECONOMY

In spite of the fact that concern about oil and other resources has eclipsed other international economic concerns, there remains an underlying international economic reality and a fairly coherent set of international economic preferences; notwithstanding the surface turbulence. There are some who believe that we are undergoing a historic crisis like that described by Ortega y Gasset.[1] An open world economy is still largely preferred; we have seen this frequently during the oil and petrodollar crises.

The underlying economic reality consists of an economic system and certain institutional and legal norms that relate to certain practices in trade and to monetary affairs. To a degree these norms are exemplified by the principles and operations of the International Monetary Fund (IMF), and the General Agreement on Tariffs and Trade (GATT). Changes are taking place in the international economy, and not all have been fully perceived. The basic "internationalization" of production that is associated with multinational corporations, the multi-state assembly of products, and many other developments have not been so widely perceived as they might have been. We have already seen that the Bretton Woods system did not provide institutions to deal with international capital movements, multinational corporations, or internationalization of production. The proposals and initiatives described in Chapter 3 have been put forward to repair this omission. No truly coherent and precise parameters have been developed for the multinational corporation or the international investment process in which we are interested. The discussion must therefore commence within a broader context.

The expression "currently preferred" will be used instead of "current," since we do not have an entirely open or integrated and interdependent global economy. Significant government barriers or government policies exist that can be described as protectionist. The nationalism of the age is apparent, and it is the affront to this nationalism posed by the multinational corporations that has caused the problem. Notwithstanding such nationalism, the prevalent intellectual mode and current national and international policy lean toward an open and international economy. Indeed, national "protectionism" is often a reaction to this. Because it is far from wholly effective, I prefer to call it the "currently preferred" rather than the "current" international economic scheme.

Many present norms and current preferences have arisen out of, or have been reinforced by, the Bretton Woods system established at the end of World War II. In turn, the Bretton Woods system was built upon economic theories and policies that are associated with the theories of free trade and international trade, which go back at least to Adam Smith. Notwithstanding the trouble the system has undergone during the 1970s, it is fair to say that the system has worked well, since it has delivered an enormous volume of goods and services, much of it stimulated by international exchange. Needless to say, there are enormous problems in the distribution of these benefits in the international economy and within the various domestic economies.

The system has been built up from policy preferences; national government policies; international institutions; and a series of agreements, rules and norms, all of which have sought to promote international economic exchanges that include trade, investment, and financial movement. Despite the oil crisis, the petrodollar recycling problem, and the recent increase in demands for reform made by the developing countries, these policies still seem to prevail. At the international level, policies have often leaned toward a laissez fair or pure-market system.[2]

The international economic system is not presided over by central economic organizations, whether they be taxing authorities, central banks, or budgetary bodies. Instead it is a mixture of market forces and sporadic national policy and international action. Recent examples are partially institutionalized national consultations by some governments through the OECD, or special efforts such as the International Energy Agency and the Financial Support Fund, or so-called safety net, to assist the petrodollar recycling process. International discussions continue with respect to food and other subjects. The principal exceptions to this generalization are the IMF and the GATT.

INTERNATIONAL MONETARY FUND AND THE GENERAL AGREEMENT ON TARIFFS AND TRADE: INSTANCES OF THE CURRENT PREFERENCE

Although they are both concerned with important aspects of the international economy, neither the IMF nor the GATT deal directly with the problems caused by international investment and multinational corporations. These institutions reflect the economic preferences that were current at the time of their creation, and in the manner that they survive to the present day, they reflect current preferences. The operation of the IMF has been changed to some extent since the Smithsonian Agreement of 1971, and while further reform has been discussed certain principles embodied in the original and current articles of agreement have survived.

The basic principle of the IMF, as of other international institutions such as the GATT and the OECD codes, is the pressure for the "liberalization" of national controls. In the case of the IMF this is applied to current monetary transactions by moving countries from Article XIV (where restrictions on payments and transfers are permissible) to Article VIII status (where currencies are convertible and such restrictions are not permitted). In general, nations are not to adopt new restrictions with respect to current account payments and transfers if they are to stay in the good graces of the IMF. Despite the Smithsonian Agreement, this policy continues.

Another policy that continues is that against discrimination. Nations are not to have multiple exchange rates, which is to say they are not to discriminate among the different nations who are their trading partners.

The final basic principle might be called a minimum standard. Until 1971 nations were to have fixed par rates that they were not to change, except in limited circumstances, without IMF approval. This formal system has broken down, and it is this breakdown that people often have in mind when they speak of the breakdown of the Bretton Woods system. At the present time we have so-called floating rates, although in consultation with the IMF; and indeed, close to 60 percent of countries, mostly developing, still have fixed rates. IMF Article VII, section 3, contains the provisions with respect to multiple rates and nondiscrimination. The fixed-rate system then in effect imposed a minimum standard. At the present time there is a system of international surveillance, which is an important feature of the IMF system. The notion of a minimum standard is important to international lawyers.

GATT embodies principles similar to those of the IMF, the corner stone of which, the most favored nation principle, bars discrimination among different countries. The periodic tariff negotiation rounds called for by the GATT represent a basic policy of liberalization of national controls over trade. GATT prohibitions such as that against quantitative restrictions or quotas represent a clear minimum standard.

The process of liberalization and the other policies have not worked in all areas. Tariffs have been reduced more substantially in the industrial than in the agricultural area. Developing countries, through trade preferences, now seek at least a temporary exception to the most favored nation principle. Nonetheless, the general policy and effect of the GATT is clear. The new multilateral trade negotiations, the so-called Tokyo round, will carry this further. They may very well further extend GATT principles to nontariff barriers and to nonindustrial areas. The national treatment provision of the GATT is another nondiscrimination provision.

The various treaties of friendship, commerce, and navigation that the United States has entered into with various countries, many since World War II, and similar treaties among other countries, also apply the most favored nation and national treatment standards to trade and investment.

The IMF deals basically with money, trade account, and the adjustments that countries must make if there is to be equilibrium in those areas. This affects international investment and multinational corporations in a number of ways. For instance, pressure on a country's balance of payments that arises from trade may be shifted to investment. Presumably a smoothly working adjustment mechanism would remove some national pressures from investment, although the money and multinational corporation problems have probably been unduly confused. Some of the movements of short-term capital, or hot money, that occurred under the fixed-rate system prevailing before the Smithsonian Agreement were excessively blamed on the multinational corporations.[3]

Multinational corporations do hold in their treasuries large sums of money, although not all of this money is liquid or available for transfer to different currencies. Under the fixed-rate system, defensive movements were made by the corporations to protect their positions. Other actors, such as banks, central banks, and governments, probably were more active on a large scale, and the multinational corporations have largely been exonerated.[4]

The "gap" in the IMF articles with respect to capital movements is such that, when under balance-of-payments pressures, countries are free to control capital in situations in which they might not be free to control current account. The attempt in the late 1940s to create an international trade organization, which would have contained restrictions on national action with respect to investment, failed. Governments have been free to impose national controls on capital, investment, and multinational corporations; and they have done so, although they have met with resistance.

SOME NATIONAL CONTROLS

Possibly because economic theorists, and also the IMF, have been more concerned with current account, or possibly for other reasons, the history of national controls with respect to capital movements is poorly documented, although some documentation has been done in recent years. The motive and operation of national controls has often been ambiguous. The foreign direct investment controls exercised by the United States between 1968 and 1973 for balance-of-payments reasons did not in fact prevent foreign direct investment overseas, since it remained possible to borrow funds abroad. Similar controls imposed by the United Kingdom at various times seem to have had the same effect. The impact of controls on inward capital movements has not always been clear; for example, some controls imposed for balance-of-payments reasons may in effect have been used to bar foreign direct investment and the consequent creation of foreign controlled business. Some French controls may have been of this kind. Recent suggestions in the United States that Arab and Iranian, and previously Japanese, investments be regulated or barred, did not have balance-of-payments motives; on the contrary, the United States would like to have the foreign exchange, but what has been feared is the foreign control. The basic distinction seems to be between balance of payments or exchange controls on the one hand and investment controls on the other.

At various times Germany and Switzerland have imposed controls on inward movement of capital. In the case of Germany, which welcomes foreign direct investment and foreign business, it is clear that the reason has been to dampen domestic inflation and balance-of-payments effects, that is, to prevent an excessive foreign exchange surplus.

Because they are IMF Article XIV countries, developing countries, which have extensive exchange controls, many on current account, impose controls on inward as well as outward capital movements for balance-of-payments and investment reasons.

For investment and business reasons the Japanese have in the past imposed controls on inward investment in order to avoid foreign business participation in their economy. At the same time, they have imposed inward and outward controls for balance-of-payments reasons.

The investment legislation in Canada and Australia resembles that of developing countries, with the explicit purpose of controlling foreign business participation in their economies.[5]

The OECD codes impose, subject to the relevant derogations and reservations, limitations on OECD members' controls with respect to both inward and outward capital movements, whether for exchange or investment reasons; it is not always easy to disentangle the motivation behind particular capital controls, however. Some controls seem to be imposed explicitly for exchange reasons; an example of this is the divided foreign exchange markets that Belgium has sought to maintain with respect to current and capital account. Many observers believe that the separation cannot be effective, and even that it is difficult to control capital movements, whether inward or outward, given free movement on current account as mandated by the IMF.[6]

THE CURRENT PREFERENCE IN THE INTERNATIONAL INVESTMENT AND MULTINATIONAL CORPORATION AREA

In Chapter 7 the relevant treaties and international agreements will be discussed as they apply to the international investment and multinational corporation process. In this chapter it will be useful to discuss those instruments that have emerged to fill the gap left by the IMF in implementing the current preference for an open world economy. One of the original purposes in establishing the International Bank of Reconstruction and Development (IBRD), or World Bank, at the end of World War II was to revive and strengthen capital markets and the movement of private capital. The function of the World Bank has shifted almost entirely to the financing of infrastructure in developing countries, albeit in part with funds raised in private markets. Presumably this infrastructure has facilitated some private investment in developing countries, as also have the activities of the International Finance Corporation (IFC), the sister institute of the IBRD, which finances private projects in developing countries. Another arm of the IBRD, the International Center for the Settlement of Investment Disputes (ICSID), has as its ultimate purpose, through facilitation of the resolution of investments disputes, the promotion of private investment. However, ICSID has not yet finally adjudicated a dispute. While the IBRD has probably contributed more to the movement of private investment than it has discouraged, its activities are now limited to developing countries and its exact impact with respect to private capital movements would be hard to measure. It does not regulate such movements in any way.

There have been suggestions that the IBRD should, in effect, certify the fairness of foreign direct investment deals in developing countries. The bank has resisted this suggestion, although, like other lending agencies such as the Agency for International Development (AID), the IBRD probably does pass on the fairness of the private deals it finances. The IBRD does not finance many private deals; the IFC, which does, considers fairness to some degree. The IBRD has canvassed the possibility of a multilateral investment insurance agency, but this has not made much progress. At an earlier stage it considered the possibility of an investment code much like the Abs and OECD codes.[7] It is too early to say how effective ICSID will be in promoting the investment climate of the developing countries that are its members.

The Treaty of Rome, which established the European Economic Community (EEC), calls for complete freedom of movement for capital and related services; as a legal matter this has kept at least intra-European investment open. The network of treaties of friendship, commerce, and navigation that has been entered into by the United States and many other countries often provides for freedom of establishment and protection against expropriation. The OECD codes also push in this direction. All these instruments reflect the currently preferred system, with its predisposition to openness and freedom of movement and its resistance to national control. Unfortunately, their coverage does not extend to all countries. The provisions vary from country to country; some allow for reservations and derogations. At best the development is not complete.

THE UNDERLYING INTERNATIONAL ECONOMIC THEORY

In relation to economic theory, the most relevant basic intellectual field seems to be that of international trade. Much more of the theoretical writing on foreign direct investment in multinational corporations has been built on trade theory than on the international monetary theory, which deals directly with money, the adjustment mechanism, and the balance of payments. In this there is a certain irony, insofar as the IMF, which is the custodian of international monetary matters, seems to have been more important in the development of the post World War II economy in which the multinational corporations have flourished than the GATT, which is the custodian of international trade matters.

The apparent difficulties of the multinational corporation and investment flows may be blamed on the fact that the most fully developed theory deals with trade and to a lesser extent with money flows, rather than with international investment and multinational corporations. The reasons for this are not difficult to find; they are rooted in history.

The basic principles of international theory are built on the basic factors of production; of land, which includes natural resources; of labor; and of capital. Of these, only capital has been thought to be mobile, and there have always been assumed to be, and still are, restrictions on it.

The Euro-dollar market has provided much greater mobility than the earlier, more isolated national capital markets of Europe, many of which were quite small in contrast with the large capital markets in New York and London, which were fairly accessible to foreign borrowers and investors, subject to interest-rate differentials, exchange risks, and taxes.

It has been suggested that capital is industry specific, and that money which is available for investment in a particular industry is not freely available for investment in all other industries.[8] Labor was always thought to be immobile in spite of the mass immigrations, including the present migration of "guest workers" to Germany and "illegal aliens" to the United States.

Since the factors of production were thought to be largely immobile, trade among the several national economies was supposed to optimize the allocation of resources among them and thus maximize the global welfare. The theory of comparative advantage was adduced, to suggest ways in which that trade might be conducted for the greatest benefit. Trade within a large national market is to some extent akin to trade between national markets, although a national market would be subject to a national government, taxation, and budget.[9]

Economists and civil servants dealing with economic matters in the developed and also in the developing countries, having been educated in this theory, tend to accept its prescriptions; for them it is the preferred system. To have free trade, we must have an open system, free of government restrictions. Were we to attain this system, an equalization of all factor prices, including the price of labor, which is to say, of income, would follow.

Unfortunately, economists tend to ignore what I will refer to in the political setting as the "Lockean chasm," by which I mean the difference between a domestic economy and an international economy. In both economics and politics, the difficulty is that nations relate to each other in a way that is different from the way individuals do. This has many consequences, one of which is government measures that distort what might otherwise be the effects of free trade, with the result that resources are not allocated in the best possible way on a global basis. Nations are not usually prepared to accept an optimal allocation of resources if they can obtain more for themselves instead. International trade theory, which is derived from a domestic economy model, does not fully grapple with this problem, although the currently preferred economy is the open system based on free-trade ideas.

Liberal economists tend to think that such a system will also maximize economic development in each country. As for income distribution effects, they believe that government policy, which in a sense is arbitrarily imposed on the otherwise perfectly working economy, can take care of this.[10]

The process of international investment and multinational corporations confounds the assumptions of international trade theory, which are based on the essential immobility of relevant factors, whereas the process is based on substantial mobility of capital, management, and production. The multinational corporation depends on free movement of raw materials, capital goods, other goods and services, but the final product may be produced locally, and not actually traded, exported, or imported. The process suggests new factors, including management and technology, that do not neatly fit into the simpler versions of international trade theory. Besides this gap in traditional trade theory, there is also a gap or paucity of information.[11] The lack of information makes it difficult to completely develop the theory, and at the same time the gap in the theory has to an extent contributed to the gap in the information.[12]

Although traditional international trade theory does not deal fully with international investment and multinational corporations, inevitably it would lean toward a preference for free capital movement and freedom for international corporations. This is true because the theory advocates (1) optimization of the allocation of resources, which arises from the free play of market forces; (2) increased mobility of factors, which increased competition can only enhance; (3) government intervention only as a second or third best choice; and (4) free trade. It carries a built-in objection to bureaucratic controls, either national or international. The only theoretical construct that it has developed with respect to investment is the so-called optimal tax, which is analogous to the optimal tariff.[13] The optimal tax, which is a rather minor device, would compensate for interest differentials that would not exist in a perfect economy. This is to be distinguished from the issues associated with normal income taxation, such as tax neutrality or equity.[14]

Traditional trade theory has developed no principle that would justify the national or international control of long-term capital movements that an international investment organization might comprehend. Nonetheless, economists recognize that a belief in free trade does not necessarily entail a belief in free capital movement, although the reasons may not be wholly clear. One reason may be the simple historic fact that traditional trade theory did not fully focus on international investment and multinational corporations, which have had their greatest development since that time. More and more editorial writers and rigorous economists include free international investment and multinational corporations within their free-trade preference. Cairncross suggests that free capital movement is not inevitably entailed by free trade.[15] The reason for this is the greater political resistance to free capital movement, partly because of the greater visibility of the foreigner, the presence of foreign people, the greater intrusion of foreign life styles, and the sense of domination by foreign corporate headquarters that are established on a more permanent basis than would be the case with exports.[16]

I do not believe that an absolutely open system with no national controls is necessary to preserve the essence of the process. Opinions about the essential core of the process may also change. For example, more and more companies accept joint ventures with local private and state partners. Production sharing and work contracts replace concessions in the oil industry. Contracts for technological and engineering services are accepted by some companies in lieu of equity investment.

While no coherent theory appears to have been developed as part of international trade theory to explain the process of international investment and multinational corporations, a number of theoretical explanations have been put forward, and there has been a great deal of writing, pro and con, about the benefits of foreign direct investment and capital movement, both inward and outward from a national economy.

Part of this theory is associated with capital movements and with money seeking its maximum return. As we move toward foreign direct investment as associated with management and control, we encounter theories related to the growth of the firm. More generally there are theories that suggest that all economic factors seek a maximum return when given the opportunity to do so, such as Raymond Vernon's writings with respect to the product cycle[17] and to the suggestion that corporations invest abroad to preserve their market share within an oligopoly structure. Yair Aharoni has also written about the various elements, both rational and otherwise, that enter into the foreign investment decision process of individual companies.[18]

Numerous attempts have been made to fit the multinational corporation into these theories, although many of them would apply to any foreign direct investor. The multinational corporation is seen as having a monopoly, whether permanent or short lived, on certain technology or on the combination of technology and the personnel to utilize it; or a monopoly with respect to a differentiated product market or in certain scale advantages with respect to a mixture of such factors as capital, personnel, and markets. In my view none of these theories is fully persuasive, and some are too academic.[19]

The multinational corporation, using the corporate legal or a comparable form, can combine the dynamism of the entrepreneur with the facilities of large accumulations of capital and exploit economic opportunities on a scale that others cannot, thereby gaining a competitive advantage.

Eric Stein has referred to the corporation as the "central institutional device for large scale organization of energies and resources" in the modern world.[20] Seymour Rubin has written the following about these corporations:

> The preoccupation of the owners, organizers and managers of multinational enterprises, or those of enterprises aspiring to a multinational or transnational state, is fairly clear. They seek, in general, more and more profitable business. They seek sources of raw materials, efficient production, and secure markets. They look for profits; and the closer the after-tax income can remain to the pre-tax earnings, the better they like the situation. They therefore expand abroad to protect their positions in the industry, or to get into and establish industrial production or access to raw materials. They seek to deploy their technology, capital and managerial skills profitably. In so doing, they look for corporate advantages. These may be tax or other concessions: utilization, to the extent that increasingly sophisticated tax collectors still permit, of base companies in tax havens, low cost labor, etc. In the search for optimum profitability, they establish transfer prices which benefit the enterprise as a whole, increase production at efficient plants and slow down or close inefficient ones. They act as responsible businessmen whose job is to produce effectively, and hence, to benefit their shareholders.[21]

Some of the writing about multinational corporations seems almost apologist; the dynamism of the corporations, however, is unmistakable.

From country to country there is widespread debate about the impact of foreign direct investment, especially inward, and the multinational corporation, and the literature on the topic is vast. On one side it is argued that the multinational corporation brings in capital; creates jobs, provides a continuous flow of technology that would otherwise be unavailable; and supplies management, entrepreneurship, access to foreign markets, and the demonstration effect of skills on local suppliers, customers, and competitors. On the other side are cited undue foreign exchange costs, truncation of local economies, a branch-plant mentality, frustration of local research and development, imposition of alien consumer tastes, and suppression of local competition and entrepreneurs.[22] R. Vernon, incidentally, suggests that the net balance-of-payments effect on the host country, including that arising out of savings from import substitution and export earnings, may be slightly positive, although he admits the equivocal nature of the issue.[23]

It is sometimes said that foreign direct investment is not a zero sum game, that it assists both the investor and the host country, contributing to a dynamic process of growth, the benefits of which exceed normal economic calculations. In Keynesian, but global, terms, the multinational corporation as investor promotes the economy and sustains the multiplier effect on a global basis.

THE LIMITS OF ECONOMICS

Overwhelming though the economic arguments and preferences may be, multinational corporations trouble many people. Even exports and imports are often resisted by unions and others; and in the case of local subsidiaries of foreign corporations, the foreign presence is more visible. There are more individual foreigners present; a foreign style is in evidence; and there is the feeling that decisions important to one's own country are being made abroad. Liberal economists, the relevant civil servants, and sophisticated politicians accept the arguments for international investment and multinational corporations and for free trade and free capital movement, but they cannot ignore local objections, some of which they may share. The corporate process is one thing; but the individual multinational corporation and its subsidiaries may be another.

In Canada the U.S. presence is so overwhelming that the basic cultural nationalist feelings are aroused. In developing countries one hears the old infant-industry argument: free trade and free capital movement will kill native industry in the bud and thus deprive the developing countries of the ultimate benefit of free trade and free capital movement, based on a comparative advantage that can only be realized by protecting infant industry. There are those who put local social and cultural requirements and national autonomy above economic benefit, even though that benefit may assist the nation in the long run; one might think of this as Gaullism, although the French have accepted a fair amount of foreign direct investment in order to develop their own industry.

We are left with the Churchillian phenomenon: free investment, relatively free foreign direct investment, and multinational corporations all have drawbacks, but the alternatives may be worse. Thus the process of international investment and multinational corporations is accepted within the currently preferred open global economy.

AN INTERNATIONAL INVESTMENT ORGANIZATION

The spread of multinational corporations continues. There are countervailing national measures, but the corporations seem to be able to survive them. No one is certain what form a reformed International Monetary Fund might take. Trade negotiations have begun that may include modification of the GATT. It is hoped that the Bretton Woods system, revived and refreshed, will survive. Not much thought has been given within the system to the need for an international investment organization to preserve the benefits of the preferred open system, even for the multinational corporation.

NOTES

1. J. Ortega y Gasset, *Man and Crisis* (1958).

2. See for example, R. Cooper, "Towards an International Capital Market," in *International Investment* (J. Dunning, ed., 1972). R. Caves, "International Corporations: The Industrial Economics of Foreign Investment," in *International Investment*, op. cit. at 265. H. Johnson, "The Efficiency and Welfare of the International Corporation," in *International Investment*, op. cit. at 455.

3. *Implications of Multinational Firms for World Labor and Investment and for U.S. Trade and Labor: Report to the Committee on Finance of the United States Senate and its Subcommittee on International Trade on Investigation No. 332-69, under sec. 332 of the Tariff Act of 1930*, at 531-46 (Comm. Print 1973).

4. Ibid.

5. A. Cairncross indicates the paucity of the literature in A. Cairncross, *Control of Long-Term International Capital Movements* 81-86 (1973).

6. See, for example, M. Cordon, "Protection and Foreign Investment," Econ. Record 209 (1967).

7. See H. Steiner and D. Vagts, Transnational Legal Problems (1968); S. Rubin, Private Foreign Investment, Legal and Economic Realities (1956).

8. R. Caves, op. cit., at 265, 267.

9. R. Cooper, The Economics of Interdependence: Economic Policy in the Atlantic Community 49-110 (1968).

10. See, for example, R. Caves and R. Jones, World Trade and Payments: An Introduction 561-64 (1973).

11. See, for example, A. Safarian and J. Bell, "Issues Raised by National Control of the Multinational Corporation," 8 Colum. J. World Bus. 7, 19 (Winter 1973); J. Dunning, The Determinants of International Production (1973).

12. With respect to the "factors" involved in international investment and multinational corporations, see Z. Hirsch, "Multinationals: How Different Are They?" in La Croissance de la Grande Firme Multinationale 91 (G. Bertin, ed., 1973).

13. See, for example, O. Carreau, "The Interest Equalization Tax," 2 J. World Trade L. 47, 54 (1968).

14. See R. Caves, op. cit.; A. Cairncross, op. cit.

15. A. Cairncross, op. cit.

16. See Wash. Post, Oct. 10, 1974, sec. A at 14, col. 1.

17. R. Vernon, Sovereignty at Bay (1971), p. 65.

18. Y. Aharoni, The Foreign Investment Decision Process (1966). See also R. Aliber, "A Theory of Direct Foreign Investment," in The International Corporation: A Symposium 17 (C. Kindleberger, ed., 1970); E. Penrose, "Foreign Investment and the Growth of the Firm," in J. Dunning, op. cit., at 243; J. Stopford and L. Wells, Managing the Multinational Enterprise: Organization of the Firm and Ownership of the Subsidiaries (1973); P. Drucker, "Multinationals and Developing Countries: Myths and Realities," 53 For. Affairs 121 (1974); C. Kindleberger, American Business Abroad: Six Lectures on Direct Investment (1969).

19. See, for example, H. Johnson, op. cit.

20. E. Stein, Harmonization of European Company Laws, National Law Reform and Transnational Coordination 75 (1971). Compare J. Hurst, The Legitimacy of the Business Corporation in the Law of the United States, 1890-1970 (1970).

21. S. Rubin, "Multinational Enterprise and National Sovereignty: A Skeptic's Analysis," 3 Law and Pol. Int'l Bus. (1971). Drucker, op. cit.

22. For literature treating the benefits, see R. Vernon, Sovereignty at Bay: The Multinational Spread of U.S. Enterprises (1971); J. Dunning, op. cit. note 2, at 377. D. Brash, "United

States Investment in Australia, Canada, and New Zealand," in Direct Foreign Investment in Asia and the Pacific (P. Drysdale, ed., 1972); A. Safarian, "Perspectives on Foreign Direct Investment from the Viewpoint of a Capital Receiving Country," J. Finance, Papers and Proceedings (1973). For literature dealing with disadvantages, see C. Vaitzos, "Bargaining and the Distribution of Returns in the Purchase of Technology by Developing Countries," in Underdevelopment and Development 315 (H. Bernstein, ed., 1973); M. Watkins, Foreign Ownership and the Structure of Canadian Industry (1968).

23. R. Vernon, op. cit. at 172-78.

CHAPTER

6

THE NATION-STATE AS MANAGER OF THE NATIONAL ECONOMY

Is national sovereignty really at bay? Is the nation-state in its position of management of the national economy really threatened? I think the answer to these questions is no.

Conditions are difficult for the nation-states. The modern economy, with its deliberate investment decisions by society, and the rise of the welfare state, with its expectations, impose domestic pressures on the state. At the same time, economic interdependence imposes external pressures. These pressures are not always easy to reconcile.[1]

FUNCTIONS AND PRETENSIONS OF THE NATION-STATE

The principal functions of the nation-state are not economic, but cultural. Nations field athletic teams. They are the social arenas in which values are resolved. As such, they have gained in importance as religions have declined, as empires have expired, and as subnational groups have remained repressed.* Society is policed by nation-states. Nation-states are conservative forces. They galvanize pride, patriotism, and loyalty in a way that no multinational company, without the history, continuity, prospects, or range of activities of a nation, can do. Nation-states provide external defense against other nation-states. In the face of the 1973-74 oil embargo, each nation-state sought its own oil supplies.

---

*Great Britain, if sufficiently determined, will probably survive the Welsh and Scots; Canada will probably survive the French and English Canadians.

Traditions of mercantilism, of a trade surplus for each nation-state, survive. Even within the European Economic Community, each nation tries to secure its own access to raw materials and its own markets, and to have its principal industries in its own hands; cross-border mergers have been fairly rare.

On top of this basic nationalism, a structure of national economic decision making is now superimposed in almost all countries. This probably has an additional, inevitably nationalistic effect. I refer to the kinds of economic policy associated with John Maynard Keynes, his disciples, and his rivals. Almost all modern nations have moved, in one degree or another, from a policy of domestic laissez faire to a degree of conscious and social state intervention in the economy, although the same may not be the case with respect to their international economies. This contrast is the source of the tension between governments and international business. Briefly, all governments now pursue policies that restrain business cycles in order to minimize unemployment, stabilize and increase incomes, and further other social and economic aims. Governments use a number of measures to attain these ends; these include tax, budgetary, and monetary policies. For many countries, trade policy and the operation of foreign exchange rates is also vital. Above all, as Keynes made clear, the maintenance of the overall investment level in the economy is crucial.[2]

Some states are more interventionist than others. The French have been thought to favor a dirigiste approach, in which the government, the unions, and businessmen consciously and periodically work out investment levels and directions. Possibly for cultural reasons, but also because of such necessities as the need for securing an access to markets and raw materials, the Japanese are thought to use "administrative guidance" more than most countries. The developing countries that seek to accelerate their economic growth almost all use economic plans of one kind or another. In the United States and the United Kingdom there is more talk of economic planning than formerly. The Soviet Union and many other countries have resorted to state ownership of industry and other economic activities. All these developments encourage the state, which is one of the repositories of nationalism as a rule, to seek to control the economic fate of the national society.

INTERDEPENDENCE

I have referred to the development of economic interdependence in Chapter 1. The flourishing of the multinational corporation has merely been a part or manifestation of this broader development.

Someone has described the corporations as big fish in a sea; nevertheless they are visible, concrete, and more permanent than other aspects of international economic exchange. In fact, they have themselves become vehicles of this exchange, which was created by the Bretton Woods system and by rapid technological developments in transportation, communications, and computation.

The exact degree of interdependence is debated. The rise in the volume of exports and imports has had an effect on domestic competition, incomes, prices, and other policies; this rise has made exchange-rate policies important. It can be argued that the shift from fixed to floating rates produces interdependence, although governments do not permit a wholly free float. The argument over exchange rates is an argument about a mechanism intended to achieve equilibrium in a situation of underlying interdependence. The problem of access to supplies, whether petroleum or commodities, and the need for foreign capital that has been induced by development policies are two examples of this. In the case of the more developed countries, the open Bretton Woods system has led to a closer relationship among the capital markets. This has also led to increased mobility of funds shifting from market to market because of changes in interest rates. Multinational corporations themselves, with their related activities in various countries, accelerate the interrelationship of economies. Tourism is a minor, although not negligible development. The increased universalization of material standards is certainly relevant, as is the desire in each country for the latest technology, no matter where the technology has been developed. The developing countries want to share in this system; hence their need for capital and technology and their desire for the foreign aid and other assistance that contribute to this. Although I would not be prepared to state that the nation-state system has been transformed into a transnational system, multinational corporations have transformed the possibilities of domestic economies, and the fact is that interdependence is considerably increased.[3] Seymour Rubin has referred to multinational corporations as fish in a sea of interdependence.[4] R. Muller goes so far as to suggest that the emergence of multinational corporations had made it impossible for nation-states to pursue traditional economic policies.[5]

PROBLEMS PRESENTED BY INTERDEPENDENCE

There is no question that increased economic interdependence presents problems for governments, especially in their role as post-Keynesian managers of the domestic economy, usually of the welfare state variety. These have been the subject of much literature. One need only think of the problems of the United Kingdom, a deficit country; of West Germany, a surplus country; of Japan; of any number of developing countries; and of the United States itself. There are the problems of the balance of trade, of the terms of trade, of access to resources, of the balance of payments, and of the adjustment mechanism. Fixed rates bring short-term movements of capital. The floating rate must be managed or reserves found and husbanded. All are aggravated, indeed by definition almost created by international economic exchange. The freer movement of capital makes it more difficult to use the interest rate as a means of managing the domestic economy; this has been discovered by Germany and other countries. When interest is raised in order to dampen the economy, it attracts foreign capital, which stimulates the economy instead.[6] The greater mobility of labor can make economies more dependent on foreign workers. Examples of this are Germany with its guest workers and the United States with its illegal aliens.

The multinational corporation should be seen as part of this pattern of interdependence. There are many who think that multinational corporations complicate matters. It has been suggested that, during times of threatened devaluation under the fixed exchange rate system the multinational corporations have aggravated the movements of short-term capital. Multinational corporations are blamed for plant closings and said to have adverse effects on employment, although this seems relatively minor when compared with the large number of jobs "created" by the multinational corporations when they have moved abroad and employed local labor. Trade unions in the home countries of multinational corporations suggest that this represents the "export" of jobs; others suggest that there is a net creation of jobs in both home and host country.

The practice of transfer pricing, with its many supposed consequences, which is made possible in some cases through the existence of tax haven countries, is often cited as an evil of the multinational corporation. However, this is a relatively minor aspect of the operation of multinational corporations and is incidental to the economic activity they create. It can be regulated by appropriate tax laws and possibly by discouragement of the tax havens that are permitted by certain countries.

Some groups in developing countries believe that multinational corporations represent a threat to their traditional values; to a large extent, however, the corporations are just a small part of the general process of modernization that many developing countries are undergoing, this process being an aspect of the increased interrelatedness of all countries today.[7] It may be that multinational companies do affect values in the developing countries to some extent, although they are subject to the economic plans, laws, and regulations of each country.

AMBIGUITIES

Most governments are of two minds about multinational corporations: this applies as much to home countries as to host countries. Host countries criticize multinational corporations and foreign direct investment, but at the same time many of them provide incentives to attract them. They wish to exercise control over their own domestic economies, but at the same time they wish to derive the benefits of international trade and international economic exchange. The purpose of both is to enhance the living standards of their people. This ambiguous situation does in fact impose limits on the complete freedom of choice of governments, in that they must be prepared to make trade-offs.

National economies vary widely in their degree of openness to the world. Completely closed economies have become extremely rare. The Soviet-bloc countries increasingly engage in trade and even joint ventures with non-bloc foreigners. Burma and one or two other countries are fairly closed to the world's economy. Nicholas Katzenbach has suggested that the multinational corporations present political rather than economic problems to the nation-states; he believes that nation-states can cope with multinational corporations and derive all the benefits they wish without having to pay any unacceptable cost.[8]

All national economies, whether closed or open, are confronted with the necessity of making these choices. Which trade-offs will be made will depend on how certain economic goals are valued, how great the desire for modernization is, and how the nation-state decides it is to be achieved. Different groups within the society, and especially its elite groups, will have different views about this.

DEFENSES AVAILABLE TO STATES

Nation-states, if they behave sensibly and realistically, can handle the problems of the international economy. They need not panic, but they must decide what they want; this may be difficult, given the different interests that exist within a country. In light of the development under the Bretton Woods system, it appears that most nation-states will not wish to seal themselves off from the current global economic system. Many of the Communist countries have increasingly involved themselves in the open economic system, although there are newly communist countries, Viet Nam for example, that have not. The People's Republic of China has avoided this entanglement to a large degree. There are other countries that will do so also. The pressure of developing countries for reform and for a new international economic order does seem to presuppose participation in the global economic system if only on more advantageous terms.

A developing country can certainly resist many external economic pressures if it wishes to do so, although there are limits imposed on the freedom of the nation-states because of the fact that the world economic system is rather open and competition among the states for the world's resources, markets, and goods is toughening. For example, the government of Turkey has a very cautious attitude toward foreign direct investment, consumer imports, and tourism.

A nation-state can deal with multinational corporations if it wishes. I am thinking not only of the power of a group such as the Organization of Petroleum Exporting Countries (OPEC), but also of the power of an individual national state. It is not merely legalistic to suggest that multinational corporations, certainly in all aspects of their local operations, are subject to the jurisdiction of the host state and that the host state can exercise such jurisdiction. It is not merely weakness, corruption, or confusion that prevents many nation-states from doing this, but simply the fact that they are not as well organized as they should be. The crux of the problem lies in the ambiguity that surrounds the multinational corporation, that is, the ambiguity related to a nation's participation in the open world economy. I am not an apologist for the individual multinational corporation, but I do believe that many of them are in fact the "good citizens" they claim to be. The multinational corporations are large, visible, and subject to frequent domestic criticism. It is likely that their tax-paying records in most host countries compare very favorably with the tax-paying records of local companies.

Local officials and planners can handle many of the "threats" perceived to be created by the multinational companies they have invited into their countries. To some extent they can regulate the consumption patterns induced by the multinational company; in many cases they actually wish to foster these changes, which is of course why the corporations were invited in. Existing international organizations and bilateral arrangements can handle other problems, such as that of extraterritoriality. Interestingly, one of the assertions of U.S. economic regulatory power that has bothered some developed countries has been the antitrust laws, which are pre-Keynsian devices for regulating the economy. (See Chapter 8.)

If the alternative to nation-state jurisdiction is a sense of panic and an inability to control events, governments can impose capital controls. The United States has imposed its foreign direct investment controls and Canada its Foreign Investment Review Act; Switzerland and Germany have imposed controls on the inward flow of short-term capital, which was feared to have an inflationary effect; the developing countries have imposed their foreign investment review machineries; and other countries have imposed state-control mechanisms. I am not arguing for or against these, but merely pointing out that they are available and in fact have been used and that there is no indication that the multinational corporations need overwhelm individual nations. The tax incentives and tax havens that governments provide are largely voluntary. Without tax havens the abuse of transfer prices would not take place easily. If nations wish to impose laws that make it difficult for a local employer, whether part of a multinational enterprise or otherwise, to close their plants, they can do so; though the economic cost may ultimately be a high one. Mergers and takeovers, especially by foreign companies, bother many governments, and a nation can prohibit or control them.

Although tax incentives are voluntarily offered, it may not be easy to withdraw them, though many governments, including, for example, Indonesia, have modified such incentives downward. Incentives are sometimes offered by provincial governments, even in the face of central government objections. Also, within the EEC certain governments wish to offer incentives that the EEC would like to discourage. The OECD is examining this question. Transfer prices are a much-debated subject; not enough is known about them.

In the simple taxing situation of an investment in Country A with remittance of profits to Country B, a tax credit system in Country B, given a tax rate in Country A that does not exceed that of Country B, eliminates the desirability of artificial transfer pricing. There may be management, and other, reasons for this practice; local custom duties may have an effect. International guidelines might be useful in this area. (See Chapter 10.) With respect to mergers and takeovers, it can be argued that certain mergers are less desirable on an international basis than others are. Thus the acquisition of the French company Machines Bull by GE or Minneapolis Honeywell may be more acceptable, in terms of global competition, than its acquisition by IBM. The French, however, would see this issue from a different perspective.

THE POSSIBILITY OF "EXCESSIVE" NATIONAL CONTROLS OF THE INTERNATIONAL INVESTMENT AND MULTINATIONAL CORPORATION PROCESS

I do not wish to underestimate the difficulties that international economic exchange and multinational corporations may present to certain countries at certain times. Unquestionably there is uncertainty and the risk that governments may "overreact," which raises the question of whether there is a risk of excessive national control. To national control might be added regional controls if the Andean Pact and the EEC are considered. The first impact of these controls, especially the Andean ones, has been a reduction in foreign investment. To the extent that such investment is beneficial it is possible that the benefits of interdependence are lost and local peoples hurt. The question is, to what extent is the process of international investment and multinational corporations hurt by national controls. The companies have shown considerable flexibility in adapting themselves to local requirements, whether they be local majority control, hiring of local personnel, use of local components, or a shift from an equity to a contract basis. Different companies in different home countries have different interests, whether it be access to supplies, market shares, or profits or merely the case of a dynamic company and restless management looking for new opportunities. While individual subsidiaries in individual countries may be hurt by national controls, a single multinational corporation, multinational corporations as a group, and therefore the process of international investment and multinational corporations would only be hurt by the simultaneous rise of excessive controls with respect to a number of major markets. It would be at this point that companies might wish to retaliate and seek to persuade their home governments to retaliate on a major basis as well.

The extraterritorial assertion, principally by the United States, of economic regulatory laws has led to retaliation by other governments.[9] Examples that are often cited include legislation passed by Ontario that is designed to prevent companies that are subject to its jurisdiction, which include Canadian subsidiaries of U.S. companies, from delivering documents to U.S. authorities without Ontario approval; this was provoked by the assertion of the U.S. antitrust laws. The pending Canadian corporation law contains a similar provision. The United Kingdom and the Netherlands have passed similar provisions applicable to antitrust, shipping, and other investigations. Canada, Argentina, and other countries have been involved in the application of U.S. export controls to local subsidiaries of U.S. companies. A dramatic example is the case of Societe Fruehauf v. Massady, in which the French subsidiary, although controlled by the U.S. parent corporation, was freed by the French court from the operation of U.S. export controls.[10]

It is highly unlikely that the sum total of national and regional controls will become such that companies will not be able to survive them, given at least the ambiguous appeal of international economic interdependence and the multinational corporations themselves for a majority of governments. One possible analogy has been the OPEC, but it can be argued that the OPEC merely seeks to obtain a larger share of the benefits of an economically interdependent world for its own members. It is true that some of its actions have severely shaken the fabric of the international economy; yet that effect was probably not intended; OPEC was testing the limits of its power. I do not believe that OPEC is particularly against the multinational corporations, in this case the oil companies. The OPEC members and the other oil-producing countries have sought a larger share of the international income and also participation in the local crude extraction companies. However, international investment and multinational corporations may have an increasing effect on the petroleum market, quite apart from the fact that the oil companies can pass along increased oil prices and profit from the inflated levels in the oil industry.

If national controls really began to hurt the multinational companies, their governments might retaliate by endorsing a strong international investment organization such as that which I referred to in Chapter 1. However, before taking this action the governments would think in terms of unilateral, national retaliation.

There are some precedents for this. The United States has used the lure of its market for Japanese exports to induce Japan to open itself to foreign direct investment, but the process has been a slow one. So too, Canada must be aware that its exclusion of U.S. investment must inevitably affect U.S. policy toward Canadian imports and other economic interests in the United States. French exclusion of some U.S. investment has offended the United States, although on the whole France has been reasonably free in allowing U.S. companies to operate in France. Expropriation by developing countries has led to the Hickenlooper Amendment to U.S. foreign aid legislation and to similar laws with respect to sugar quotas and U.S. votes in the World Bank and other lending agencies. This was a congressional and not an executive initiative and has not been applied very much. Even if this amendment were applied to U.S. foreign assistance, which the United States thinks of as an act of largesse, the attitude would not be the same about barring inward investment from foreign countries. The countries that are likely to restrict U.S. multinational corporations are not the same ones that would be the home countries of multinational companies coming into the United States. There may, however, be reciprocity with respect to the Arabs, Iranians, and Venezuelans, which are sources of some capital, with our interest in investing in their countries.

Fred Bergsten and J. J. Boddewyn have suggested that there would be investment wars, that is, retaliatory restraints on outward and inward investment,[11] but it is hard to see how these would come about.

NOTES

1. A. Cairncross, Control of Long-Term International Capital Movements 1 (1973).

2. With respect to trade policy and exchange rates see R. Cooper, The Economics of Interdependence: Economic Policy in the Atlantic Community (1968); J. Behrman, National Interests and the Multinational Enterprise: Tensions Among the North Atlantic Communities (1970).

3. For discussions of the degree of interdependence that has actually been achieved compare R. Cooper, op. cit.; K. Waltz, "The Myth of National Interdependence," in The International Corporation: A Symposium 220 (C. Kindleberger, ed., 1970); R. Keohane and J. Nye, "Transgovernmental Relations and International Organizations," 27 World Pol. (Oct. 1974). See also R. Keohane and J. Nye, Transnational Relations and World Politics (1972), with respect to the emergence of a transnational system.

4. In conversation with the author sometime in 1975.

5. R. Muller and R. Barnet, Global Reach: The Power of Multinational Corporations (1974).

6. See R. Cooper, op. cit.; J. Behrman, op. cit.

7. With respect to the closing of plants, see J. Behrman, op. cit.; also Comm'n of the European Communities, Multinational Undertakings and Community Regulations 7-15 (Comm'n Communication to the Council, Nov. 7, 1973).

8. N. Katzenbach, "The Realistic Prospects for Political Integration and Organization of Developed Countries Related to Investment," in International Control of Investment 66 (D. Wallace, ed., 1974).

9. P. Goldberg and C. Kindleberger, "Toward a GATT for Investment: A Proposal for Supervision of the International Corporation," 2 Law and Pol. Int'l Bus. (1970); J. Corcoran, "The Trading with the Enemy Act and the Controlled Canadian Corporation," 14 McGill L. J. 174 (1968); New York Times, Mar. 18, 1974, at 45, col. 8; Business Week, April 13, 1974, at 80-81.

10. Societe Fruehauf v. Massady (1968) D.S. Jur. 147 (1965) J.C.P. II 14, bis (Cour d'appel, Paris), 5 Int'l Legal Mat'ls 475 (1966).

11. F. Bergsten, "The New Economics and U.S. Foreign Policy," 50 Foreign Affairs 199, 204-07 (1972); J. J. Boddewyn, "EEC Policies toward U.S. Investors," Moorgate and Wall St. Rev. 44, 62 (1973).

CHAPTER

7

THE CURRENT INTERNATIONAL POLITICAL SYSTEM AND THE CURRENT LIMITS OF INTERNATIONAL LAW AND ORGANIZATIONS

I will briefly review some aspects of the international political system and also of international law and organizations, especially as these relate to the process of international investment and multinational corporations. Although cooperation among the Western industrial nations and Japan, and also between them and the developing countries, has probably increased since World War II because of the operation of the international economy and the threats posed by the Soviet Union, there are still very definite limits to the extent of cooperation possible. Basically this is because of the manner in which the nation-state system, which is the bedrock of the current international political system, operates. It is important to be reminded of this in considering the prospects for an international organization in the area of international investment and multinational corporations. The nature of the international political system inevitably imposes limits on the possibilities for international law and for international organizations. An international organization exists at the sufferance of the nation-states that are its members, and this imposes a confederal maximum on international organizations. Though they can coordinate national policy, international organizations cannot create their own policy and impose it on nations. There is a continuum of degrees of cooperation among nation-states, whether within international organizations or otherwise. The nations may be moving slowly along that continuum, but they have not gone far or progressed rapidly. With respect to an international investment organization, there are not only the inevitable limits of the confederal maximum, but also the limits imposed by the difficulties associated with the substantive problems that such an organization would seek to regulate.

THE CONFEDERAL MAXIMUM

To the extent that law, whether in treaty or customary form, is tougher on a nation-state, being more exactly spelled out and binding, the limits on it will be even greater than those on an international organization, which to some extent can be thought of as a weaker substitute for law in which final agreement on specific norms is postponed and things are left to be worked out.

One of the basic principles of the international political system that are relevant to international organization and law is the "Lockean chasm," by which is meant the profound distinction suggested by John Locke, that although domestic society is largely subject to the rule of law, the relations among societies, or nation-states, resemble a jungle and are subject basically to the rule of force. This observation presupposes that the independent nation-state is the bedrock of the current political system; I do not believe this can really be disputed.

Raymond Aron has spoken convincingly about the operation of this nation-state system. Nation-states are uncertain about their relationships with other nation-states, and within this uncertainty they seek to survive and to defend their essential interests, as they perceive and define them; they also seek advantage with respect to other nation-states.[1] Although this concept is normally applied to the political, military, and diplomatic relations among states, it also applies to economic relations. Some of the basic economic relations are the grist of political relations. Wars have been fought, and diplomacy practiced, in order to gain access to land and resources. To the extent that the international economy is perceived by a state as securing its essential interests, the state will behave toward it in a predictable manner.

How might this concept be applied to multinational corporations? To the extent that multinational corporations enable the home state to secure its essential economic interests, the state will behave toward them as it behaves toward the more traditional instruments of state power. Beyond this point things become more complicated. The basic national identity of multinational corporations can still be determined, and whether or not the corporation's chief executives are citizens of, or loyal to, such particular nation-state, such nation-state will continue to exercise jurisdiction over the multinational corporation as if it were national. A home country may wish for inward investment in order to provide "hostages" and a sense of reciprocity with foreign host countries as well as to provide the basic economic benefits of inward investment. It may also believe that the free operation of the international economy is basically beneficial to itself and its allies. This is the mid-1970s position of the United States.

Although the operations of multinational corporations are complicated, we have not reached the stage at which the basic nation-state system has been transformed by the multinational corporations into a transnational system in which the corporations have become independent centers of power, beyond the control of nation-states. This is a complicated point. Many countries as a matter of policy wish to preserve the independence and autonomy of their economic sectors. Furthermore, in the United States there is the belief that sovereignty resides in the people. To some extent the economic sector is in alliance with the needs of the people, rather than with the concerns of the state. If states wish to exercise power over multinational corporations, they are in a position to do so, as was shown by the events associated with the oil crisis. Even where companies are flexible, are able to act autonomously, and can make independent contacts with foreign governments, this does not alter the basic position that the system is a system of nation-states that can exercise control over all private actors, to the extent that they wish or need to.

The fact that a Swedish company, Ericsson, was able to get a contract from the British government in 1974 for telephone equipment, in opposition to British companies, by lobbying with the unions representing the workers in the United Kingdom does not indicate that this transnational operation has upset the basic nation-state system as it applies to relations between the United Kingdom and Sweden, between their respective societies, or among any other nations, societies, or companies.

A fair appraisal of the operations of existing international organizations will bear out the confederal maximum principle. Thus a fair reading of the history of the General Agreement on Tariffs and Trade (GATT) and the International Monetary Fund (IMF) suggests that while these specialized agencies have achieved much, they have done no more than their members wished to do. This has been evident in specific measures dictated by their members. It has been true in the case of the GATT, which resolves disputes by means of special working groups that in effect mediate and conciliate, and in the case of the IMF, which has over the years resorted to such devices as the General Agreement to Borrow (GAB), the Committee of Ten, the Committee of Twenty, and other devices reflecting the interests of its most powerful members. This is equally true of other specialized international agencies of the United Nations. N. T. Wang, an influential staff member to the Group of Eminent Persons, suggests that no more could be expected of an international organization in dealing with multinational corporations.[2]

There are a number of organizations, in both the military-political and economic areas, that deserve special mention: the

International Energy Authority (IEA), the European Economic Community (EEC), the Andean Pact, and the Organization of Petroleum Exporting Countries (OPEC). The accomplishments of these organizations show that governments can cooperate closely if the interests in question are important. The IEA, which was developed after the oil crisis of 1973-74, is, in the rather narrow area of petroleum supplies an economic analogue to NATO; it is an economic defensive organization. The EEC, which is thought of as a successful international organization, is a grouping of a limited number of countries that is most effective in limited economic areas.

The EEC has been most successful when it has limited itself to the technical and confederal, rather than when it has moved toward the political and federal. This bears out the suggestion made in 1946 by David Mitrany that international organizations will be much more likely to succeed at the technical and confederal level, rather than the political and federal.[3]

It is too early to see whether or not the Andean Group will be successful. The OPEC seems to have been successful, but it may be no more than a higher form of the confederal maximum. The OPEC secretariat does not impose decisions on the member governments; on the contrary, the more powerful member governments determine the policy of OPEC. Therefore the confederal maximum is the furthest that international organizations have gone on the continuum of cooperation. Divisions between developing and developed countries do not override this basic nation-state fact: the blood of like-minded nationals is thicker than the water of like-minded countries. Most people realize that nation-states are more quick to resort to diplomatic negotiation than they are to third-party adjudication, as in the International Court of Justice or the International Center for the Settlement of Investment Disputes. Governments claim almost exclusive jurisdiction over their own nationals and do not allow other governments, or international law, to intervene.

INTERNATIONAL LAW: THERE IS NO DISTRIBUTIVE JUSTICE

The limitations of international law, in this as in all areas, are merely confirmation of the limits of the nation-state system. This is especially obvious with respect to international investment and multinational corporations, for which very little law has been developed. The paucity of international law in arbitrating among the nation-states is in itself a confirmation of the limitations of the system. To the extent that there is international law, its limited extent may be seen as a further confirmation of this: there is no international government, welfare state, tax, or budget; the normal attributes of a governmental or legal system are not present. Many jurisprudentialists and jurists would suggest that a key to law is acceptance and that force is not necessary as a means of sanction. Nonetheless, acceptance depends on an ultimate and credible international sanction.

It is more difficult to get law accepted, whether in the form of custom or treaty, than it is to raise support for an international organization, though the latter will also require a treaty for its establishment. Because of the required agreement on particular rules and norms, an international organization might also be a truer test of the nation-state system. We have seen that international organizations work under the rule of confederal maximum. The world is nowhere near the framework and order Max Weber posited as necessary in order to minimize the risk and uncertainty necessary to induce regular behavior, for nation-states, individuals, or multinational corporations in the international setting. The proliferation of international agreements and treaties must always be examined in terms of their actual effectiveness before new areas are projected from them.

States, their foreign offices, and their legal advisors and legal staffs are aware of international law and are to some extent guided by it.[4] International institutions may well be creating a more cooperative attitude, going beyond the prior, defensive structure of international law.[5]

Possibly most crucial for our purposes is the fact that internationally there is no agreement with respect to the standards of distributive justice, as there is in some domestic societies. Redistribution of income and other benefits does not take place voluntarily even in domestic societies, but it does come pursuant to the political process. It might be argued that the OPEC oil price increase was an effort at redistribution, although to a limited number of countries with a relatively limited population with disparate internal social structures. Both the manner of the increase, that is, the absolutely rudimentary nature of the isolated step that was taken, and the result, which has been a possible reduction of living standards among the poorer classes in industrial countries and in the developing countries, plus an increase in the living standards of sheiks and of the upper classes in certain countries, reflects the almost total absence of any mechanism or set of standards for distributive justice in the international setting. The Lockean chasm is often overlooked by those who think of the world in global terms: most citizens of most countries do not think very far beyond national borders when thinking of their economic interests. The world is not a consolidated balance sheet in the minds of the people or of the leaders of their countries.

MULTINATIONAL CORPORATIONS AND INTERNATIONAL INVESTMENT

Just as there is no standard of distributive justice in international law, so the multinational corporation is not a legal reality. International law is too undeveloped to deal with this subject; moreover, the multinational corporation is new. Essentially the nation-states enact laws and regulations with respect to issues, some of which touch the multinational corporation. To my knowledge there are very few national laws referring to multinational corporations as such, although this is beginning. Thus the Trade Act of 1974 imposes certain antidumping duties on multinational corporations.[6] The multinational corporation is not yet become much of a legal concept or category.

What, then, is the relevant international law? International law, at least public international law, is the law that limits nation-states. If we begin the process of international investment and multinational corporations, in legal terms, with entry into a particular country and carry it through to long-term security of the resulting investment, the law is slight. In fact, the multinational corporation, like other non-state actors, is not technically a subject of public international law. This is a subject of some debate.[7] Multinational corporations have entered into investment agreements with governments that call for the application of international law.[8] There is also a problem in private international law, or conflicts of law, with respect to which national law would apply. The European system revolves around the question of the location of the siege sociale.[9]

There are additional structural problems. Typically, international law does not govern the relations between nations and their own nationals. As a result, there can be no international law with respect to the relationship between the multinational corporation and its home state. To the extent that subsidiary corporations are deemed to be nationals of the host state, this would also be the case with respect to the relationship between the local subsidiary and the host country.

The sole exception is of cases in which the law has viewed the nationality of the shareholders of the subsidiary as relevant, thus bringing the subsidiary within the rules that govern the responsibility of a state for injury to aliens. In fact, this is the only body of public international law that has been relevant to multinational corporations. This body of law deals only with a fraction of the process of foreign direct investment and multinational corporations, that is, with protection against expropriation, repudiation of contracts, and like acts. Even in this area the law has been only moderately developed, and it is not gaining strength.

Under this body of law a state is entitled to espouse the claims of its nationals against other states and treat them as injuries to itself. However, it requires that the local judicial remedies be exhausted in the state committing the alleged injury. Technically, once the state has espoused the claim of a corporation of which property has been expropriated by a foreign government, that claim becomes the legal claim of the espousing government and ceases to be the claim of the multinational corporation. In practice, the multinational corporation would presumably benefit from the espousal of the claim, to which international law might be applied. In cases in which the relationship between the multinational corporation and the host country is covered by a concession, by another investment agreement, or by a local investment law calling for adjudication or arbitration under international law, then a similar claim might be applied.

This law, as it relates to the taking or expropriation of property and to the repudiation of contractual arrangements, appears to be in a state of decline. Many developing nations, while accepting the existence of a body of international law, do not accept the key standard of prompt, adequate, and effective compensation with respect to a taking of property, although many would subscribe to the view that a taking should not be discriminatory, that is, that it should apply equally to foreign and domestic property owners. Even the Supreme Court of the United States, in the Sabbatino decision, found, for technical "act of state" reasons, that a U.S. court should not review the adequacy of the compensation for, or the legality of, a taking of U.S. property by a foreign government.[10]

It is this at least temporarily declining area of international law that has given rise to the model of a minimum standard, no discrimination, and possibly procedural due process.

There has never been much customary law with respect to the ongoing operations of a company, although treaties of friendship, commerce, and navigation do sometimes provide for most favored nation and national treatment with respect to the administration of local antitrust and other laws. Similarly, there has been no customary international law with respect to the right of entry, and therefore nations have been completely free to bar foreign nationals from their economies. Treaties of friendship, commerce, and navigation and similar treaties (there are few between industrial and developing countries) very often provide for national treatment with respect to entry and establishment of new companies. The Treaty of Rome explicitly provides this national treatment for the member states of the EEC, and the OECD codes, to the extent that they are not derogated or reserved, do provide considerable restrictions on member governments that affect the financial operations of companies.

However, these restrictions have not been enforced as private rights in courts but rather are seen as restraints on governments.

Cutting against customary international law protection with respect to expropriation and repudiation of contracts is the Calvo doctrine, which is largely limited to Latin American countries. This doctrine would deny a government the right to espouse the claims of its nationals, thereby restricting the injured national to the law of the host country, which might include international law protection as locally construed.

The Sabbatino ruling has been somewhat restricted by the second Hickenlooper Amendment, and U.S. courts now do apply international law to expropriations.[11] The nature of espousal has been somewhat confused by the Barcelona Traction case, which suggests that a claim may not be espoused by the government of the shareholders of a corporation but only by the government of the place of incorporation.[12] This is not current U.S. practice. The Calvo doctrine is Latin American in origin, although its principle may be spreading.[13] Incidentally, Latin American countries do apply international law in their courts, although they do not accept the minimum standard and the measure of prompt, adequate, and effective compensation. Instead they apply a standard of nondiscrimination, as well as local constitutional standards, which often do not call for compensation.

As already noted, the law of "responsibility of states for injuries to aliens" by definition does not apply to treatment by a state of its own nationals. This body of law is sometimes also subsumed under the expression "denial of justice" and applies not only to interference by a state with the property of a foreigner but also with a foreigner's personal liberty. The phrase has a procedural implication, and there is some suggestion that there is also a minimum standard of procedural law implied.[14]

Although the relevant public international law is thin, it is all that there is in the area of regulation of multinational corporations. We have already seen that the articles of agreement of the International Monetary Fund (IMF), which do limit the authority of nation-states with respect to international monetary affairs, leave a gap with respect to the process of international investment and multinational corporations.

There is no international law of corporations, of taxation, or of economic regulation such as antitrust law. There are no restrictions on nation-states; nor are there international norms governing multinational corporations with respect to these matters. The only remotely relevant body of law would be private international law or conflicts of law principles, and certain jurisdictional principles of public international law that would determine what particular national law would apply to such corporate or regulatory matters. On an analogous note, there is no international law restricting the OPEC cartel.[15]

It is the essential void in the international order with respect to these matters that may partly explain the almost total lack of legitimacy at the international level that people instinctively seem to ascribe to multinational corporations. In the eyes of a lawyer, the multinational corporation tends to break down into a collection of national corporations, each of them incorporated under a particular national jurisdiction. The totality or enterprise--"enterprise" being the phrase favored by economists and some politicians, does not really exist for lawyers. In the truest sense, the multinational corporation is a legal nonentity that confronts nation-states with great economic power. Some of the states believe they have less economic power and seek countervailing power either of their own or in some cases at the international level, at which there is almost no public law.

NOTES

1. R. Aron, Peace and War; A Theory of International Relations (1966, translated from the French by R. Howard and A. Fox).

2. N. T. Wang, "Towards an International Code of Conduct for Transnational Corporations," paper presented to the Conference on the Nation States and the Transnational Corporations in Lesser Developed Countries in Aspen, Colorado, Dec. 13-18, 1974, at 13-14.

3. D. Mitrany, A Working Peace System (1946).

4. L. Henkin, How Nations Behave; Law and Foreign Policy (1968).

5. W. Friedmann, The Changing Structure of International Law (1964).

6. Trade Act of 1974, Pub. L. No. 93-618, 88 Stat. 1978, sec. 321, adding 19 U.S.C. sec. 2371.

7. P. Jessup, The Price of International Justice (1971); see also P. Jessup, "Non-Universal International Law," 12 Colum. J. Transn'l L. 415 (1973).

8. E. Stein, Harmonization of European Company Laws, National Reform and Transnational Coordination 29-31 (1971).

9. The state of the law as it applies to multinational corporations is well summarized in D. Vagts, "Multinational Enterprise: A New Challenge for International Law," 83 Harv. L. Rev. (1970).

10. Banco Nacional de Cuba v. Sabbatino, 376 U.S. 398 (1964). It is possible that the Supreme Court may, at some point, retreat from this position. See Alfred Dunhill of London, Inc. v. The Re-

public of Cuba and Daniel Solano Pinera, Supreme Court Docket No. 73-1288.

11. First Nat'l City Bank v. Banco Nacional de Cuba, 400 U.S. 1019 (1970), vacating Banco Nacional de Cuba v. First Nat'l City Bank, 431 F. 2d 394 (2d Cir. 1970).

12. Barcelona Traction, Light and Power Co. (Belgium v. Spain, 1970) I.C.J. Rep. 3, 9 Int'l Legal Mat'ls 227 (1970).

13. R. Lillich, "The Diplomatic Protection of Nationals Abroad: An Elementary Principle of International Law under Attack," 69 Am. J. Int'l L. 359 (1975).

14. American Law Institute, Restatement of the Foreign Relations Law of the United States (second), sec. 165, comment c at 502-503 and secs. 178-82 at 534-48 (1965).

15. M. Joelson and J. Griffin, "The Legal Status of Nation-State Cartels under United States Antitrust and Public International Law," 9 The Int'l Lawyer 617 (1975). For a divergent view, see "Report and Recommendation of the Comm. on Int'l Econ. Organizations," American Bar Association, Section of International Law (April 1975).

CHAPTER

8

MATTERS BEYOND THE SCOPE OF ANY PROSPECTIVE INTERNATIONAL INVESTMENT ORGANIZATION

Even if an international investment organization were to be created in the foreseeable future, which is unlikely, there are certain subjects that probably would not be included within the scope of its powers. This is evident from experience with, and principles developed by, the existing nation-state system and the international law that it supports.

In summary, because of the primacy of the nation-state, diplomatic methods are certainly preferred to third-party adjudication, and bilateral methods are preferred to multilateral ones. There is a confederal maximum to the continuum of cooperation among nation-states and the operations of international organizations. Within this broader reality, the narrower area of the regulation of multinational corporations is even less organized; so far as law is concerned it is an unformed area.

Besides the fact that the multinational corporation is unknown to the law, there is also, apparently, insufficient data for policy makers. There is very little consensus about what the policy should be toward the multinational corporations, and there is less cooperation among governments about the application of policies. There is also the inevitable inertia of preference for the current, and in this case thin, legal approach; certainly the broader the proposed changes the more difficult it will be to achieve them. Beyond this, many prefer the relatively laissez-faire international arrangements. Combined with the inertia I have mentioned, there is a preference for issue by issue solutions, either limited to multinational companies or including other matters, and an apparent instinct to work through the existing international organizations.[1]

EXCLUSIONS BECAUSE OF DEFINITION OF THE PROBLEM

Certain subjects would not be covered by an international investment organization as I have defined it. The parameters I have placed on the relevant activities of the process of international investment and multinational corporations, as defined in Chapter 2, exclude coverage of the total subject of capital flows, even though these are not at the present time subject to the International Monetary Fund (IMF). It also excludes, entirely, the subject of public aid or foreign assistance.

Similarly, because of the definition of the problem, other international systems, although related to the phenomenon in which we are interested and although not covered by other international organizations, are excluded. These include the operations of all national capital markets and also any regulation of the international capital market or securities market that should emerge. Similarly, international commodity markets as such are excluded, although many multinational corporations obviously deal in commodities.

Problems such as those created by the increase in oil prices (and the recycling of petrodollars), which of course impinge on the operations of the multinational oil companies, would be excluded. The IMF deals with certain aspects of this problem; the producing countries have provided some assistance to countries affected by the increase in oil prices; and there will be further national steps. In the United States these national steps may include deregulation of oil prices and windfall taxes on oil companies. Someday gasoline (that is, oil) will in one way or another be rationed and we will embark upon a search for alternate fuels.

The EEC, as well as Japan and others, have investigated the operations of the oil companies during the 1973-74 oil crisis. Undoubtedly there has been much bilateral diplomatic negotiation between the United States and its consumer "allies" and between them and the oil-producing countries, and there will be more general discussions between consumer and producing nations. The Financial Support Fund (the so-called safety net of $25 billion) may be established.

The oil-producing countries will look for ways to secure their oil prices against inflation, whether by linking them to Special Drawing Rights (SDRs) or to industrial price indexes or otherwise. Similarly, those in surplus will seek security for their investment in industrial countries; although similar to the long-term security that foreign direct investors, that is, multinational corporations, seek, this kind of security will be different to the extent that the investment is placed in portfolio, private and public, instruments. Much of this is intimately related to the world in which multinational corporations operate, but none of it is within the scope of the problem as I have defined it in this book. Hence it would be beyond the scope of any prospective international investment organization as discussed here.

Similarly, a prospective international investment organization would not deal with the question of statistics with respect to capital flows or possibly, indeed, even with statistics as related to multinational corporations. Many national governments, especially that of the United States, collect statistics with respect to investment and multinational corporation activity. The IMF collects a great deal of information with respect to capital flows, some of which pertains to multinational corporations. The Organization of American States (OAS) and the new UN Commission on Transnational Corporations may collect more statistics. Even if a strong international investment organization were to be created, and even if some of the existing organizations and their functions as they relate to multinational corporations were to be combined with it, the statistical gathering still might not be within the international investment organization, although there is nothing in principle to prevent it.

A prospective organization would not be expected to deal with matters that are dealt with by existing international organizations or that would be dealt with by such organizations if further reformed. Thus it is possible that the IMF might deal with certain short-term capital movement problems, although the floating rates seem to have mitigated them. If the Euro-dollar market were ever to come under international control, it might very well be under the IMF; it would not be under an international investment organization with the parameters I have defined. The securities industry is yet another field that is not yet covered by any international organization. The industry is not covered by the OECD codes.

The General Agreement on Tariffs and Trade (GATT) may be further reformed. Its powers with respect to governmental procurement may be increased, and it may come to deal with certain pollution controls and environmental matters, which may be treated as nontariff barriers. There has been an occasional suggestion that regulation of the location of processing, presumably in the developing country in which the raw materials are found, should some day come within the GATT. Certainly this latter subject could be within an international investment organization, but it would not be so if the GATT were to deal with it. The UN Environmental Organization in Nairobi, which was set up by the 1972 Stockholm Conference, may deal with some of these matters at some point.

The EEC and the OAS may develop certain measures. To the extent that these measures deal with multinational corporations, it may very well be that they would be subject to any prospective international investment organization that would be seeking to apply its standards on a universal basis and that would somehow have to come to terms with "subordinate" regional organizations.

THE LADDER OF INTERNATIONAL COOPERATION

The nation-state is the basis of the international political system. States tend to act independently to further their individual interests, but they do cooperate. The progression from individual action to cooperation develops by stages, although instinctively states will tend to the lowest stages. Briefly, the progression is from (1) individual national policy, to (2) individual national policy that takes into account other nations' policies to (3) various degrees of consultation on a temporary and informal basis with respect to the formulation of such national policies to (4) more formal, regular, and continuous cooperation that is provided for by agreement, treaty, or otherwise to (5) regional or international organizations in which this process is further regularized to (6) some international body that has a measure of supranational authority.[2]

THE MARKET AND AD HOC DEALS

As we have already seen, there are many people who believe that the operation of international business and multinational corporations should be left alone and that market forces, the price mechanism, and a spirit of laissez faire are what is called for. This attitude would apply to proposals for any strong government policies, not only a policy promoting an international investment organization. This is a matter of conviction that may be supported by the habit of inertia but goes beyond it. It is related to a belief in the open economy, which it is believed allocates benefits and resources with the greatest efficiency. National and international controls are seen as endangering this system.

If host governments will not accept this approach, the next most acceptable approach, from the point of view of those sympathetic to market forces, is that of specific deals between investors and host countries, which are very common, especially in developing countries. To some extent individual concession agreements are yielding to investment decrees and more standard arrangements under local investment laws or mining or petroleum laws, although the individual deal, including tax, foreign exchange, and other provisions is still common.[3] Special arrangements are made between investors and governments when expropriation or similar measures are threatened. Renegotiation of concession and other investment agreements is increasingly common.

Related to this approach is the increased desire on the part of the governments of developing countries for more information, assistance, and training with respect to the negotiation of investment deals. Basically the governments wish to make better bargains. The Report of the Group of Eminent Persons recommends that the United Nations become more active in this area, as the developing countries are also doing.[4]

A possibly analogous development is the codes of conduct that various bodies in the industrial countries, and individual companies themselves, have imposed upon themselves in their dealings with host countries, especially developing countries. Examples of this are the International Chamber of Commerce (ICC) code and the code of Caterpillar Tractor.[5] These codes are voluntary and essentially without sanctions. The codes of the UN, OECD, and OAS may prove to be similar.

Another reinforcing tendency in this area is the distrust that many economists seem to have, almost as a matter of theory, for bureaucrats, who might interfere with the working of economic forces. This distrust probably applies equally to national and international bureaucrats, whether in existing or potential institutions. Since the economists are an important constituency in the development of policy with respect to international economic matters, this distrust reinforces the workings of the principle of the confederal maximum, which we have considered in Chapter 7 and which in turn is reflected in the everyday suspicion that politicians and administrators in many countries have for international institutions.

INEVITABLE NATIONAL CONTROLS

Inevitably, estimating the prospects for international organizations involves guesswork, as does predicting what areas of social control will remain with individual nations. An international organization will be carved out of the total field of social control, and to the extent that the controls remain national, they will not be available to the international organization.

This is the large field of social control, of legislation, regulations, and the like. It is generally agreed that we have a "horizontal" order in international affairs, in which nation-states are the source of any international control that might be imposed upon them, rather than a "vertical" order, in which a central governing authority imposes controls on the nation-states regardless of their wishes. This will inevitably continue to be the case on an even larger scale with respect to the disparate and traditionally "private" (in the sense of being outside the public law sector) activities of the multinational corporation. This may also be the case with respect to matters that are largely national, such as the operations of banks and insurance companies within domestic economies, although these operations may impinge on the process of international investment and multinational corporations and similar international matters, which will be seen more in terms of domestic impact than from a global point of view. This will be equally the case with respect to host countries, home countries, and third-party countries. It is possible that an international organization will provide guidance to nations in shaping these controls, but many of the controls will remain largely national.

This applies to laws, regulations, and other controls, actual, emerging, or proposed, that are handled at a national level and that in my view will continue to be handled at this level, whether or not an international organization emerges.

HOST COUNTRIES

In the first place, the enormous field of general economic, tax, and social legislation will remain local in all countries, as will a great deal of the legislation that is more specifically related to corporations and multinational corporations. Each country will continue to establish its own joint-venture policy; for instance, each country will decide whether the local government must have a share, whether a certain percentage of shares must be held by nationals, and whether directors or managers must be nationals.

Each country will also decide what incentives to provide to foreign investment, although one can deplore the national competition in incentives. The OECD is considering how its members might bring their incentives more into line. It has also, in the past, studied the problem of competitive incentives by developing countries.[6] The most severe problem in this area is probably that of tax havens, which typically are small countries that obtain considerable foreign exchange because of their advantageous tax laws.

Countries will continue to determine what their basic foreign investment policies are and what their policies are with respect to reinvestment by foreign investors. Although this is most obviously true of the developing countries, it is also hard to believe, although conceivable, that the United States would allow an international organization to determine or influence its policy with respect to investment by Iranians, Arabs, or Japanese in the United States, or that Germany would allow its policy with respect to Iranian investment to be so influenced. This is true in spite of the fact that both the United States and Germany have followed essentially internationalist and open-economy approaches to these matters.

Notwithstanding the existence of the OECD Code of Liberalization of Capital Movements, the OECD member countries reserve the right to determine their policy with respect to inward and outward long-term and short-term capital movements controls. If an international investment organization is established, to the extent that it does not deal with these matters and explicitly make them part of its jurisdiction, they will remain a matter of national legislation.

Economic planning, to the extent pursued, will remain national. Essentially national control over petroleum and mining development also seems inevitable. Expropriation is a difficult problem; it will sometimes be resolved by specific renegotiations between companies and governments. There will continue to be negotiations between governments on specific subjects such as those that were induced by such provisions as the Hickenlooper Amendment, which required the suspension of foreign assistance until an expropriation and its compensation were resolved. The OPIC investment-guarantee bilateral agreements call for government negotiations in cases in which the Overseas Private Investment Corporation (OPIC) has compensated an expropriated U.S. investor.

National programs of investment insurance such as that of the OPIC will of course remain part of the approach to this problem, while multilateral guarantee programs of any value seem distant. Nonetheless there would clearly be a role for an international investment organization with respect to expropriation, to which I will return in Chapter 10, inasmuch as the long-term security of investments is one of the most important aspects of the process of international investment and multinational corporations.

Possibly less dramatic, but much more inclusive, are the normal corporation laws that cover the internal governance of business enterprise. When a Robert Vesco or a Bernard Cornfeld is charged with cheating shareholders, it is the government of the place of incorporation that will probably pursue the matter. I doubt that even the most sweeping of George Ball's proposals would alter this.

It is possible that nations have reached out too far with this kind of regulation; some people believe that some national authorities and courts have gone too far in "piercing the corporate veil" by finding the parent corporations of local subsidiaries liable to jurisdiction and for damages. However, it is unclear whether the integrity of the process of international investment and multinational corporations has been endangered by this.

Private international law has sought to mediate in this area through the development of certain predictable techniques for choosing which national laws will in fact govern which aspects of corporate activity. Thus in the European jurisprudence the law of the seat or principal offices of the company, the siege sociale, often governs questions involving the internal governance of a company. Within the EEC, treaties have been developed to solve some choice-of-law problems.

The attempt to go further and actually harmonize national laws has moved slowly. Attempts to go even further and develop a law that might be available, at least on an optional basis, for all companies in Europe, at least those doing business in more than one country, have also progressed slowly.[7]

The European experience suggests the enormous intractability of the problem and the reluctance of governments to yield their individual authority in these matters. Large areas of taxation, too, must inevitably remain in the national domain, and not just for simple revenue-raising reasons. Different countries have different methods of raising taxes, whether through turnover taxes, income taxes, or excise taxes. They have different legal cultures and different theories of jurisdiction. Thus the United States would be reluctant to abandon its own notions of tax equity, which dictate that all taxpayers in similar brackets pay a similar tax, and tax neutrality, which calls for a similar tax rate on all similar transactions, whether foreign or domestic. These policies would make it difficult to agree to a uniform tax rate for all multinational corporations, irrespective of their nationality.

Labor legislation will also retain national characteristics that are responsive to the peculiar relationship between management and labor in each country and to the peculiar preferences of national labor unions, and to different wage levels. The international "solidarity" of labor unions is not very much in evidence. There are few examples of strong international union secretariats and fewer of multinational bargaining by unions. This probably results from the economic situations of the industries concerned. There is increasing divergence of Canadian and U.S. workers within what were joint Canadian-American unions.[8] On the other hand, one sees in Europe some movement toward codetermination, that is, the representation of workers on company boards.[9] Nonetheless, each country will inevitably develop its own unique legislation in this area.

With respect to antitrust and restrictive practices legislation, it has often been noted that every country seems to have its own theory of economic regulation, its own peculiar purposes in developing antitrust law, and certainly its own economic interests, such as the protection of its own home-based corporations.[10]

HOME COUNTRIES

Much of what has been said about host countries applies to home countries. Thus in the tax area it is unlikely that the United States will allow to be removed from national controls such questions as the operation of its foreign tax credit, sub part F and deferral, or its depletion allowances, all of which are in the process of reform. It is conceivable, but highly unlikely, that the United States would give up the authority to impose foreign direct investment controls or an interest equalization tax. It is also unlikely to relinquish the power to reimpose the Reserve Bank guidelines on the foreign lending activities of its banks, which were imposed in spite of the U.S. subscription to the OECD Code of Liberalization of Capital Movements. The United States obtained a derogation from the code for the imposition of mandatory foreign direct investment controls in 1968.[11]

There might be some national controls that the United States would be willing to give up. Liberal economists, at least, might happily sacrifice the proposals associated with Hartke-Burke, which would have authorized the federal government to restrict foreign patent licensing and foreign direct investment in order to save jobs and technology, to the jurisdiction of an international investment organization. If there were proposals for adjustment assistance with respect to the jobs exported by multinational corporations, the United States would certainly wish to retain the national right to give such assistance.

In another area, it is highly unlikely that we would give up the right to espouse the claims of our corporations against foreign expropriation or interference, as we would if we were to accept the Calvo doctrine. That is one reason why the proposal of George Ball that corporations be chartered internationally, and thus presumably deprived of national protection with respect to investment and other disputes, seems so unrealistic at this time. Extreme though the Hickenlooper Amendment approach may be, it is probably more acceptable to the United States than that taken in the Barcelona Traction Case.[12] The United States is also backing away from the Banco Nacional de Cuba v. Sabbatino, which seems to deprive U.S. courts of jurisdiction in cases in which U.S. investments have been expropriated abroad.[13] Even in the area of export and investment insurance, which is administered by OPIC and the Export-Import Bank, it is unlikely that the United States will agree to binding uniform rules for maximum or minimum terms.

The United States would also be unwilling to give up its right to develop a national policy to stimulate investment in developing countries. The U.S. attempt to develop uniform standards of export credits with the EEC and Japan has gone very slowly.[14] Although the United States is not at the present time particularly interested in developing an investment credit for investment in developing countries or agreeing to, for example, tax sparing arrangements, it would wish to preserve flexibility even in this rather marginal area. Proposals for a multilateral guarantee agency have moved very slowly because of the different criteria of different investor countries, although this is not the only obstacle.[15]

There are more difficult questions. How can Canada, or any country of which a large part of the national economy is dominated by foreign investors, ever change this situation should it desire to do so? Should it not be allowed to promote local investors? Will doing so discriminate against foreigners? Must such local promotion remain within national control? Certain limits could be imposed on such a process; we will return to these in Chapter 10.

Of course there will be other domestic pressures for more national control, some of which may in fact be political, for example socialist, but also possibly antiinternationalist in nature. There are also pressures for extraterritorial control associated with U.S. economic regulation. Presumably these latter developments should be within the sphere of an international investment organization, although their status will be enormously difficult to determine.

What of regional efforts, whether through the EEC, in its competition policy or its policy with respect to multinational companies, or through the Andean group, the OPEC, the International Energy Agency, the Consultative Group Coordinating Committee (COCOM), or the OAS? Here we enter the realm of those political developments that if carried far enough might begin a train of events that would lead to an international investment organization. Just to mention these suggests, however, how much of the activity in this area can never be brought within an international investment organization at any time in the foreseeable future.

BILATERALISM AND DIPLOMACY

Much is being done, and will almost inevitably continue to be done, at a national level, and much is also being done through bilateral and diplomatic means; this is likely to continue. The volume of diplomatic activity, bilateral and multilateral, is enormous. Examples of multilateral activity abound in the trade and international monetary areas, in the GATT and IMF, some of which do touch on multinational companies. We are interested only in those more legal aspects that impinge on the process of international investment and multinational corporations.

Thus tax treaties, and the consultation among the competent authorities of national tax services that is provided for in these treaties, might be used to resolve problems of competing and overlapping tax policy. Some transfer price problems might lend themselves to this approach. The extraterritorial assertion of antitrust authority by the United States has to some extent been moderated by provisions for coordination between the U.S. and Canadian authorities and on a more widespread basis through the OECD Restrictive Practices Committee; not all this relates to multinational companies. Some of the extraterritorial assertions of export control in the United States might be handled in this way.

Canada, Argentina, France, and other countries have objected to this.[16] This probably is no longer a major problem, but it is annoying and should have been moderated.[17] This does not warrant the creation of a GATT for investment.[18] It is generally believed that the competing assertion of jurisdiction can be mediated case by case, diplomatically.[19] However, by internationalizing some of the issues previously handled on a national basis, an international organization might further contribute to amelioration in this area.

Most exporpriation disputes, if not privately resolved, have been, and probably will continue to be, handled on a bilateral, intergovernmental basis based on the espousal of claims; on the exercise of good offices; and regrettably on such pressures as those associated with the Hickenlooper Amendment, since the approach of the Calvo Doctrine is unlikely to gain major ground. Treaties such as those of friendship, commerce, and navigation can moderate some of the disputes in this area and provide other bilateral diplomatic channels with respect to issues relevant to multinational corporations.

THE ISSUE-BY-ISSUE APPROACH

Not all national controls can be reconciled; diplomatic and bilateral approaches do not eliminate all disputes among nations. Even so, a broad-scale international organization is not the next inevitable approach; rather, the approach may be to tackle issues one by one. This approach might conceivably be limited to multinational corporations, but instead it would probably tackle a range of problems in an issue area, for example a variety of international tax problems, that would not all necessarily be related to multinational corporations. Even the United Nations proposals to deal with the multinational corporation in its totality reveal the belief that an issue by issue approach may be more feasible and that specific agreements in certain areas may have to be made before a general agreement dealing with multinational corporations can be achieved.[20]

The issue by issue approach antedates the global approach to the process of international investment and multinational corporations. On the other hand, the fact that this approach has not achieved much suggests the possibility that it may not necessarily survive the more global approach. The OECD has had more than 30 working groups on international tax problems since the mid-1960s. The United Nations has been working on double tax treaties for several years. Indeed, as long ago as 1929 the League of Nations proposed a model bilateral tax treaty dealing with a number of double tax issues and issues of allocation of tax between two jurisdictions. So too, the OECD has proposed a code with respect to expropriation and compensation and has done work in the area of restrictive trade practices. The OECD Code of Liberalization of Capital Movements and Code of Liberalization of Current Invisible Operations, which deal with discrete activities such as dividends, interest, access to security markets, and freedom to make loans, are in a sense issue oriented. Some believe this is still the way of the future.[21] Seymour Rubin once suggested creation of a number of informal forums.[22] These could deal with the full range of issues confronting multinational companies on an informal basis and need not be inevitably limited to particular issues. N. T. Wang suggests that specific arrangements will have to come before a general multinational company treaty.[23] Compare the suggested approach of the OAS. Deliberation over tax treaties and double taxation continue. Historically, attempts to tackle antitrust problems at the international level have not been limited to international companies. The attempt to coordinate national environmental controls represents an example of the issue by issue approach. Harmonization of national laws takes place on an issue by issue basis and applies equally to national and multinational companies and other affected actors.

In a sense the issue by issue approach represents a further refinement of the functionalism that some have said is the inevitable approach to international problems, given the nation-state system and the confederal maximum pressures I have mentioned, and represents no more than a further refinement of the approach seen in specialized international agencies and the approach to commodity agreements. On the other hand, although tax, antitrust and other issues are analytically very separate and although each is enormously difficult of resolution, they are not very separate politically. There may be a danger that the separate approach to each issue will result in a trivialization and a lack of coordination, with the result that the possibility of a solution at the political level, where much of the problem arises, may be lost.

GROWTH IN THE COORDINATION OF GOVERNMENT POLICIES

Nations are reluctant to create strong international organizations, although undoubtedly some movement is taking place. The progression tends to be from (1) exclusively national policies to (2) national policies that are more outward-looking, that is, sensitive to both the domestic and outward-looking policies of other countries to (3) the cooperative formulation of national policies to (4) the creation of international machinery ranging from committees that may be no more than the regular meeting of officials to (5) more regular cooperative formulation of national policies through international organizations and finally to (6) genuine supernational agencies, which we do not have. Akin to genuine supernational agencies is binding third-party adjudication.[24] An example of cooperative formulation of policies can be found in the area of exchange rates since World War II, although perhaps this has not gone far enough.[25]

Many international organizations provide no more than an occasion for diplomatic negotiations, which are in a sense a lower rung on the ladder of cooperation. There is often greater coordination, however, especially at the OECD, although to be sure the OECD consists essentially of like-minded industrialized nations. In a sense its activities might be assimilated into a regional defensive organization like NATO, the International Energy Agency, or the OPEC.* However, OECD does seek to have its members coordinate policies, which are otherwise disparate in their aims. This coordination ranges from macroeconomic policy through more specific legal measures, as exemplified in the Code of Liberalization of Capital Movements. In the area of international investment and multinational corporations and in closely related areas, discussions are going on with respect to the coordination of the terms of export credits, tax incentives, and tax havens, as well as discussions on multinational companies and on international investment in the tax and antitrust committees of the OECD. These latter committees are the Fiscal Affairs Committee and its working groups, the Restrictive Practices Committee, and the Committee on International Investment and Multinational Enterprises. The Executive Committee has also taken a hand in the area. A measure of the increased coordination taking place through the OECD is the fact that officials from domestic departments or agencies, such as treasury, agriculture,

---

*The EEC does represent something more akin to a supernational entity; the OAS, however, seems to be little more than occasional forum, leading to very little definite action.

and commerce officials, often participate instead of foreign service officers.

Unfortunately, this increased coordination of governments that are largely like-minded in their aims is taking place at the same time as nations seem to be further splitting into blocks. Thus coordination within the OECD seems to take place at the same time as increased discussion within the United Nations Conference on Trade and Development (UNCTAD), but a division of opinion between the two groups has been increasingly reflected in U.N. deliberations. It is too early to know what results the September 1975 initiatives of Henry Kissinger, to commence a detailed dialogue on specific international economic problems with the developing countries, at the UN General Assembly special session will have.[26] The split between OECD and UNCTAD raises the most profound questions, although there are others, about the viability of an international investment organization.

The upshot of this chapter is that these existing realities must condition the emergence of an international investment organization and may delay or possibly prevent it. The organization would inevitably be carved out of the field covered by this reality; nonetheless, international issues, which are possibly solvable only by an international investment organization, remain.

NOTES

1. N. T. Wang, "Towards an International Code of Conduct for Transnational Corporations," paper presented to the Conference on the Nation States and the Transnational Corporations in Lesser Developed Countries in Aspen, Colorado, Dec. 13-18, 1974. The issue by issue approach of the EEC is shown in Comm'n of the European Communities, Multinational Undertakings and Community Regulations (Comm'n Communication to the Council, Nov. 7, 1973).

2. Compare R. Cooper, The Economics of Interdependence: Economic Policy in the Atlantic Community 260-68 (1968).

3. D. Smith and L. Wells, "Mineral Agreements in Developing Countries: Structures and Substance," 69 Am. J. Int'l L. 560 (1975).

4. The Impact of Multinational Corporations on the Development Process and on International Relations: Report of the Group of Eminent Persons to Study the Role of Multinational Corporations on Development and on International Relations, UN Doc. E/5500/Add. 11, Rev. 1-ST/ESA/ 6.

5. Int'l Chamber of Commerce, Guidelines for International Investment (1972); Bus. Int'l. (Oct. 18, 1974).

6. G. Reuber et al., Private Foreign Investment in Development (1973).

7. See E. Stein, Harmonization of European Company Laws, National Law Reform and Transnational Coordination 27-32 (1971) for a comprehensive discussion of these problems.

8. See B. Jones, "Labor Unions Role at Multinationals Found Still Limited," New York Times, April 21, 1975, at 45, col. 4.

9. See G. McIsaac and H. Henzler, "Codetermination: A Hidden Noose for MNCs," 9 Colum. J. of World Bus. 67 (1974).

10. C. Edwards, Control of Cartels and Monopolies: An International Comparison (1967).

11. "OECD's Code of Liberalization of Capital Movements," reprinted from the OECD Observer at 4 (Dec. 1971).

12. Barcelona Traction, Light and Power Co. (Belgium v. Spain, 1970), I.C.J. Rep. 3, 9 Int'l Legal Mat'ls (1970).

13. Banco Nacional de Cuba v. Sabbatino, 376 U.S. 398 (1973); First National City Bank v. Banco Nacional de Cuba, 400 U.S. 1019 (1970). Alfred Dunhill of London, Inc. v. the Republic of Cuba and Daniel Solano Pinera, Supreme Court Docket No. 73-1288.

14. See, for example, Bulletin of the European Communities Commission 12-1974, at 70, and 5-1975, at 55.

15. See H. Steiner and D. Vagts, Transnational Legal Problems 357-58 (1968).

16. P. Goldberg and C. Kindleberger, "Toward a GATT for Investment: A Proposal for Supervision of the International Corporation," 2 Law and Pol. Int'l Bus. 295 (1970); J. Corcoran, "The Trading with the Enemy Act and the Controlled Canadian Corporation," 14 McGill L. J. 174 (1968); New York Times, Mar. 18, 1974, at 45, col. 8; Business Week, April 13, 1974, at 80-81.

17. S. Rubin, "Of Cuba and Our Foreign Subsidiaries," letter to the Editor, New York Times, Mar. 13, 1974.

18. See P. Goldberg and C. Kindleberger, op. cit.

19. Lowenfeld, "Book Review," 65 Am. J. Int'l L. 853 (1971).

20. "The Impact of Multinational Corporations," op. cit., and the follow-up document, UN, at 7-8,(Feb. 28, 1975).

21. D. Vagts, "Multinational Enterprises: A New Challenge for International Law," 83 Harvard Law Review 739 (1970); and S. Rubin, "Multinational Enterprises and National Sovereignty: A Sceptic's Analysis," 3 Law and Pol. Int'l Bus. (1971).

22. S. Rubin, op. cit.

23. N. T. Wang, op. cit.

24. See R. Cooper, The Economics of Interdependence: Economic Policy in the Atlantic Community (1968).

25. See G. Halm, A Guide to International Monetary Reform 99-112 (1975).

26. See 73 Dept. State Bull. 425 (1975).

PART III

A MODEL FOR AN INTERNATIONAL INVESTMENT ORGANIZATION BASED ON AN OPEN WORLD ECONOMY, INTERNATIONAL LAW, AND MINIMAL SOCIAL CONTROL

CHAPTER

9

THE OPEN WORLD ECONOMY, INTERNATIONAL LAW, AND MINIMAL SOCIAL CONTROL

Chapters 7 and 8 have defined some of the limitations of the international political system and also outlined some of the existing economic and other policy preferences. In Chapters 11 and 12 I will further particularize these possibilities and preferences. Unless there is a substantial shift in the economic policy preferences that are detailed in Chapter 5, possibly because of the increased impact of some of the values that were suggested in Chapter 4, the realities of Chapters 7, 8, and 6 will not be easily overcome.

No real consensus has developed, especially at the international level, for a new policy with respect to foreign direct investment. Similarly, no real consensus has developed on this subject in the United States or in most other countries. So too, because of the realities of the confederal maximum, which is discussed in Chapter 7 and in Chapter 8, one must acknowledge that it is still too early to expect a new kind of international cooperation, although progress is being made. We have seen in Chapter 8 that many subjects will inevitably remain in the national sphere or be handled on an individual basis or by diplomatic negotiation, or possibly on an issue by issue basis, and that an international organization will have to carve out its jurisdiction from this reality. The international handling of an inherently international and limited issue, such as standards for some aspects of the transfer price issue, is more likely to occur than a full-bodied system of international supervision of corporations. Even this limited-issue approach is unlikely. It will be interesting to observe the activities of the recently established United Nations Commission on Transnational Corporations, although it apparently will initially work on a "code of corporate behavior," a possibly nebulous enterprise, instead of developing rules that would be binding on corporations and states alike.[1]

Nevertheless, in this chapter I will describe a possible model for an international investment organization, although I do not think such an organization is likely in the foreseeable future, even on the modest lines of the model I will discuss here. However, it is useful to have a concrete model, if only to appreciate the extent of the difficulty.

This model incorporates the principles of open world economy, international law, and minimal social control. Many of the advocates of an international organization for regulating multinational corporations and foreign direct investment believe that multinational corporations, or certain of their practices, should be controlled. Were control ever to become necessary, it would probably be control of some nation-state practices as they relate to the international economy, including the activities of the multinational corporations, rather than direct control over the multinational corporations. The corporations would largely be controlled by nations, and it would be some of the excesses of national controls that might be subject to scrutiny on the international level. It is in the world's interest to promote international investment and multinational corporations, at least within certain reasonable limits.

The model builds on an open world economy because the process of the core of international investment and multinational corporations, within the parameters outlined in Chapter 2, fits into the operations of this most widely preferred international economy; in effect, I accept the premises and presumptions of the Bretton Woods system.

The principle of international law is included because it allows for a limited number of rules applied to nation-states, rather than a world government with a full panoply of powers. It suggests limitations on nation-states instead of on multinational corporations because that is the way international law operates.

There is no consensus about the substantive rules that might be applied to multinational corporations. States do not have enough confidence in international organizations to delegate enough power to a new organization to enable it to regulate a large number of corporations. There is no real precedent within the current international legal system for an international organization that would directly regulate corporations, which are "nationals" of nation-states, without dealing through the nation-states in the first instance.

The principle of minimal social control is necessary because, notwithstanding the severe limitations on the international system and the absence of any strong consensus about multinational corporations, there is a widespread feeling that something should be done. Some minimal, moderate, or reasonable controls, in addition to the national controls that are already in existence, may be needed. The requirements of the Keynesian state that are discussed in Chapter 6, as well as some of the emergent values that are touched upon in Chapter 4, suggest the origins of this need.

Additional national social controls will certainly be imposed, and an international organization should to some degree permit these. International guidelines with respect to the permissible limits of national controls may be necessary. These national controls would presumably be directed against multinational corporation excesses or abuses. Each nation-state will experiment in drawing the line between the core of the international investment and multinational corporation process that is to be preserved and the excesses and abuses. Under the present international system there will be mistakes, and international controls will have to tolerate these.

Minimal social controls might be imposed by the international machinery itself. An international body could establish standards for determining transfer prices with respect to certain transactions and might also establish certain international accounting standards to be applied to certain kinds of transactions. More ambitiously, it might develop standards for allocating the total tax revenues derived from a multinational corporation among the various nations in which that corporation is active. The practical problems would be great. Different nations have different taxes, including income, customs, and turnover taxes. The possible approaches to this problem are briefly discussed in Chapter 10. Of course, the allocation of the tax "cake" of a particular company is not to be confused with a global welfare state that would have powers of taxation and a budget. The international organization would do no more than provide guidelines to nations and enable them to share equitably the tax revenues of particular companies the revenues of which, although large, should not be confused with global income.

Another area might be that of international mergers, with international standards to determine which mergers might be globally beneficial and permitted and which not. The number of mergers with global impact might not be many. The antitrust area is one in which efforts have been made in the past, including the Havana Charter, the 1953 United Nations attempt, and later the OECD and GATT proposals.[2]

THE NORMATIVE SHAPE OF THE MODEL INTERNATIONAL INVESTMENT ORGANIZATION

Although the basic principles of the international investment organization would be open world economy, international law, and minimal social control, this says very little about its organization or basic norms. Consistent with the international political system, the state of international law, and the prevailing international economic preferences, the basic norms might be progressive liberalization, minimum standards for states, nondiscrimination, temporary safeguards, minimization of jurisdictional overlap, and minimal procedural standards.

Progressive Liberalization

The principle of progressive liberalization that is evident in the IMF, GATT, and the OECD codes would be further applied to the process of international investment and multinational corporations as defined within the parameters of activities previously discussed. As this principle has operated in other organizations, it would involve, (1) a collective, international review of national actions, such as the IMF conducts with respect to the application of Articles XIV and VIII, and (2) the application of the "ratchet principle," pursuant to which national restrictions can be removed but new ones cannot be added. Moreover, these restrictions may not be discriminatory.

The ratchet principle is operative in the IMF and the GATT, and also under the OECD Codes of Liberalization of Capital Movements and Code of Liberalization of Current Invisible Operations, although the OECD has permitted a fair amount of backsliding. (See Appendixes C and D.) The European Monetary Authority and European Payments Union, which led to convertibility of European currencies, operated in a similar fashion. The provisions of the Treaty of Rome, which established the EEC, that are applicable to capital movements operate in the same fashion.

A detailed definition and application of the concept of the process of international investment and multinational corporations is extremely complex and involves issues of varying political intensity. For instance, the topic at issue may be something as abstract as freedom of capital movement. We have already seen that this general principle is not so firmly established in the rhetoric of contemporary economic preference as free trade.

On the other hand, the issue may be as specific as the possibility of direct investment in certain sectors of Japanese industry. The general attitude appears to be permissive to free capital movement and investment, possibly because of the difficulty of recycling petrodollars. At the same time there is in evidence the nationalist objection to foreign investment, whether direct or otherwise and whether in the United States against Arabs or in the Andean Pact countries against the United States. The petrodollar problem seems to have overwhelmed the others. Germans seek Iranian investment, and the U.S. executive branch seeks Iranian, Arab, and Japanese investment, at least within the limits of consultation with the federal government.

Australian and Canadian objections to foreign investment seem almost to be forgotten, as do those of the EEC. Mexico also pushes ahead with inward foreign investment, and the same is true of many other countries.

I think it is still fair to say, with Herbert Gray, that there is a "tendency toward liberalization" of capital investment, but "the pace is slow and uneven."[3]

Minimum Standards for States

The notion of minimum standards to be imposed by international law on states with respect to their behavior to foreigners is one of the classic approaches of international law. It would not be easy to apply this standard to the process of international investment and multinational corporations, but there are a number of ways in which it might work that can be suggested.

Governments might wish to bar foreign investment from certain key sectors; in fact, almost all governments do so. A minimum standard might prohibit governments from designating certain sectors as "key." The type of sector varies from country to country; for instance, Arthur Burns has suggested that the Arabs should not be allowed to dominate certain key U.S. defense industries, yet he would have no objection to Arab domination of General Foods.[4] Other countries might consider the food sector as a key sector.[5]

Some governments may feel that although foreign investment is allowable there should be limits on the total percentage of foreign investment in the economies of their countries or in particular sectors. Similarly, they may believe that there should be limits on the investment of particular countries. Thus (this is pure hypothesis), the Canadians might wish to limit foreign investment in the automobile sector to 50 percent of the total investment stock in the sector and the investment of the United States to 30 percent.

Very few governments have developed policies with respect to this issue. It is doubtful whether a government would be willing to discuss its policy with an international organization or accept a minimum standard. For example, an international standard might prevent a government from restraining foreign investment in a particular sector if total foreign investment did not exceed 25 percent and the investment of a particular country did not exceed 15 percent.

M. Watkins has suggested that there should be an upper limit to foreign investment in Canada and certain sectors of its economy.[6] A rule in this area would be difficult to apply. It would also have implications for national policy with respect to takeovers, expansion of existing investments, and reinvestment.

I would distinguish rules that specify the maximum percentage of equity that a foreign investor may hold in a particular company or enterprise, which is frequently the subject of host-country legislation. (See the fifth section of Chapter 8.) The exigencies of investment in particular enterprises and various other local pressures can resolve this matter, whether or not there is great variety with respect to particular investments. Countries will insist on retaining autonomy over this matter.

The volume of permitted petrodollar investment in a particular country is not within the parameters of the process of international investment and multinational corporations as I have defined it.

Another aspect of the process of international investment and multinational corporations to which the minimum standard might be applied is one to which it has been applied in the past, namely the question of expropriation of property and compensation, and to a lesser extent, repudiation of agreements. It is reasonably clear that unless there is a certain long-term security supporting the investment process, the risks involved in it will ultimately abort parts of it. An adaptation of the traditional Western standard of prompt, adequate, and effective compensation may be required. Other means, such as national investment insurance programs, effective negotiation and renegotiation of contracts, and selective exclusion of foreign investment, are available and are being pursued.

Nondiscrimination

Part of the classical approach of international law, including protection of property, is nondiscrimination, which is sometimes described as a requirement for "national treatment," that is, treatment of foreigners that is no worse than the treatment of nationals. Sometimes nondiscrimination takes the form of the lesser requirement that all foreigners be treated equally, as in the most favored nation requirement of the GATT. The IMF applies the rule of nondiscrimination when it bars multiple exchange rates or different rates for traders of different nationalities.

Nondiscrimination should be a basic rule, although there might be an occasional exception. The OECD Code of Liberalization of Current Invisible Operations permits the reservation of 25 percent of the local film manufacturing market to local producers and requires nondiscrimination only with respect to the remaining 75 percent. An example of discrimination would be the treatment by the Andean group of various classes of foreign investors.

The OECD has been discussing a convention for its members that would require national treatment, or nondiscrimination, with respect to (1) entry, that is, the right of establishment as it may be subject to local investment screening laws and (2) operations insofar as they are subject to tax measures, antitrust, labor, pollution, accounting, and other standards. In effect, foreign investors and foreign multinational corporations would have to be treated the same as nationals.

Those familiar with the equal protection clause of the Fourteenth Amendment to the U.S. Constitution will realize that reasonable classifications distinguishing companies of different sizes and characteristics might still be possible. A national-treatment standard with respect to entry would certainly affect the operation of screening laws such as Canada's Foreign Investment Review Act or similar laws in many developing countries, only a few of which are members of the OECD. It would also affect proposals to restrain takeovers of existing enterprises by foreigners.

Existing international law, as propounded by the West, also bars discrimination with respect to the taking or expropriation of property and the compensation for the same. The OECD Code of Liberalization of Capital Movements and Code of Liberalization of Current Invisible Operations bar discrimination, as does the Treaty of Rome.

An area in which the application of the nondiscrimination standard would be difficult is that which relates to governmental promotion of local industry. This is an important matter; if governments wish to minimize the impact of foreigners on their economy, they will wish to promote investment by their own nationals. There has been talk of this in Canada and in the EEC; the Canadians have established the Canadian Development Corporation for this purpose. A most favored nation standard that allowed the nations to favor local investors over foreign investors without discrimination among foreigners of different nationalities might be appropriate. However, this would not solve the Canadian problem, which is that of a preponderance of U.S. investment. Perhaps preferences for local investors should be allowed, though with a limit on what the preference might be.

For example, developing countries give preference to local contractors under IBRD procurement rules, but the preference is usually limited to 15 percent. Canada and Australia have indicated that they will not subscribe to the proposed OECD national treatment proposals with respect to entry and operations. Government procurement policies in the EEC raise similar questions. For example, should the Italian government be allowed to discriminate in favor of Italian or EEC contractors? Should all contractors, of whatever nationality, be treated equally? Various incentive and subsidy programs raise the same questions.

One approach to the problem of promotion of local investment might be to treat it like the infant industry problem and permit preference for locals temporarily.

The application of international standards to national controls would, like the application of rules in other areas, raise many technical issues. Presumably the rules related to foreign investors would also apply to local subsidiaries of foreign investors. However, the Treaty of Rome, which established the EEC, requires that local subsidiaries of foreign companies be treated like other local companies.[7] Would countries be completely free in deciding which companies were local instead of controlled by foreigners? There are many criteria for determining whether a company is of foreign derivation, including share ownership, share voting power, management, and directors.[8] The courts of different countries have different standards for determining whether a local subsidiary is controlled by foreigners. If relevant, how would sectors of the economy be defined, and how would investment stock be measured?

To permit discrimination, the reasons for which may be appealing, is to encroach on the open system, at least in its pure form.

J. Rawls suggests that society may prefer certain inequalities, by way of an incentive device, but suggests that they will not be "just" unless they are perceived to be "fair."[9] National discrimination would somehow have to seem "fair" in the light of the underlying purposes of a global system in which the predominant preference still seems to be for openness, on the ground that encroachments will be less objectionable than the evils they seek to correct.

Temporary Safeguards

The concept of temporary safeguards might be a companion to the notion of minimum standards and also to the operation of the nondiscrimination standard. We have seen this concept at work in the area of trade where, for example, the United States has asked Japan to limit its exports to the United States temporarily so that they can be more readily absorbed. At the same time the United States has indicated that it will not ultimately discriminate against Japan. This notion of a "temporary safeguard," as opposed to a permanent restriction or discrimination, has been suggested as one that should be included in a reformed GATT framework.

In the area of the process of international investment and multinational corporations, it may be that minimum standards might be remporarily suspended with respect to certain countries and that exceptions to an absolute nondiscrimination standard might be allowed temporarily. The temporary safeguard notion might set a time on the working of the ratchet principle, establishing the maximum period after which there would have to be a move forward to greater liberalization.

With respect to maximum foreign investment in a particular sector, the ultimate minimum standard might provide that a nation could not object to foreign investment if the investment did not exceed 50 percent of the total investment stock in the sector. However, the country might keep foreign investment below that figure temporarily, or it might impose an absolute dollar ceiling on foreign investment. As the local economy grew, this figure might have to be raised to fit the minimum standard, or as the host country increased its own foreign direct investment in other countries, it might have to raise its local standard.

The problems associated with the limits of growth are relevant here. If an economy were growing vigorously, with foreigners and nationals sharing in that growth, many of the problems associated with foreign investment might not seem so acute. It is the domination by foreigners of a stagnant local economy, in the face of local ambitions, that is the heart of the problem. A temporary restriction on foreign investment that is intended to facilitate local investment is akin to assistance to infant industry.

Temporary permission for a country to promote local investment in preference to foreign investment might be deemed a temporary safeguard, although the permissible margin of preference given to the local investor might decline over time. Article 73 of the Treaty of Rome permits temporary exceptions to the rule of free capital movement.[10]

Minimization of Jurisdictional Overlaps

If international control were the only control of international matters, the problem of jurisdictional overlaps would be nonexistent. However, almost all control of international transactions is national. The problems of conflict created by such national controls are probably less than is commonly assumed. We have already seen in Chapter 8 that these problems can be solved issue by issue or through bilateral and diplomatic means. The importance of certain isolated episodes of the assertion of U.S. export controls or antitrust laws has been exaggerated.[11] Countries other than the United States assert their jurisdictions extraterritorially; with the exception of one or two EEC assertions, not much of this seems to affect the United States.

Although there are principles of jurisdictional restraint that are often imposed by national courts on their own authority, the present state of international law does not provide many principles for reconciling jurisdictional overlap. The problem can be mitigated if the governments consult each other before asserting their jurisdiction with respect to matters that are of interest to more than one government or that may be deemed offensive by another government. Cases in which the outward reach of U.S. antitrust laws have been considered to be in conflict with the laws of another country include U.S. v. Imperial Chemical Industries and U.S. v. The Watchmakers of Switzerland Information Center.[12] The Hague Treaty on Hijacking lists six or seven bases of national jurisdiction with respect to hijacking and suggests certain priorities.[13]

It may be necessary to develop principles that would establish the order of priority in which nations would assert their jurisdiction over certain transactions, since the absence of a consensus about the substantive policies in an area such as antitrust makes it unlikely that there would be harmonization of different national policies, not to mention development of international substantive rules.

Minimum Procedural Standards

As long as most controls remain national, it may be necessary for international minimum procedural or due-process standards to be established for the benefit of multinational corporations in dealing with national authorities. There are few precedents in international law, although the concept of denial of justice, which is the minimum standard that states are not to violate in their treatment of aliens, suggests that the notion is not alien to international law.

Some national courts have suggested that, as a matter of international law or of both local constitutional law and international law, a nation may not assert its jurisdiction over the person of an individual if the means used to bring him or her within the jurisdiction violate a standard of due process. Examples are the abduction of individuals from ships, airplanes, or foreign countries in order to prosecute them for violation of national laws.[14] However, there have been cases, such as that involving Adolf Eichmann, in which national courts have asserted jurisdiction over defendants regardless of the means by which they were brought before them.[15]

The Canadian Foreign Investment Review Act requirement that, to be approved, a foreign investment must be of substantial benefit to Canada, has proven to be a vague standard. Under international due process, Canada possibly should be required to define this in some way that would make it possible to apply it consistently to foreign investors. Canada might therefore be required to produce definite enough standards and apply them equally to comparable classes of investors within a limited period of time. This might hinder Canada in using this vague standard as a "bargaining chip" to get more from the foreign investor, which in fact has been described as one of the purposes of the law and its generality.[16] In another context, it has been suggested that the investment laws of developing countries should not provide as much discretion as they do to officials giving investment approvals and incentives.[17]

Canada is of course unlikely to agree to subject the procedural operations of its Foreign Investment Review Act to an international organization. Similarly, the U.S. companies, confronted with an array of Canadian legislative and regulatory measures, are unlikely to be sympathetic to the idea that they must give up their right to seek the protection of their government in dealing with the Canadian authorities, as the approach of the Calvo Doctrine or of a comprehensive international investment organization might require.

IS THE NORMATIVE SHAPE TOO LIMITED?

Basically, the above principles assume a model of international guidance to nation-states and a few restrictions on national controls, which include social controls. I am inclined to think that there cannot be a more substantive international code with a minimum of international social control within the foreseeable future because of the priorities of national governments, which are not likely to allow the benefits of the open system to be jeopardized. There is not sufficient data about the process of international investment and multinational corporations, and there is no consensus about the governing economic theory. Most important, there is no consensus about the policies that should govern particular substantive areas. Nationalism limits internationalism; the international system is not thought of as one that can confer legitimacy. There is no consensus that would make possible any real international accountability, nor any real international machinery or basis for faith in it. Certain areas that might lend themselves to international-level scrutiny are accounting standards, the international tax pie for each multinational corporation, international mergers, and transfer prices. In these areas international guidance might be provided or standards developed to permit the harmonization of national policy and national enforcement by both developed and developing countries.[18]

We will not, in the foreseeable future, have an international welfare state with budget, economic plan, and *dirigiste* capacity. The United States has not even agreed to such planning within its own country.

Governments are not going to allow an international organization to regulate their nationals, whether they are individuals or multinational corporations. Although they are interesting and intended to liberate from national control the multinational corporations and indeed the entire process of international investment and multinational corporations from national control, the proposals of George Ball are not realistic under these circumstances. Also unrealistic is the suggestion that corporations become anational and therefore free of national control or that they set up their headquarters on an island, again to be free of national control. This is evident if only from the deliberations at Geneva and elsewhere with respect to the proposed deep sea bed authority. Since an international organization is not likely to emerge, the companies will not be willing to give up their right to seek the protection of their national governments, as suggested by the Calvo Doctrine.

Since there is at present no effective international standard of distributive justice, a prospective international investment organization could not principally be an instrument for the redistribution of wealth, although the multinational corporation, through the promotion of economic activity and the transfer of technology, may contribute to this goal. In this sense an international investment organization, by regulating and smoothing the corporate process, might facilitate some redistribution. For this reason it is premature to speculate on the ultimate values to which an international investment organization might contribute. Some of these values might be greater equity in the distribution of benefits, greater participation, and greater national autonomy. No foreseeable international investment organization is going to become the promoter of global employment and of research and development, the eliminator of the branch-plant mentality, the preventer of vertical integration, or the promoter of a Canadian or European counterattack on American or other multinational companies.[19]

Even if it were possible for an international organization to emerge that would actively promote international policies and priorities, the organization would not be popular. Many developing countries would object to such a strong international organization. It might well be seen to overly legitimize the multinational corporation and the process of international investment and multinational corporations. Moreover, given current economic preferences, these countries might well fear that the organization would be too liberating of the process and too supportive of the status quo; many might fear that it would be too much dominated by the United States.[20] In a word, I return to my view that it is too early for an international investment organization with a substantive code with any specificity or effectiveness.

NOTES

1. Res. 1913 (LVII) par. 7; see also Draft Program of Work on the Full Range of Issues Relating to Transnational Corporations, UN Doc. E/C.10/2 (1975).

2. S. Rubin, Private Foreign Investment, Legal and Economic Realities (1956); C. Edwards, Control of Cartels and Monopolies: An International Comparison (1967); B. Bittker and L. Ebb, United States Taxation of Foreign Income and Foreign Persons (1968).

3. Canadian Government, Foreign Direct Investment in Canada (1972).

4. Statement of Arthur Burns, chairman of the Federal Reserve Board, "Hearings on the Kissinger-Simon Energy Crisis Program Before the Joint Economic Committee," 93d Cong., 2d Sess. 40 (1974).

5. See L. Brown, World Without Borders (1972), ch. 6.

6. M. Watkins, Foreign Ownership and the Structure of Canadian Industry (1968).

7. Treaty Establishing the European Economic Community, Mar. 25, 1958, 298 U.N.T.S., art. 58.

8. D. Vagts, "United States of America's Treatment of Foreign Investment," 17 Rutgers L. Rev. 374, 396-97 (1963).

9. J. Rawls, A Theory of Justice (1971).

10. Treaty Establishing the European Economic Community, op. cit.

11. See Bulletin of the European Communities Commission 12-1974, at 70, and 5-1975, at 55; H. Steiner and D. Vagts, Transnational Legal Problems, 357-58 (1968); P. Goldberg and C. Kindleberger, "Toward a GATT for Investment: A Proposal for Supervision of the International Corporation," 2 Law and Pol. Int'l Bus. 295 (1970); J. Corcoran, "The Trading with the Enemy Act and the Controlled Canadian Corporation," 14 McGill L. J. 174 (1968); New York Times, Mar. 18, 1974, at 45, col. 8; Business Week, April 13, 1974, at 80-81; A. Lowenfeld, "Book Review," 65 Am. J. Int'l L. 853 (1971).

12. U.S. v. Imperial Chemical Industries, Ltd., 100 F. Supp. 504 (S.D.N.Y. 1951); U.S. v. The Watchmakers of Switzerland Information Center, Inc., (1963) Trade Cas. par. 70, 600 (S.D.N.Y. 1962). Compare First National City Bank v. Banco Nacional de Cuba, 400 U.S. 1019 (1970), vacating Banco Nacional de Cuba v. First National City Bank, 431 F. 2d 394 (2d Cir. 1970); A. Lowenfeld, op. cit.

13. Convention for the Suppression of Unlawful Seizure of Aircraft, Dec. 16, 1970, art. 4, 22 U.S.T. 1641, 1645 (1971) part 2, T.I.A.S. No. 7192 (effective Oct. 14, 1971).

14. U.S. v. Toscanino, 500 F. 2d 267 (2d Cir. 1974). See Treaty with Japan on Friendship, Commerce and Navigation, April 2,

1953, art. II, par. 1, 4 U.S.T. 2065 (1953), part 2; T.I.A.S. 2863; 206 U.N.T.S. 143 (effective Oct. 30, 1953).

15. See Attorney-General of the Government of Israel v. Adolf Eichmann, Text of Judgment of the Supreme Court, par. 13 (May 29, 1962), reprinted in 36 Int'l L. Reps. 277, 304 (1968); Report: 16 Piske Din (1962), at 2033, in Hebrew.

16. Canadian Government, Foreign Direct Investment in Canada (1972).

17. See J. Russin and R. Brown, "Automatism v. Discretion: The Industrial Incentive Law of the Dominican Republic," 3 Law and Pol. Int'l Bus. 366 (1971); J. Heller and K. Kauffman, Tax Incentives for Industries in Less Developed Countries (1963).

18. N. T. Wang, "Towards an International Code of Conduct for Transnational Corporations," paper presented to the Conference on the Nation States and the Transnational Corporations in Lesser Developed Countries in Aspen, Colorado, Dec. 13-18, 1974.

19. J. Behrman, "Supranational Control of the Multinational Enterprise," in International Control of Investment 66 (D. Wallace, ed., 1974).

20. D. Wallace, op. cit. at ix.

CHAPTER 10

SPECULATION UPON FURTHER DETAILS

If an international organization of the variety suggested in Chapter 9 were to emerge, more detailed questions would arise. In Chapter 11 I will speculate about how politically realistic the prospects are for the devopment of the situation that would give rise to an international regulatory organization. The UN, the OECD and other agencies are starting to move into this area, but we do not yet have the critical mass of forward motion that would make it possible to predict that a strong organization will appear. The evolution of international controls in an area as new and as complicated as the process of international investment and multinational corporations must be slow. Goldberg and Kindleberger suggest that this slowness is inevitable.[1]

Any proposal to create a new international organization would raise many questions about what it would be and how it would be created. A prospective international investment organization would raise the same questions. Among the principal questions would be the following:

1. What would be the mix between a political and a technical approach to international control of the process of international investment and multinational corporations and how would these two approaches be related? Control would involve technical issues of great complexity; yet the multinational corporation is a subject of great political sensitivity.

2. What would be the outer parameters of a prospective organization?

3. Would it deal with all economic sectors or only some?

4. How legal would the organization be?

5. Would it be created by treaty?

6. Would a treaty contain precise rules governing the process of international investment and multinational corporations?

7. Would it provide for third-party adjudication of disputes between the organization and the nations and corporations subject to it, as well as of disputes between nations and of disputes between a nation and a multinational corporation?

8. What sanctions would there be for violations?

9. Would the treaty be self-executing or would it require further implementing legislation in each country?

10. Possibly more important, would the members be developed countries only or would they also include developing countries?

11. Would the organization have jurisdiction over both nation-states and multinational corporations?

12. What would be the precise role of the multinational corporation in the organization?

13. What would be the precise machinery of the international organization?

14. What organs, such as executive or legislative, would the organization contain?

15. Would it be divided into separate parts, or chambers, dealing with different substantive areas?

16. What would be the voting arrangements?

17. Would all parts of the treaty be equally obligatory?

18. What would be the relationship of an international investment organization to other international organizations such as the IMF and GATT?

19. How would the treaty, or other controlling instrument, be amended?

These are all fairly obvious points, but merely to note them is to suggest the variety of issues upon which one must speculate.

THE MOST INTERESTING SPECULATIONS

Political versus Technical Focus

Would the emphasis of the international organization be political, considering general issues such as the relationship of the multinational corporations to nation-states, not to mention such political episodes as ITT's adventures in Chile; or technical, handling the myriad complexities of taxation, accounting, transfer pricing, antitrust, and other restrictive practice issues? The answer to this question would affect not only the timing and the manner in which the actual establishment of an organization might begin, but also the evolution of the organization once it was commenced upon. The answer would obviously be found in the concept of the organization and the level and nature of the personnel that would staff it. The answer would also aid in determining how support for its creation might be developed within different countries. The answer to the question would determine the shape of the strategy that the organization would have to undertake as it developed. Examination of what has happened in the UN, the OECD, and the OAS is relevant. There has been an attempt in the UN to straddle the political and technical emphases. Many believe that a political emphasis, biased in favor of the problems of the developing countries and away from details and norms, has so far often prevailed.[2]

To answer this question it will be necessary to discuss what the organization would be and also how it would emerge.

Degree of Legality of the Organization

Probably the most basic question about the nature of the organization is that of the degree of its legality. Here we should keep in mind not only the shape of the organization at its commencement, but also the shape it would take as it evolved. This question might be considered in terms of the possible forms the organization might take, in descending order from the most to the least comprehensive and binding forms.

Neither the United Nations nor the OAS considers it possible to formulate a comprehensive treaty instituting such an organization in the mid-1970s. This treaty, which would include fairly detailed rules and standards that would be applicable to all the relevant economic sectors and substantive areas within the parameters of the process of international investment and multinational corporations, would be a general agreement for multinational corporations similar to the General Agreement on Tariffs and Trade.[3]

If the treaty were complete, precise, and self-executing, it might be enforced by international litigation between states or by private parties or states in national courts, and would be a code of international law. No one seems to think that this is possible in the foreseeable future.

If the treaty did not include an extensive code of substantive rules, it might be possible for it to establish an international organization merely defining in broad outline the outer parameters of the scope and powers of the organization. As for the kind of an international organization it might be, it might resemble the IMF or the GATT, or it might, as some have suggested, be merely a forum or series of forums, that would be basically devoted to discussion, some consultation, and possibly some information gathering.[4] It is not clear whether the UN Commission on Transnational Corporations will become even that.

If there is no tight and comprehensive treaty or substantial international organization, then there is no question whether the organization, or another body implementing the treaty, would have the authority to prescribe rules and regulations. There is also no problem of whether the treaty and these rules and regulations would be self-executing, and there is no question of sanctions for their violation.

At a possibly lower level, there might be a code of conduct governing nation-states; the OECD is seriously considering this possibility. Presumably it would be hortatory rather than legally binding. It is not clear what aspects of conduct would be governed or whether the code would be general or specific. It has been suggested that third-party binding adjudication is the key to the solution of the problem of the multinational corporation.[5]

Issues cannot be justiciable unless there are norms or standards, that is to say laws that can be applied to those disputes. Someone has suggested mediation, the results of which would be compulsory and binding on the parties. At a slightly lower level is the possibility of further coordination, presumably of the policies of different nation-states, such as the United States, Canada, and to some extent the members of the OECD through their Restrictive Practices Committee, which have coordinated the enforcement of their respective antitrust laws. Coordination would extend to the formulation of national policies, including legislation, regulation, and general economic policy. A more likely method might be consultation among governments with respect to the enforcement of existing laws, regulations, and policies. Consultation seems less binding on governments than coordination. Again, the international organization might merely investigate multinational corporation practices, or it might propose to give them publicity with the idea that adverse publicity would lead to changed practice. An organization might also monitor or subject to surveillance the multinational corporations.

Some writers have suggested that an international organization would merely gather information, an activity that may be quite effective legally or quite ineffective. Part of this activity would be an increased dialogue between nation-states and multinational corporations with respect to foreign direct investment practices. Dialogues have been conducted in the past under the auspices of the United Nations and the OAS and have not applied to specific transactions or even to proposed government policies, but have been limited to the discussion of various outstanding concerns.

Relevant to all of the above would be the level, extent, and efficacy of the machinery that would be established to run the organization.

How Would the Organization Develop?

Without deciding when the events might begin that would lead to the creation of an international investment organization, we can posit a time when something resembling the model that is discussed here might be said to commence. After this commencement, the development of the organization would be a progression toward more, and more definite, norms; a greater binding quality; more elaborated sanctions; and provision for adjudication.

It is important to be clear about what each particular measure would entail. Quite a number of the suggested measures in this area are ambiguous and may in fact not be as easy as they seem. The suggestion that an easy first step would be the gathering of information can conceal many ambiguities and may be more difficult than is evident, depending on the kind of information that would be gathered, the manner in which it would be gathered, and the uses to which it would be put. The information might run from general statistics to far more specific corporate disclosures, which might be used for purposes of publicity, investigation, or negotiation or as a base for political action that would be inimical to a corporation. Words such as monitor, consult, coordinate, and mediate need not necessarily involve easy procedures. Dialogue may be a less ambiguous way of settling disputes than information gathering.

It is probably not worthwhile to speculate on the precise steps by which the organization would evolve toward greater specificity and sanctions. It is likely that the organization would evolve by stages, as the EEC has done. Possibly the organization would commence its activities in a number of subject areas, such as tax, antitrust, and capital flow. The precise nature of its approach, along the political-technical spectrum would be important, as would the level and quality of its personnel, and many other such factors. A mediocre organization, a "parking lot" for political hacks, would not be useful.

An effective organization would provide the organized impulse that would lead to a further definition of the problem and to measures that might be realistically taken.[6]

An effective international investment organization would probably divide its operations into separate parts or chambers, each of which would address different technical issue areas, such as tax and transfer prices, antitrust laws, patents and technology transfer, capital flows, and screening laws. In spite of these divisions there would have to be some overall political organ to direct and pull together the work. It is difficult to project how the development within each chamber would relate to the stages of the overall development of the organization.[7] It is conceivable that work in different areas would lead to agreements of different binding qualities, although the exact relationship of these to each other is difficult to envision.

It seems reasonably clear that as the organization evolved there would have to be continuous consideration and refinement of the parameters of the activities within its scope. Presumably it would continue to focus on the problems of the multinational corporation from its entry into particular countries through the problems of long-term security. Presumably it would concern itself with activities in various economic sectors. These activities would be subject to review, as would some of the exclusions from the scope of the organization that I have assumed would be made. It is not clear how much of the process of international investment and multinational corporations must be preserved, and with what degree of intactness, if its economic and other benefits are to be maintained.

It may be asked whether the international law model is the practical maximum attainable. The exact position of the organization on the political and technical spectrum would be continuously considered, although practical politics might dictate the result. The implicit emphasis on function, because of organization into chambers or parts dealing with different technical subjects in relation to an organization that is based on different economic sectors, might become an issue.

The degree that the charter of the organization is binding might determine whether it is divided into, (1) formal parts or chambers, with staffs, investigatory powers, the capacity to draft conventions, and the like, or possibly (2) more informal forums, each dealing with a particular subject matter but in a less legal way.

SUBJECTS TO BE COVERED BY ORGANIZATION

What issues might the organization concern itself with? Because of the technical complexity of the issues, they must be tackled separately by experts. However, the work of the organization would be unified by the overriding focus on the totality of the process of international investment and multinational corporations, and impelled by the political reality that had given rise to the creation of the organization, which would be reflected in the top political organs of the organization.

The issues I will discuss below represent my own assessment of issues that might be considered interesting and important.[8] I will begin with issues that I think are important and urgent, and possibly more feasible of investigation than others. In listing and discussing these issues I am to some extent redefining the parameters of the activities with which the international investment organization is to be concerned, which were first mentioned in Chapter 2. Given a preference for an open world economy, the limits of an international law model, and a preference for at least minimal social control, the following subjects lead to an organization that would essentially guide and limit nation-states in their dealings with multinational corporations rather than directly control the multinational corporations themselves. These subjects are described as functions, or chambers, of the organization.

Capital Flows

The chamber of capital flows would deal with the issues embodied in the existing OECD Code of Liberalization of Capital Movements and Code of Liberalization of Current Invisible Transactions. It would concern itself with the capital movements that are essential to the functioning of the process of international investment and multinational corporations within the parameters that have been defined, and it would presumably redefine these parameters. It would develop standards to govern national capital controls in order to permit the process to continue.

Establishment

The chamber of establishment would deal with the problems of entry into and establishment in host countries and with the screening laws of host countries. It would be involved with takeovers to the extent that these raise entry questions; they may also raise questions of antitrust and securities law. Certain issues of reinvestment would certainly come within its scope. The treaties of friendship, commerce, and navigation, the Treaty of Rome, and the OECD codes touch on this subject.

New investment laws in Argentina and Mexico, as well as the Andean Group, touch on the question of reinvestment. The proposals in the William's Bill to authorize the U.S. president to bar any foreign equity holding of more than 5 percent in a U.S. company, directed against Arab investors, would be within the scope of this chamber.

Tax

A major chamber would be tax. The issues covered might include the suggestion that the corporate tax pie of multinational corporations be allocated among the relevant home and host countries according to certain objective criteria such as assets, employees, and sales in each country. R. Vernon has suggested this.[9] Some such arrangements have been proposed for the allocation of taxes between states in the United States. In 1929 the League of Nations proposed an approach in tax treaties to avoid double taxation and to allocate taxes between two tax jurisdictions in cases in which no other approach was feasible.

Transfer price issues would be another subject for this chamber. The issue here is the fair allocation of income among the different units of a multinational corporation that Section 482 of the United States Internal Revenue Code and the regulations thereunder seek to achieve. The issues are manifold and complex and can involve the proper treatment of such matters as goods bought and sold, monies loaned, services rendered, and overhead. Each taxing jurisdiction will seek to gain as much of the income of a multinational corporation for itself as possible. Thus, under 482 the United States would in theory seek to maximize the income of the parent and hence the tax on it, whereas a host country would seek to maximize the income of the subsidiary within its jurisdiction.

Investment and other incentives, as well as the operation of tax havens, would be a subject of this chamber. The OECD is now seeking to determine how incentives between different nations and regions of nations can be harmonized.

Work in the tax area, as in other areas, would prove to be extremely difficult. Different countries depend on different types of taxes: income taxes, customs taxes, and turnover taxes. The countries assert different theories of jurisdiction: territorial jurisdiction or universal jurisdiction. They define terms, income, and deductions differently, and they enforce their laws with different sanctions and achieve different levels of efficiency.

Antitrust

It has been suggested that cross-border, or international, mergers would be a suitable subject for international scrutiny. I have already cited the example given by P. Goldberg and C. Kindleberger, that the acquisition of the French corporation Machines Bull by IBM would be of much greater international significance than its acquisition by GE or Minneapolis Honeywell. Kindleberger also cites the example of the Norwegian aluminum company Aardal, which was acquired by Alcan, and suggests that its acquisition by a smaller aluminum company would not have been as significant in its anti-competitive effect on the global market. The EEC has been considering the establishment of new merger guidelines that involve companies with a combined total turnover of more than one billion European units of account.[10]

Presumably such cases of international mergers of major significance are relatively rare. There is much greater interest in many countries in the issue of any takeover of a local company by a foreign company. It might very well be that standards might be developed that would limit the power of nations to bar certain takeovers.

The United Nations Conference on Trade and Development (UNCTAD) has criticized many practices of multinational corporations as restrictive, including tie-ins, allocation of export markets, certain restrictions on "technology transfer," and others. Some international code might be developed in this area, although the history of prior attempts has not been promising. The Havana Charter contained a section on restrictive trade practices, although, like all prior international initiatives, it was not focused on the multinational corporation, but rather proceeded from the premise that private barriers to trade were as offensive as governmental barriers. It would have applied in the same way to exporters and national companies as it would have been to multinational investors. An early draft of the charter would have permitted complaints by private parties. The Havana Charter did not fail because of the inclusion of the restrictive practices provision; however, in 1953 when the United Nations sought to revive an international restrictive practices code that would have been largely based on the provisions of the Havana Charter, it failed because the United States believed that other countries should develop their own antitrust laws before an international treaty was attempted. Subsequent OECD and GATT efforts have not met with any greater success.[11] The final draft of the Havana Charter eliminated private antitrust complaints.

In this area, more so than in the tax area, inasmuch as different countries have different purposes and policies, all countries raise taxes. The United States still places unique emphasis on antitrust laws as a means of regulating its economy. The EEC is giving more and more emphasis to its competition policy. Beyond that, very few countries attach the importance to tax laws that the United States does. As with all laws, nations will be very reluctant to curb the economic interests of their nationals, including the multinational corporations based in their own countries.

Long-Term Security

Although highly controversial, the subject of long-term security must be within the parameters of the process that an international organization would regulate, not so much in relation to individual expropriations, contract repudiations, or other breakdowns, as in relation to the cumulative effect of a failure to protect investment on the overall process of international investment and multinational corporations. Long-term security is crucial to host countries. The greater the perceived risk for investment, the greater the pressure to increase the rate of return and fast payout.

The history of international efforts in this area is, again, not very hopeful. In 1929 the League of Nations proposed a code for the protection of foreign investment. Chapter 12 of the Havana Charter, added at a fairly late stage in its drafting and entitled "economic development," in fact dealt with the protection of foreign investors. The weakness of this provision was one of the reasons that the Havana Charter failed in the U.S. Congress. Since that time there have been a number of proposed investment protection codes, including the Abs Code, an OECD draft and others.[12] The ICC Investor Guidelines also seek to impose "obligations" on the investor.[13] National measures such as the Hickenlooper Amendment, which calls for the termination of U.S. foreign assistance to any country that expropriates property and does not take certain steps to compensate,[14] are a reflection of the absence of international measures.

Governments have taken practical steps to handle this problem by establishing national investment insurance programs. Proposals to establish a multilateral-guarantee authority have not yet made progress. There is disagreement on the substantive international law standard in this area, whether related to compensation for the taking of property or to protection of investment contracts. The U.S. courts have seemed confused about what their position on the matter should be. There is an absence of consensus between the developed investor countries and the developing host countries. This problem must continue to be worked on.[15]

Accounting Standards

There have been frequent suggestions that more uniform accounting standards should be developed for the operations of multinational corporation in different countries, presumably to enable governments, unions, and others to deal with them more effectively. The demand for international accounting standards touches on a different system, which impinges on the process of international investment and multinational corporations but is not limited to it, in much the same way as capital markets, insurance companies, and banks do. This is part of the demand for greater disclosure and more information about multinational corporations. It is a subject with which the international investment organization might legitimately be concerned.[16]

OTHER CHAMBERS

There are many other subjects that an international organization might concern itself with, including patent and technology transfer problems, pollution, labor relations, problems of a social audit, and government procurement.

Labor-management relations represent a vast subject, varying from country to country, that cannot be central to an international investment organization concerned principally with the process of international investment and multinational corporations. At the same time a number of unions are very concerned about multinational corporations.[17] Similarly, multinational corporations are concerned about problems of worker participation in management.[18] In one or two industries, international secretariats of unions have been set up with a view to facilitating multinational bargaining with multinational corporations by their employees. This movement has not progressed very far.[19]

The notion of the social audit, which arises out of the corporate responsibility movement, is that corporations should report, not only on their economic results but also on the social consequences of their actions, to a number of constituencies, including shareholders, employees, and society at large. This movement has not developed very much nationally or internationally. Procurement may be for the GATT. (See first section of Chapter 2.)

Information

Presumably there would be a chamber dealing with all manner of questions related to corporate disclosure and information. The kind of information that would be gathered would be crucial. This might run the range from statistical information, some of which might be gathered by other, already existing organizations, about inward and outward gross capital flows for countries, global flows, data for particular industries, and information about individual companies and their plans. Such information could serve many purposes. Companies might be required to complete forms that would be turned over to the international organization for any purpose it wishes. Developing countries have spoken of data banks containing information that would enable them to negotiate more effectively with multinational corporations. Information might be useful for law enforcement purposes or merely to focus the light of publicity on a corporation.

The EEC mentioned various kinds of information in its resolution of November 1973.[20] The UN Commission on Transnational Corporations and the related Center on Transnational Corporations will concern themselves with information. The OECD is also considering this matter. The Culver-Inouye Act requires the U.S. Departments of the Treasury and Commerce to collect information about direct and portfolio investment in the United States from all foreign investors.[21] The SEC collects such data. Trade unions also seek such data to assist them in their negotiations.[22]

Guidance

Another chamber might assist developing countries in their negotiations with foreign investors by developing technical assistance for them. Such an approach is consistent with the status quo and the better operation of market forces. The UN has made available the services of experts to assist with negotiations.[23] Harmonization of host country laws might be another function for this chamber.

THE EXACT STATUS OF MULTINATIONAL CORPORATIONS IN AN INTERNATIONAL INVESTMENT ORGANIZATION

One of the most important questions about any prospective international investment organization is what role the multinational corporations would themselves play in that organization. In theory and in practice, multinational corporations, like other private parties, have not been the subject of international law or participated in international organizations directly. The operation of the UN Commission on Transnational Corporations reflects this approach. The code of conduct that the commission will work on, although addressed to the delinquencies of multinational corporations, would presumably operate through the national states.

In a sense this is one of the manifestations of the principle of the confederal maximum. Governments will not delegate much authority to an international organization at all, much less authority to deal directly with their own nationals. There are very few exceptions to this. The European Human Rights Convention does permit private complaints in certain limited circumstances.[24] The proposed deep sea bed authority might deal directly with corporations, but it is highly unlikely that such an authority will be agreed upon. The International Air Transport Authority (IATA), has, as its members, governments and airlines, many of them government airlines, which agree on rates that are subject to final national regulation. The proposed UN Liner Conference Convention would provide for arbitration between governments and conferences. The European Coal and Steel Community and Euratom have had some authority over companies, pursuant to treaty.

Should multinational corporations have a role in an international investment organization? Should they be represented in the organization with votes? This question has nothing to do with the suggestion that the nation-state system has yielded to a transnational system, but merely applies to the potential efficiency of the organization.

A related question is whether the multinational corporations should provide personnel to assist in the management of the organization, a contribution that might very well upgrade the organization and render it more serious but that would have its own inherent dangers. Presumably multinational corporations would not, individually, join the organization. This would present too many problems; for example, there would be very narrow questions about the definition of the term "multinational corporation," and there would be problems about corporations that were dissolved or merged.

The corporations might instead join the organization through elected representatives of various federations and professional bodies to the governing body of the international organization. The exact nature of the role of the companies would be important; employers do participate in the International Labor Organization, but this has not necessarily given that body any added clout. The Communications Satellite Corporation (COMSAT), and the proposed seabed authority if it ever materializes, might be examined for precedents.

Would the corporations or their representatives share in the voting power of the organization? I suspect that most people would feel that the multinational corporations should not have so strong and direct role as these questions suggest. Almost all of us carry in our minds the nation-state model of the international system, in which regulatory power inheres in nation-states, which in turn may participate in an international organization. The idea seems strange of private actors, nationals of nation-states, participating in this power.

The United Nations Commission on Transnational Corporations is composed of representatives of governments. An earlier proposal by the Group of Eminent Persons that the commission be composed of individual experts selected in their individual capacity, although by governments, was rejected by the United Nations Economic and Social Council (ECOSOC).

Multinational corporations might play a lesser part as advisors to an international investment organization. They have done this, as have trade unions, with the OECD, acting through the Business International Advisory Committee (BIAC), and it is contemplated that they will do so with the United Nations Commission on Transnational Corporations. UNESCO already has many private organizations as consultants.

There is a more technical, legal question about whether an international investment organization, if it should ever develop to the point at which it would have the power to adjudicate disputes, could give multinational corporations sufficient standing to institute or participate in such procedures. Almost all international claims are presently espoused by states.[25]

UNIVERSALITY OF AN INTERNATIONAL INVESTMENT ORGANIZATION

In addition to the question of whether multinational corporations would be members of an international investment organization, there is the basic question about what countries would be members. I assume that membership would be taken up only by countries that actively participate in the open economy and are already members of the institutions established by Bretton Woods; at least initially, many Communist bloc countries would not be active members. A more basic question is whether developing countries would join freely with developed countries. My feeling is that the organization must be as universal in this respect as possible. Although the bulk of multinational corporation investment is in developed countries, the bulk of protest about multinational corporations comes from developing countries, suggesting that the volume of multinational corporation investment in their countries is also substantial. The politics of the two groups of countries is somewhat different. Most developed countries are both host and home countries, whereas many developing countries are primarily host countries and are not sources of outward foreign direct investment by their own multinational corporations.

Iran and a few Arab countries, Venezuela, and other places such as Hong Kong and Singapore are sources of outward foreign investment, although it may not yet be through multinational corporations. Brazil, Mexico, and other countries may become bases for their own multinational corporations. Statistics can be misleading. Regardless of the fact that 70 percent of U.S. investment is in Europe and Canada, the remaining 30 percent, although much of it is in natural resources, can have a substantial impact on developing countries. The figures for investment by other capital exporting countries are not so lopsided. Moreover, countries such as Canada have some problems akin to those of developing countries.

The extent of the problems of a developing country may be greater than the extent of the problems of a developed country. The developing country will have a more severe balance of payments problem; it will be far more dependent on external technology; and it will not itself be a source of outward foreign investment or a base for multinational companies. The developing country will not have as large a market as most developed countries, and unless it is able to use control over its own natural resources in some relevant way, it will feel itself to be in a weaker bargaining position. The developing country is a sovereign state, however, and presumably its markets or other factors related to it appeal to multinational corporations, since the multinational corporation in question is seeking to invest in it. It may therefore be argued that the attitude of the developing country need not be all that different from that of a developed host country.

It may be that, in developing specific rules, some of the earliest and most active chambers of an international investment organization might deal with problems of greater interest to developed countries, such as certain tax and antitrust problems. However, the organization would probably be working in many relevant areas simultaneously, many of which would be of equally great interest to developing countries. Depending on the bias of the organization, it might even be of greater interest to developing countries in its initial stages.

The organization should embrace both developing and developed countries in its work, and both should have the option of joining the organization at its commencement. The ability of a country to choose particular chambers to join might weaken the effectiveness of the organization, inasmuch as countries might join only those chambers in which they saw a clear benefit but no sacrifice. This question would have to be considered carefully. In the IMF and the GATT, developing countries have not initially taken on the full obligations of membership. In the case of the GATT many did not join, while in the case of the IMF many remain in Article XIV status.

An international investment organization would have to have authority over regional organizations and not merely coexist with them. Thus the rules of an international investment organization would have to override and control, for example, the EEC and the Andean Group. As a realistic matter, the international investment organization would probably arise partly in response to the excesses of both national and regional controls. There is an analogy here to

Article XXIV of the GATT, which makes certain exceptions for customs unions. It has been suggested that the growth and abuse of these, for example in some of the Mediterranean pacts of the EEC, are undermining the GATT and that if the GATT is to be restored to effectiveness it must in some way check such regional practices.[26]

To the extent that a regional organization such as the European Coal and Steel Community, which is now merged in the EEC, has authority over individual iron and coal companies, such jurisdiction would have to be related to the jurisdiction of the international investment organization. This again raises the question of the status of the multinational corporation in an international investment organization.

OTHER ORGANIZATIONAL QUESTIONS

A few of the other questions concerning an international organization are as follows: What would be the administrative organs of the organization? How would the notion of "chambers" be related to the structure of the organization? Would there be a legislature?

How strong an executive would the organization have? We have already touched on the question of whether there would be multinational corporation membership.

What would be the voting arrangements? Would there be weighted voting for member nations, as in the IMF and IBRD, or a one-nation, one-vote approach, as in the GATT? This feature of the GATT has been cited as a reason for its present weakness. There have been suggestions that a further layer of more developed countries be created within the GATT, to function through a special council.[27]

Would there be machinery for third-party binding adjudication? What would be the sanctions for violation of the rules? If there were a link to GATT or the IMF, might violations of the international investment organization rules trigger IMF or GATT sanctions? (This would be an unlikely prospect.)

How would the organization be funded? How would the provisions of its governing instrument be amended? How would it be related to the GATT, to the IMF, and to other organizations?

LOCUS

Where would an international investment organization be placed? Would it be part of the UN, and thus, regrettably, rendered suspect in the eyes of most developed countries, or would it be part of the IBRD, and thus, perhaps, rendered somewhat suspect in the eyes of many developing countries.

The OECD has been suggested as a possible locus, as it has sought to complement the IMF and the GATT. Unfortunately, OECD membership is restricted to 24 developed countries. Its membership could be expanded to include developing countries, but then it would cease to serve the purpose that it now does, which is to coordinate the economic strategy of developed countries.[28]

As noted, the OECD is undertaking many studies with respect to international investment and multinational corporations. It has prepared draft documents dealing with the national treatment and the operation of multinational companies. It has been the author of the Code of Liberalization of Capital Movements and the Code of Liberalization of Current Invisible Operations. Its Fiscal Affairs Committee has over 30 working groups on international tax problems. Its Restrictive Practices Committee has been at work on antitrust problems.

Presumably a new organization would have to be created. It could draw on the statistical and other work of existing organizations. A question, especially for the United States, is whether any such new organization could be created that would not be excessively U.S. dominated. Still to be answered is the question of when, and under what circumstances, such an organization might in fact arise.

NOTES

1. P. Goldberg and C. Kindleberger, "Toward a GATT for Investment: A Proposal for Supervision of the International Corporation," 2 Law and Pol. Int'l Bus. 295 (1970).

2. N. T. Wang, "Towards an International Code of Conduct for Transnational Corporations," paper presented to the Conference on the Nation States and the Transnational Corporations in Lesser Developed Countries in Aspen, Colorado, Dec. 13-18, 1974.

3. <u>The Impact of Multinational Corporations on the Development Process and on International Relations: Report of the Group of Eminent Persons to Study the Role of Multinational Corporations on Development and on International Relations</u>, UN Doc. E/5500/Add. 11, Rev. 1-ST/ESA/6 (hereinafter known as the Eminent Persons Report); OAS Resolution, "Organization of American States, Behavior of Transnational Enterprises Operating in the Region and Need for a Code of Conduct to be Observed by Such Enterprises," CP/Res. 154, at 167-75 (July 10, 1975).

4. Seymour Rubin has written on the subject of forums. See S. Rubin, "Multinational Enterprise and National Sovereignty: A Skeptic's Analysis," 3 Law and Pol. Int'l Bus. 1 (1971).

5. See J. Behrman, <u>National Interests and the Multinational Enterprise: Tension Among the North Atlantic Communities</u> (1970).

6. E. Stein, Harmonization of European Company Laws, National Law Reform and Transnational Coordination (1971).

7. Eminent Persons Report, op. cit.; N. T. Wang, op. cit.; OAS Resolution, op. cit.

8. The UN has listed issues with respect to the prospective work of its Commission on Transnational Corporations in UN document UN E/C 10/2, Feb. 28, 1975. The OECD has a comparable agenda.

9. R. Vernon, "The Multinational Enterprise: Power versus Sovereignty," 49 For. Affairs 736, 747 (1971).

10. P. Goldberg and C. Kindleberger, op. cit., p. 304.

11. C. Edwards, Control of Cartels and Monopolies: An International Comparison (1967).

12. S. Rubin, Private Foreign Investment, Legal and Economic Realities (1956); The Conference Board Report, The Search for Common Ground: A Survey of Efforts to Develop Codes of Behavior in International Investment (1971).

13. S. Rubin, op. cit., note 4.

14. U.S. Foreign Assistance Act, sec. 620(e).

15. See, for example, First Nat'l City Bank v. Banco Nacional de Cuba, 400 U.S. 1019 (1970), vacating Banco Nacional de Cuba v. First Nat'l City Bank, 431 F.2d 394 (2d Cir. 1970).

16. This has been suggested by the Eminent Persons Report, op. cit.

17. See, for example, Organization for Economic Cooperation and Development, note by the Trade Union Advisory Committee on Multinational Corporations, RE/TUAC/75.1, Paris, Mar. 14, 1975.

18. See, for example, the protest of the U.S. Chamber of Commerce in Germany with respect to proposed changes in the German worker participation law, New York Times, Oct. 13, 1974, at 17, col. 1.

19. See B. Jones, "Labor Union Role at Multinationals Found Still Limited," New York Times, April 21, 1975, at 45, col. 4.

20. See Comm'n of the European Communities, Multinational Undertakings and Community Regulations (Comm'n Communication to the Council, Nov. 7, 1973).

21. "Foreign Investment Study Act of 1974," Pub. L. No. 93-479, 88 Stat. 1450 (1974).

22. Organization for Economic Cooperation and Development, op. cit.

23. As suggested in the Draft Programme of Work on the Full Range of Issues Relating to Transnational Corporations, prepared by the Commission on Transnational Corporations, UN Doc. E/C. 10/2.

24. European Convention for the Protection of Human Rights and Fundamental Freedoms, Nov. 4, 1950, 213 U.N.T.S. 221, Eur. T.S. No. 5, art. 25.

25. Compare the early proposal in the Havana Charter, op. cit., and the limited role of the individual before the European Court of Human Rights, op. cit.

26. J. Jackson, *World Trade and the Law of GATT* 586-92 (1969).

27. The Atlantic Council of the United States Policy Papers, *GATT Plus a Proposal for Trade Reform Council* (1975).

28. See S. Rubin, op. cit.

PART IV

HOW REALISTIC ARE THE PROSPECTS FOR AN INTERNATIONAL INVESTMENT ORGANIZATION

CHAPTER

11

THE POSSIBLE DEVELOPMENT OF THE SITUATION AND THE PROSPECTS IN COUNTRIES OTHER THAN THE UNITED STATES

The chances of setting up an effective international investment organization, which means not merely a code of conduct or behavior, or a set of guidelines, are not very great at this time. It is reasonably clear that both the multinational corporations and the politicians and civil servants who make government policy prefer the current muddled situation as being the best approximation available of the preferred international economy described in Chapter 5. It is middle-level policy-making civil servants as much as politicians, and not popular sentiment, that determines national policy toward international organizations, their creation, and their operation. Many civil servants, whether in developed or developing countries, seem to subscribe to the views of the liberal economists with respect to international exchange and its benefits.

The present situation provides a balance. It is possible that the approach suggested in Chapter 8 of national, diplomatic, and possibly issue by issue measures will always suffice. Especially when one appreciates that the absence of any real consensus with respect to the process of international investment and multinational corporations reinforces the inevitable tendency among nation-states to inertia, that is, to not moving toward a greater development of institutionalized international coordination. Why should countries go beyond the present efforts of the United Nations, the OECD, the OAS, the ICC, or the voluntary codes of conduct of the Caterpillar Tractor Company? There is some development in these areas, but it is easy to think of reasons why both multinational corporations and various nation-states would resist a strong international investment organization.

The world has come a long way without an international investment organization. The overall and long-term framework of security for foreign investment is far from ideal, though it may still be sufficient for multinational company purposes. Also, the opportunities for many of the companies seem to continue to expand to accommodate their global views. It was Max Weber who brought out the enormous importance of contractual security for trade and investment.[1] This is also needed, subject to the necessary changes on a global scale. In a sense the multinational corporations need "lebensraum," although they appear to have it, whether in the West and the Third World through investment and contract or in the East through contract alone.[2]

What could change the situation in such a way that, notwithstanding the continued global economy, the growth of interdependence, which will be uneven over time and space, and the continued operation of the principles of the GATT and the IMF, an international investment organization would become more attractive?

One would have to envision the situation in which too many nations with important markets begin to enact too many, and possibly too inconsistent, restrictions with respect to the process of international investment and multinational corporations. If the investment laws and decisions of the Andean Group, Canada, Mexico, and Brazil become too difficult and not susceptible to handling by the normal diplomatic, national, and bilateral means, this might cause concern. Relevant in the past was the French attempt to push the EEC into imposing community restrictions in opposition to continued penetration by foreign multinational corporations and foreign direct investment.

Another relevant development would be that of U.S. laws imposed on inward foreign investment, leading to retaliation. I am skeptical of this development. It is possible that the United States might pass laws authorizing its executive branch to limit, for example, inward Arab investment. It has been suggested that such laws would lead to retaliation and investment wars, but there is little evidence that this would happen. What countries would retaliate? Would Switzerland, the source of inward foreign investment into the United States, retaliate? There have been earlier examples of actual or threatened retaliation: the Hickenlooper Amendment; the Australian reaction to U.S. foreign direct investment controls; attempts by the United States to use its market to force Japan to liberalize its inward investment rules; Canadian and other objections to U.S. export controls; and the celebrated Chicken War, which led to retaliation, under the GATT, by the United States against the EEC because of its ban on U.S. frozen chickens. In each case the mechanism has been different. At least in the developed world, there are not many existing national capital controls, whether with respect to inward or outward investment, especially controls with an investment, as opposed to a balance of payments, motive. We have seen the rise of Australian,

Canadian, Mexican, and Andean Common Market (ANCOM) measures, which are, in effect, no more than extensions of the investment controls all developing countries have had for many years. The United States, Germany, and other countries have shown concern about inward Arab investment and have examined their legislative and regulatory instruments. The Arabs have been moderate in their direct investment policy, and it is hard to see what nation that is a base for multinational corporations would retaliate against such measures. Article 8 of the OECD Code of Liberalization of Capital Movements bars retaliation in capital controls. (See the last section of Chapter 6.)

Retaliation is not the key to the developments that might lead to an international investment organization; rather, the key might be the example of the rise of national restrictions, inconsistent with each other, that might disturb multinational corporations. Multinational corporations unquestionably worry some people; it is therefore not unlikely that there will come to be a crosshatch of overlapping laws and regulations directed principally at their operations. The sum total of these laws and regulations may create a climate that overrides the present Weberian feeling that the international economy is sufficiently hospitable to the process of international investment and multinational corporations.

It would have to be felt that this climate was becoming so poor that the traditional national, bilateral, and diplomatic measures could not cope with it. This may have been the feeling with respect to the problems in the oil industry in 1973 and 1974, but by 1975 this feeling had abated. It would have to be believed, for example, that U.S. legislation with respect to the U.S. multinational corporations lacked credibility abroad. Related to this overseas view that American controls were not sufficient, and to increased overseas national controls, there would be further developments within the United States. These might take the form of renewed labor union pressure, as seen in the proposed Hartke-Burke legislation of 1972, or in tax measures designed to restrict foreign investment abroad.

The investigation of the oil industry reflected a comparable sentiment. Most of the response to the panic brought about by the oil embargo and the initial increased oil prices, which certainly seemed to be a true crisis, has subsided. The more "socialist" interest in controlling the multinational corporations in order to control the domestic economy is an untypical variant; Ronald Muller believes that the increased influence of multinational corporations makes such control of the economy much more difficult.[3]

Were these various developments to come together, it is possible that multinational corporations and economically liberal civil servants in the West would value the use of an international investment organization to control domestic pressures in various countries.

Of course, there can be no uniformity of interests among multinational corporations or among civil servants.

Robert Hudec has suggested that one of the principal purposes of the GATT is to control protectionist domestic pressures.[4] Is it possible that an international investment organization could be strong enough to put down such domestic pressures as the 1975 pressures in the United States against Arab investment, or at least strong enough to strengthen the hand of the executive? We have seen an increase in the congressional role in various provisions in the Trade Act calling for congressional approval or disapproval of particular trade measures. Given the considerable confusion in the domestic mood, an international investment organization that was actually established in reality might have some effect. Whether that confusion could be overridden to create an international investment organization in the first place is a more difficult question.

What of developing countries, where there is such ambivalence toward multinational corporations? It would be difficult, if it required parliamentary action, for civil servants in developing countries to override the political problems enough to decide for establishment of an international investment organization. If the organization were to emerge from an existing organization such as the United Nations, it might be easier to establish in developing countries.

Even if the situation in the West became favorable for the establishment of a multinational organization, it is unlikely that it would become favorable in the developing countries at the same time. Unfortunately the "one world" view seems to be absent in such deliberations as those relating to the sea bed or the UN Charter of Economic Rights and Duties adopted in December 1974. In this realm, global progress is slow. The results of the Henry Kissinger initiatives at the United Nations in September 1975 remain to be seen.[5]

THE COUNTRIES

In Appendix A I will briefly look at a number of countries in order to determine what support there might be, given these developments, for an international investment organization. I have chosen the countries somewhat arbitrarily from among both the developed and the developing countries, with the EEC included as a single unit. I have excluded countries that are mere tax havens. Presumably countries with both substantial inward and substantial outward foreign investment would prove most sympathetic to an international investment organization.

The discussion of each country is superficial; in fact very few have spoken officially upon the subject of an international investment organization. To extrapolate from the factors in the economic history of each country to determine what its future policy may be with respect to an international investment organization at some indefinite time in the future, is a highly speculative exercise. Most countries do not have explicit policies with respect to inward and outward foreign direct investment; and a policy with respect to an international investment organization is one step further removed. The Grey Report on what Canadian policy toward inward foreign investment should be, included superficial sketches of the policies of other countries. It did not touch upon the subject of an international investment organization.[6]

A key to determining the policy of each country toward an international investment organization is the general policy of the country toward an open world economy and its degree of openness to it. However, this policy and openness can change. For instance, policy toward inward foreign investment became more open in 1974.

In each country I will try to determine how the preliminary series of events would come about. The basis is a policy that would favor an open world economy. There are a number of important nations that have such a policy. Through thick and thin the United Kingdom followed such a policy, presumably because over the years it has been dependent on trade and outlets for outward investment, and because more recently, it has also become dependent on inward investment. Japan and Germany seem to follow such policies. The collective EEC, although its policy is slightly more ambiguous, also subscribes to this policy. There is no reason to think that Brazil, Iran, and other countries that are moving toward an important economic status will not also follow such a policy. It seems that successful national economies prefer an open global economy. From time to time national measures for curbing excessive openness are proposed. In the early 1970s the Lebanese sought to restrict both domestic and foreign operations of foreign banks in Lebanon, although in general, until its troubles grew worse in 1975, Beirut was a veritable Mecca to such banks.[7]

Notwithstanding the apparent indifference of the IMF, truly comprehensive and rigorous capital controls, even of the balance of payments variety, not to mention controls on investment, are relatively rare except for the investment and planning controls of the developing countries, although there has been some increase. The overriding factor is still the free hand that the IMF or Bretton Woods system has given to an open world economy; a principal drawback is the absence of an effective adjustment mechanism that can gain consensus support. This absence of an adjustment mechanism gives rise to pressure for capital controls to solve balance-of-payments problems. Some believe that floating currency has ameliorated this, although many do not consider it a permanent solution. The balance-of-payments problems of developing countries, many of which are on par values systems, cannot be cured by a mere adjustment mechanism. The general factors discussed with respect to each country, while not dispositive, may be indicative of what the final "tilt" of each country would be, given the developments in each of them that would lead to establishment of a multinational investment organization.

This chapter does not pretend to be a carefully designed piece of social science research, which would select the factors carefully for their capacity to predict and employ a means of measuring the predictive capacity of each factor. Essentially I have roughly compared the relevant interests, policies, and laws, recognizing that laws may be no more than compromises of various interests. Not all laws are faithfully or consistently implemented. Also, a national policy toward something that is as speculative as a strong and effective international investment organization will evolve in a dynamic fashion and cannot be readily gleaned from the static reading of existing policies. As a political matter, coalitions of support would have to be developed in each country; such coalitions might depend on the particular issues that were linked up in the promotion of the organization, which might include such issues as tax, antitrust, labor, disclosure and bargaining, capital movements, pollution, and patents and technology transfer. State departments and foreign offices have tended to be too elitist to develop a real coalescence of underlying interests; multinational corporations, in straddling an area between politics and technology, may not be so elitist.

THE FACTORS

Each country, or region, has a thumbnail sketch that touches on as many relevant factors as possible. Not all sketches will be based on the same factors. I had initially intended to develop a chart for each country with ten relevant factors, and I had hoped to be able to suggest that if six or seven were affirmative, then the particular country would, given the evolution of certain events, be sympathetic to an international investment organization. Obviously such a hope would have suggested more definiteness than is justified. In considering each country's sketch, it is important to keep in mind the model described in Chapters 9 and 10. Thus, for example, such a model might permit Canada to restrict inward foreign investment if the investment stock of companies from one country, that is the United States, exceeded a certain percentage, such as 30 percent, in a major economic sector. The particular model of the prospective international investment organization must be kept in mind in evaluating the relevance of the total package of factors in each country. The factors picked have a wide range, but certain specific matters are excluded, such as the degree to which a country asserts its economic regulatory (for example, antitrust) or tax jurisdiction overseas. The following are the factors to be considered:

One should bear in mind general and policy factors, such as the level of development of the country. To some extent this assumes that the greater the development, the greater the inclination to an open economy. Per capita income is relevant; as it rises there seems to be a tendency toward greater openness. Reliance on foreign technology is also indicative of potential openness. Dependence on imports and other outside economic factors also leads toward an interest in openness. One has only to think of Japan and the United Kingdom. The general domestic economic history of a country is relevant. Also to be considered is the role of the state in the economy and the policy of the state toward economic planning. If the international investment organization is perceived as a capitalist organization, local planners may distrust it. There has been a comparable development within the EEC, with certain domestic groups seeing the EEC as a capitalist organization that threatens their anticapitalist domestic measures.

The general foreign economic history of the country, whether pointing toward an open or closed economy is key. This is indicated by membership in GATT and the IMF and by whether the country enjoys Article VIII status in the IMF. Whether the country is within the U.S. alliance system is also an indication, since countries that fit these conditions have been sympathetic to the U.S. lead toward an open world economy. It is also significant if the country has a history of free-trade policies. The domestic pressures in each country are also a consideration.

Another set of factors is more immediately related to the process of international investment and multinational corporations itself. It will help to study the volume of the existing stock of foreign direct investment in each country and the total volume of the existing outward foreign direct investment from that country. We should know the extent to which the particular country is a host to multinational corporations and the extent to which it is a home to them, as well as the extent to which the country is the "target" of foreign multinational corporations from a particular country. For instance, the large number of U.S. companies that are active in Canada have created a problem. A large number of Brazilian companies, if they were to invest in a particular country, might create similar problems. The current annual foreign direct investment, inward and outward, of a country is important. These "gross" figures may be more indicative than the resultant "net" figures. A country that is dependent on inward and outward investment presumably wishes to preserve the process of international investment and multinational corporations and would therefore tend to be in favor of an international investment organization. It will also make a difference whether the country has natural resources that require exploitation by companies from abroad.

The history of the capital controls in the country, both with respect to inward and outward movements, especially if a country has had explicit investment controls, will be most revealing. However, controls for balance-of-payments reasons, such as those employed by Germany and Switzerland to restrict inward short-term capital movements, will be less revealing; that is, Germany certainly believes in an open world economy, inward and outward movement of long-term capital, and foreign direct investment and would presumably subscribe to an international investment organization to preserve the process of international investment and multinational corporations. The record of derogations and reservations to the OECD Code of Liberalization of Capital Movements and Code of Liberalization of Current Invisible Transactions is highly relevant.

The policy of the country with respect to the expropriation of foreign property, compensation, and membership in the International Center for the Settlement of Investment Disputes (ICSID) is relevant, as well as whether it has treaties of friendship, commerce, and navigation with other nations that contain provisions that affect the process of international investment and multinational corporations. It is helpful to know whether it provides tax incentives for outward and inward investment and whether it has a program of foreign investment guarantees, such as those administered by the Overseas Private Investment Corporation (OPIC). An OPIC bilateral agreement with the United States would be relevant if it is a developing country.

It is important to determine where the country fits within the international law tradition, especially in the economic area, and whether it subscribes to notions of a minimum standard, or rather endorses national treatment and the Calvo doctrine, as is the case of most Latin American countries. This may be revealed by what its position was with respect to the UN Charter for Economic Rights and Duties. A country that subscribes to traditional international law protections may be more likely to accept an international investment organization of the kind described in Chapters 9 and 10, even if it is a capital importing country. Thus Canada might join such an organization despite its position in the OECD.

It is important to consider the announced general policies of a country with respect to inward and outward foreign investment, specifically foreign direct investment, at the federal and provincial, or state, level. Announced policies with respect to long-term and short-term capital movements, including portfolio movements, are relevant to a degree. It may also have announced policies with respect to multinational corporations or even with respect to an international investment organization.

Appendix A contains country sketches (some very brief) for the United Kingdom, France, Germany, other members of the EEC, the EEC itself, other European countries, Japan, Canada, Australia and South Africa, Latin America generally, and the developing countries as a group.

We have seen the ambivalence of developing countries toward multinational companies. Because of their relatively short political history, in many cases, and their small diplomatic corps, many of these countries are ignorant of the operations of many international organizations. Their capacity may be limited to the United Nations, the UNCTAD, and a few other organizations.

Once they begin to invest abroad, whether through government or private channels, the developing nations will become increasingly committed to the process of international investment and multinational corporations, as an aspect of the open world economy and also with respect to the long-term security of their own outward foreign investments. Once Brazilians invest to any degree in the United States, then any threat to these investments, in their eyes, or any undue blocking of her opportunities for future investment would make Brazil sympathetic to an international investment organization, should such sympathy protect or make possible these investments.

Appendix B contains lists of GATT members (Table B. 1); IMF members, divided into Article VIII and Article XIV countries (Table B. 2); and OECD members (Table B. 3). It also summarizes the guarantee schemes of OECD countries (Table B. 4) and lists the countries which subscribe to the OPIC program of insurance and guarantees (Table B. 5). It also contains a list of the countries that have treaties of friendship, commerce, and navigation with the United States, including provisions protecting the entry and security of investment (Table B. 6), and lists the members of the International Centre for Settlement of Investment Disputes (ICSID) (Table B. 7).

Appendix C is the text of the OECD Code of Liberalization of Capital Movements (with Annex A and summary of reservations), and Appendix D is the text of the OECD Code of Liberalization of Current Invisible Operations (with summary of reservations).

THE PROBABLE OUTCOME

At the present time there is extreme anxiety about various international economic issues. The aspirations of the developing countries continue to increase. There are distractions with respect to oil prices (a serious issue), floating rates, the recycling of petrodollars, recession, and inflation.

Confusion seems to prevail over consensus, as it has in the deliberations over the law of the sea and over the seabed authority. The discussions with respect to the UN Charter of Economic Rights and Duties did not suggest a very clear understanding on the part of governments of the impact of that charter and whether it was to be taken seriously, whether it was a negotiating position, or whether it was a sincere exercise.

This is not 1945, when the United States, and to a lesser extent the United Kingdom, enjoyed an almost total hegemony over the remainder of Europe and the developing countries. When John Maynard Keynes, hoping to avoid the domestic disasters of the 1930s, U.S. statesmen such as Cordell Hull and Harry Dexter White, hoping to avoid the exclusion of the United States from the import markets controlled by Britain and France, advocated clear and concrete ideas; many of these ideas were included in the compromise at Bretton Woods.

It was also relevant that the wartime collapse, which created the hegemony that I have mentioned, made it easier to perceive the nature of the 1930s economic crisis, a repetition of which the Bretton Woods conference sought to prevent.

No international investment organization could be created without a U.S. lead. The relative invulnerability and/or power of the United States with respect to oil and other resource problems, as compared to most other developed countries and many developing countries, has again strengthened its hand. Also, because of its size the United States is the base for the largest number of multinational corporations. Therefore we must look briefly, and finally, to the United States.

NOTES

1. M. Weber, Economy and Society 681-83 (G. Roth and C. Wittich, eds., 1968).

2. P. Drucker, "Multinationals and Developing Countries: Myths and Realities," 53 For. Affairs 121 (1974).

3. See R. Muller and R. Barnet, Global Reach: The Power of Multinational Corporations (1974).

4. R. Hudec, "GATT or GABB? The Future Design of the General Agreement on Tariffs and Trade," 80 Yale L. J. 1299 (1971)

5. H. Kissinger, speech, 73 Dept. State Bull. 425 (1975).

6. Canadian Government, Foreign Direct Investment in Canada (1972).

7. See "The Bright Lights Dim in Beirut," Bus. Int'l 322 (Oct. 10, 1975).

CHAPTER

12

RECOMMENDATIONS FOR UNITED STATES POLICY

In deciding what U.S. policy toward a possible international investment organization should be, it is useful to review current U.S. policies toward international economic affairs. Generally the United States subscribes to an open world economy, as can be seen by its promotion of the Bretton Woods system and its participation in the GATT, in the IMF, and in the OECD codes and in its response to the problems of oil and the recycling of petrodollars. Moreover, the United States has been prepared to exercise a measure of leadership with respect to all these institutions in these matters.

SPECIFIC POLICIES

We should look at more specific U.S. policies with respect to foreign direct investment and multinational corporations, both as host and home country.

Inward Investment

The most relevant fact about U.S. policy toward investment is that it is not explicitly addressed to foreign investment, and certainly not to foreign direct investment. The U.S. has a mixed economy and a variety of policies, which are not all coordinated. Inward foreign investment has been treated in roughly the same way as domestic investment.[1]

Basically, U.S. policy has been open and the U.S. has welcomed, indeed invited, foreign direct investment, although there are a few sectors that are barred to foreign investment, much as is the case with other countries.[2]

Essentially U.S. policy is one of balanced enforcement of domestically oriented policies. Sometimes there is an exception made for the foreigner; thus it is widely believed that the State Department prevailed upon the Justice Department to be somewhat more easy with British Petroleum in connection with its acquisition of SOHIO, in the application of the antitrust laws. Also there is the case of the exemption made by the SEC for certain foreign issuers.

E. Kitner and M. Joelson provide evidence of the law enforcement mentality of the antitrust division, which tends to apply the antitrust laws equally to the domestic and foreign transactions of domestic and foreign companies.[3]

In the 1970s the Department of Commerce has promoted foreign investment in the United States through its "Invest US" program. Individual states also promote inward foreign investment.[4]

There are proposals to facilitate the operations of foreign banks in the United States, including one to enable them to act as broker-dealers, something U.S. banks cannot do.

One seeming exception to this situation are the initiatives to investigate foreign investment by the Japanese, the Arabs, and the Iranians. Thus the Culver-Inouye Act requires the Commerce and Treasury Departments to catalogue portfolio and direct investments.[5] The SEC has conducted related investigations. Senator Harrison Williams has promoted a bill that would give the U.S. president the power to bar foreign investments of more than 5 percent in companies of a certain size. These measures, especially the Williams measure, have met with substantial resistance from the liberal press. It is almost as if free trade and free capital movement were a "cheap" form of internationalism that did not involve the unpleasantness and ambiguity of political internationalism.

It may be that the Williams Bill, if enacted into law, would entail a further derogation from our subscription to the principles of the OECD Code of Liberalization of Capital Movements.[6]

Outward Investment

U.S. policy with respect to outward investment, as opposed to investment within the United States, must represent an explicit policy directed toward things foreign. However, there is again a patchwork of policies, the origins of many of which seem rather accidental, that have not always been coordinated.

In the tax area the United States is experiencing some changes; there have already been some with respect to the oil industry. Tax policy presently encourages foreign investment through deferral and the operation of the foreign tax credit. The operation of the policy is essentially logical and neutral. Thus the foreign tax credit embodies the idea that income earned by U.S. companies should only be subject to one income tax; therefore if income tax is paid abroad it should be credited against U.S. taxes that are also payable. The philosophy of the U.S. system is that all U.S. entities should pay taxes wherever their income is earned; deferral is based on the notion that a foreign subsidiary is not a U.S. entity.

The application of the U.S. antitrust laws with respect to U.S. investment abroad is problematic. Basically the antitrust laws protect U.S. commerce and more specifically the U.S. domestic market. As a result, most investments abroad have not been caught up in the net of U.S. antitrust law enforcement to date.[7] As foreign markets become more important, the effect of investment abroad on other U.S. companies may become more suspect. Investments abroad that affect raw materials, if important to the U.S. market, may become suspect.

The United States has had a series of policies specifically addressed to investment in the developing countries. Thus the Overseas Private Investment Corporation (OPIC) investment insurance and guarantee programs have been designed to promote investment in developing countries, historically as part of the U.S. post World War II programs of foreign assistance to economic development. As such, they replace the earlier State Department policy, which did not especially promote U.S. investment.[8] Senator Frank Church, chairman of the Subcommittee on Multinational Corporations of the Senate Foreign Relations Committee, does not seem to subscribe to this policy of promoting investment.

The United States belongs to the International Center for the Settlement of Investment Disputes, which is expected to assist in the creation of conditions favorable to the resolution of investment disputes and therefore to investment itself. Sub-part F of the Internal Revenue Code contains provisions that were intended to at least not discourage investment in the developing countries.[9] These provisions may not have had a very great impact, however.

The U.S. foreign assistance programs have been designed to strengthen foreign economies, including their private sectors. One of the basic elements of the U.S. program has been the promotion of local private investment. The United States has agreed to generalized trade preferences for the developing countries that would further promote several economic sectors in the developing countries, including the industrial sectors. This policy of stimulating foreign investment in developing countries and generally stimulating conditions in the developing countries that are conducive to their development should be distinguished from the more massive and sustained policies that the United States pursued with respect to Europe, such as the Marshall Plan and the early U.S. promotion of the ECSC, the

EEC, NATO, and more recently the International Energy Agency. In these cases the United States probably provided much more direct political support to local leadership elements than it does in the case of the developing countries, although this may not be widely acknowledged.

The history of the Hickenlooper Amendment suggests some of the difficulties of U.S. foreign investment abroad in the face of U.S. general foreign policy interests. The problem arises with respect to expropriation and the different readings of its impact on the long-term security of U.S. investment. An expropriated U.S. investment can become a "hostage," which restrains U.S. foreign policy toward a particular country by leading the United States to cut off aid and take similar measures, thus endangering U.S. general relations with that country.

It seems as if neither side is really focusing on the process of international investment and multinational corporations or the long-term security aspect of it. Thus the congressional pressure may be intended to protect individual investments, although this may reflect a reading that protection of individual investment is important in order to preserve the process. It would be interesting to know to what degree this is analytic and to what extent it is based on a research of actual investment behavior.

On the other hand, the executive seems to be more concerned with aspects of U.S. foreign policy other than the process of international investment and multinational corporations, although the executive too may instinctively believe that, for example, total compensation for a particular investment is not that important to preservation of the process. It is not clear to what extent this is based on research and analysis. When John Connally was Secretary of the Treasury, President Nixon announced a strong, "congressional-type" policy toward investment disputes, especially in Latin America. Later Nixon and Secretary of State Kissinger announced a more lenient and traditionally executive policy and since 1973 the law has given the President the authority to waive the Hickenlooper Amendment.[10]

There are other relevant policies. Thus I have referred to export control policies that are principally related to restricting the export of certain goods and technology to bloc countries. Specifically related to balance of payments and indeed capital controls were the foreign direct investment controls, the interest equalization tax, and the federal reserve guidelines restricting lending by U.S. banks and other financial institutions abroad, all of which are now abolished. Their emphasis was on balance of payments and not on foreign direct investment. One result of these measures was that U.S. companies increased their capital abroad, even as they accelerated their foreign direct investment.[11] The operation of the foreign direct investment controls might be cited as an example of the indifference of the U.S. government to the impact of U.S. multinational companies and their foreign investment. I say this because of the often-repeated complaint that the effect of these controls was to promote local investment by U.S. companies with local funds. Large U.S. companies enjoying high credit ratings were often able to borrow money locally more readily than the largest local companies.[12]

It may be that there are gaps in U.S. policy. Thus I have suggested that particular problems of individual multinational companies may create "hostages" to U.S. foreign policy. Some of these are created by other policies of the United States. Thus the application of U.S. export controls policy to U.S. subsidiaries in Canada, Argentina, and France has created problems for other U.S. government policies.[13]

ABSENCE OF COHERENT POLICY

It is clear that the United States does not have a coherent set of policies with respect to inward or outward investment or to their combination. There is no agency charged with the development or administration of such policies. It is possible that the Economic Policy Board and the Council for International Economic Policy in the White House, State, Treasury, and Commerce among others, might all have a role here. The State Department has created an Advisory Committee on Transnational Enterprises.

The Williams Commission seemed to suggest that investment was as important an area as trade and international monetary affairs. However, it proposed few specific policies. It did suggest that incentives to inward investment might be studied by the OECD, which is now being done.[14] Secretary of State Henry Kissinger has promoted a dialogue with Latin America on multinational corporations, but it is not clear what result this will yield. The OAS does hope to develop a code of behavior for multinational corporations.[15] Kissinger has also referred to multinational corporations elsewhere.[16]

The United States has no policy with respect to the possibility of an international investment organization. The United States does participate in the work of the OECD, and would probably be more inclined to rely on its results than on those of the United Nations or on the UN Commission on Transnational Corporations. I have referred to the Abs Code, to various efforts at international antitrust arrangements, and to some discussion about multilateral guarantees, all initiatives in which there was U.S. government or private-sector interest. The Hartke-Burke and related AFL/CIO pressures, Frank

Church's assault on OPIC, and congressional pressures to increase taxes on the foreign operations of the oil and other U.S. industries, represent a dissident strain in U.S. public policy with respect to outward investment.

WHAT THE UNITED STATES SHOULD AND CAN DO

Some of the foreign policy elites have, to a degree, become confused about foreign policy, in part because of Viet Nam and the complexities and confusions that Viet Nam revealed. Most economic issues, and especially specific economic and political issues such as the process of international investment and multinational corporations and how it is to be handled, have not yet become elite foreign policy issues in spite of the interest in multinational corporations.

The status of foreign policy elites is very much in question. At a more popular level, jobs are an issue. Controversy rages over whether multinationals export jobs or not. Congress threatens tax reforms, but the abstractions of international organization are not considered. As the Williams Commission suggests, although trade and monetary affairs have been the subject of much theory and the work of many experts, and although they are within the domain of international organizations, investment is not. The new world of international production, and movement of technology, is still undeveloped.

It is difficult to speculate because it is difficult to know when the developments leading to the commencement of an international organization might begin. The foreign policy elite has not begun to think about a possible international investment organization. Congressional attention has not been drawn to it. Business does not yet see it as a lesser risk possibility. It has not yet attracted the sustained attention of the higher levels of the executive branch. Certain civil servants in the executive branch do now follow the activities of the United Nations, the OECD, and the OAS in this area.

What is the U.S. policy with respect to the process of international investment and multinational corporations, and what might it be with respect to an international investment organization? The policy would include a number of elements. Probably the United States would deliberately pursue a policy of welcome and benign neglect with respect to international production. I think the United States welcomes an independent economic life, with wellsprings and a dynamism independent of government policy; this would be a modified laissez-faire policy.

Many Americans continue to believe with Woodrow Wilson that initiative comes from outside the government and the government merely shapes and corrects.

A vital international economy outside the realm of government policy should not be confused with the notion of the "transnational" school that the nation-state, and the international political system based on it, have been superseded or transformed by the multinational corporation.[17]

This element of deliberate neglect in U.S. policy would be based on the belief that there is benefit in both inward and outward investment. It is also a realistic attitude with respect to the operation of the international political system and reflects a distrust of bureaucracy, whether international or domestic, which seems endemic to current American thinking. This element of U.S. policy assumes that the United States can live with such measures as those of the Andean group and Canada, presumably because of a belief that the strengths of the current system will be able to handle them. Presumably U.S. policy would reflect belief in the continued vitality of the principle and operation of free trade, and free capital movement, as part of a belief that an open world economy leads to a more prosperous life.

This suggests that the views associated with environmentalism, the limits of growth, and technology assessment would be fit into and subordinated to this belief, which might be modified in order to accommodate these views. U.S. policy initiatives in the 1970s have suggested a continued attachment to the free trade principle. Thus the United States is promoting the current GATT round of Multilateral Trade Negotiations, which will attack nontariff barriers and also address institutional problems of the GATT. The U.S. approach to the petrodollar recycling problem has been to leave the solution to the effects of market forces.

Basically the United States wishes to preserve an open, dynamic, productive system and to preserve the integrity of the process of international investment and multinational corporations as it relates to both freedom of investment and protection of investment. It is the process rather than the interests of any one particular company that the United States would seek to promote, to the extent that these two can be conceptually and practically separated.

Another element of U.S. policy should be the conscious promotion of the United States as a model society, as a model of modernization, and as a technological and social model. The United States has always acted as a magnet to other societies. It has been suggested that the social part of the U.S. image has been tarnished. I do not believe that this is as much the case as is sometimes believed, but certainly the United States must be more careful about this. Alistair Buchan takes the position that although the United States may continue to be a technological magnet to other societies, its social image is badly damaged.[18]

The United States has great responsibilities, and in discharging these it should remember its traditions as Yankee trader, as home of the business creed, and as practitioner of dollar diplomacy. Whether the United States likes it or not, the achievements of its large corporations are a principal basis of its national possibilities. Although what is good for General Motors might not necessarily be good for the United States, they are more closely related than is normally admitted. The United States has not as a nation, at the intellectual level, integrated its business and social traditions as much as it should. The antitrust laws represent an attempt at such integration. However, at popular and conscious levels a surprising amount of the intellectual and social tradition in the United States is in fact antibusiness, just as in the past much of U.S. business has been anti-intellectual.

The United States has both possibilities and responsibilities. Although the United States may no longer enjoy the absolute economic and other preeminence that it enjoyed immediately after World War II, its economic size is still enormous. Assuming that the United States retains even moderate economic energies, its growth relative to that of the developing countries and others remains formidable, if only because of the large base from which it began. The United States is enormously rich. It still consumes 33 percent of the resources of the world and accounts for 33 percent of its production, while having less than 5 percent of its population. Fifteen years ago the United States represented 50 percent of the world's economic production.

There probably is not sufficient public realization of these facts and their implications in the United States. Twice during 1975 Chancellor Helmut Schmidt of Germany came to the United States to urge it to abandon its deflationary policy, inasmuch as European economic recovery depended on U.S. recovery and imports. The dollar is a much more key currency than is commonly understood.[19] The OECD and the IMF have similarly urged U.S., German, and Japanese reflation since then.

Many Americans also fail to realize the full impact on the United States of the pressures associated with the Soviet Union. It is my opinion that but for these pressures the United States would have had a far more relaxed foreign policy, pursuing merely normal competitive economic policies. One has only to think back to the open door with respect to China at the end of the nineteenth century, to the policies associated with the name of Cordell Hull, or indeed to the U.S. interest in Bretton Woods to appreciate this.

However, the United States has felt under pressure from the Soviet Union. Moreover, the United States clearly needs a coherent policy with respect to the developing countries or Third World. This should be a policy that would be not merely based on dependence on on particular raw materials from certain developing countries or on sentiment. In spite of the sentimental U.S. interest in India, as a large democracy, in the 1950s and 1960s, most Americans seem to have lost their interest in India even before it veered away from democracy.

U.S. policy toward developing countries will have to take into account their enormous need to create realizable income and wealth. The developing countries, which feel this intensely, have often put this in terms of a need for redistribution of income and wealth, and this is one reason why they have supported OPEC as their champion, even though the immediate impact of OPEC policies has been to hurt those developing countries that do not have their own oil resources. It has been suggested that the requirements of redistribution not only extend to developing countries but exist also between the United States and Europe, since the European standard of living is generally less than that of the United States. The Soviet Union, Eastern Europe, and even Canada and Australia may have claims. In the case of the latter the per capita income is comparable to that of the United States, while in the case of some European countries the per capita income is greater than that of the United States. None of them, however, have the same sense of control over their economic destinies that the United States has had. The redistribution that others clamor for applies equally to per capita income and to control.

As in Chapter 4, a number of the criticisms of the process of international investment and multinational corporations as it operates today are related to redistribution. There remains an issue of whether the multinational corporation can be properly blamed for the present distribution of wealth and income and whether it can be utilized to effect a major redistribution. The possibilities of this are limited. The technology transfer that is brought on by the multinational corporations can assist in the creation of conditions for greater wealth and income in the developing countries, but it is not the multinational companies so much as the policies pursued by the governments of developing countries that will make this possible. Specifically, the developing countries will utilize their resources and the prospects of their markets as a way to attract such companies. A similar process has previously taken place in Europe, Canada, and elsewhere. More intelligent tax measures may garner a larger share of the tax revenues that multinational companies can generate, but this is a relatively minor point.

One of the paradoxes of the oil crisis, and the public sentiment associated with it, was the U.S. dismay that the oil companies did not pay much U.S. income tax but that they paid most of their taxes to the host countries.

Can the multinational corporations effect a redistribution of control? Even here I think the results will be marginal. Possibly there can be more Canadian and Australian directors on the boards of local subsidiaries. The real reason for the economic power and control exercised by U.S. multinational corporations and other developed-country based corporations comes not so much from the director-and-management arrangements of particular companies as from the fact that the home economies themselves are at a higher technological and economic level. The United States can intentionally smoothe some of the rough edges, and it can continue to promote the development of other economies, including the European and Japanese economies, but the United States should not deliberately hobble its own economy. To some extent this issue is raised by the environmental and related movements.

Should the United States urge establishment of an international organization to control multinational corporations as part of its overall foreign economic policy? I think it will be seen that such an organization, given its realistic prospects, is a fairly minor part of the overall picture.

SOME CONTEMPORARY GENERALIZATIONS APPLIED TO AN INTERNATIONAL INVESTMENT ORGANIZATION

A distinction is often made between the long-term interests of a country and its short-term interests, it being suggested that a country generally follows its short-term interests more. Since World War II the United States has considered it to be in its short-term interest to provide leadership to other countries and in its long-term interest to work with these countries. To the extent that the promotion of long-term U.S. interests and of a cosmopolitan approach that involves the interests of other countries has been thought to be idealist, the United States has been in a happy position in which idealism has had a role in its short-term and realistic calculations. This has been useful because of the idealist streak in U.S. public opinion and because of the widespread belief that the views of the public are highly relevant to U.S. policy. In order to appeal to the U.S. public, policies have often had to be simplified and "charismatic," and this simplicity in government policy can present difficulties.

It is hard to envision a popular base for an international investment organization. Baiting the multinational corporations might be more popular, although even that strikes me as a fairly sophisticated activity.

There is a broader problem. It may be that the earlier popular enthusiasm for the United Nations, which has been widespread in the United States, is fading as the earlier U.S. idealism about world government is confronted by the harsh realities of a fight over the division of the global economic pie. Moreover, a narrow and functional international organization such as an international investment organization could never have been expected, even in the best of times, to have enjoyed the popular support which the UN itself enjoyed.

This becomes relevant when we think of the problem of the locus of an international investment organization. Contemporary U.S. thinking would probably prefer the World Bank to UNCTAD, just as it might now prefer a two-tier GATT (one for the developed countries, another for the developing) if it knew more about the GATT.

There are other U.S. traditions, one of which is law and legalism, which it is hoped will survive the cynicism of the post Viet Nam period. Moreover, U.S. companies are accustomed to regulation, although they do complain about it. One also hopes that the general traditions of cooperation, as in the United Nations or the OECD, will survive, at least in the foreign policy elite if not more broadly.

It is possible that a mood of self-restraint could be generated with respect to U.S. multinational corporations. This mood might be composed of several elements. Some Americans might be prepared to restrict the spread of the corporations as a latter-day manifestation of U.S. belief in self-determination, in this case the cultural self-determination of host countries.

Other countries have restrained their multinational corporations and outward foreign direct investment, if only for balance-of-payments reasons or to avoid restrictions in host countries. As a matter of policy the United States might wish to moderate the number of "hostages" it might be giving to hostile host countries. Finally, the fear of the decline of the U.S. industrial base, asserted by the labor unions, and the fear of spreading U.S. technology to competitors are elements to be considered. In 1967 Leo Model suggested that the United States pursue a policy of restraint on foreign investment to avoid political problems, whether of the hostage or of another variety.[20] The Japanese have restrained their foreign direct investment with a view to avoiding protectionist reaction, and the Arabs have moderated some of their investments to avoid nationalist reaction in the United States and elsewhere.

Another possible element that might enter into U.S. policy is the "tithe," which has often been a tradition among rich and among religious people. The appeal of this has been evident with respect to the promotion of certain U.S. programs, such as the Marshall Plan. Whether the sentiment in support of the tithe can survive OPEC and the demands for a new international economic order is questionable.

The tithe sentiment would lead the United States to share its economic and technological advantages with others. Unfortunately this may be counterbalanced by the fear that if the United States spreads its technology too much, it will ultimately undermine the U.S. capacity to create further wealth, whether to share or otherwise.

This may be part of the AFL-CIO fear of foreign investment, runaway plants, and the so-called export of jobs. It is interesting to compare this sentiment with the mercantilism condemned by Adam Smith in The Wealth of Nations. One thinks of the British prohibition in 1856 of the export of textile equipment to India.

Another relevant sentiment may be consumerism, the movement for corporate accountability, and similar domestic analogues. However, it will be difficult to apply these automatically in the international sphere, and a poorly considered attempt to do so would probably discourage that development.

ASYMMETRY

Whatever the political difficulties that the United States finds itself in, in the economic sphere it still enjoys a dominant position. The U.S. economy and technology are very large when compared to those of the developing countries. It is U.S. technology, and food, that the Egyptians want and the Russians want. The EEC and Japan have neither the economic power nor the economic leadership that the United States has.

It will be the United States that will have to act if there is to be an international investment organization. At some point a U.S. president may feel inclined to pick up the idea, despite the difficulties already suggested, and try to sell it in the United States and abroad, much as has been done with other political issues. The initiative will have to come from the president, notwithstanding recent assertions of congressional power. A president will only do so when he believes the time is right. It is not known whether it will ever be right, in terms of the asymmetry of the U.S. relationship with developing and other foreign countries. Although the activities of OPEC may have brought home to the United States some of the limits on its power and wealth, it is unlikely that a president would voluntarily take on the task of teaching the U.S. public that there should be greater reductions in U.S. power and wealth, and some reduction in the asymmetry that I have mentioned. My guess is that matters will evolve more pragmatically.

If and when a strong, effective international investment organization were created, one consequence might be a further increase in executive power, especially with respect to the private industrial sector. Carl Kaiser has suggested that this is the inevitable effect of the increase in international organization. It is the executive that participates on behalf of its country; the legislative power is thereby reduced.[21]

Another effect of a strong international organization would be to reduce U.S. flexibility. An international organization, in order to foster an open world economy, might bar foreign direct investment controls, an interest equalization tax, or federal reserve guidelines. I think it would be some time before the United States would reach a point at which this might be possible.

For the United States the time is not yet right for some political leader to exercise his charisma within the United States to promote the formal commencement of a strong and effective international investment organization. For the time being, the United States will continue to participate in the work of the OECD, observe activities at the UN and the OAS, and consider seriously and possibly promote the various "codes of conduct" being suggested.

NOTES

1. This is documented in Legal Environment for Foreign Direct Investment in the United States (R. Rosendahl, ed., 1972), 27-30.

2. Ibid.

3. See E. Kintner and M. Joelson, An International Antitrust Primer (1974).

4. See Legal Environment for Foreign Direct Investment in the United States, op. cit. See also Foreign Investors Tax Act of 1966, 80 Stat. 1539, amending the Internal Revenue Code of 1954, reducing taxation on investment income of foreign businesses in the United States.

5. "Foreign Investment Study Act of 1974," Pub. L. No. 93-479, 88 Stat. 1450 (1974).

6. Williams Bill, S. 425, 94th Congress, 1st Session (1975).

7. W. Fugate, Foreign Commerce and the Antitrust Laws (2d ed., 1973); E. Kintner and M. Joelson, op. cit.

8. J. Wetter, "Diplomatic Assistance to Private Investment: A Study of the Theory and Practice of the United States during the Twentieth Century," 29 Univ. Chi. L. Rev. 275, 295 (1962).

9. See R. Hellawell, "United States Income Taxation and Less Developed Countries: A Critical Appraisal," 66 Columbia Law Review 1393 (1966).

10. Statement Announcing United States Policy on Economic Assistance and Investment Security in Developing Nations (Jan. 19,

1972), *Public Papers of Presidents: Richard Nixon 1972* (13) at 31 (1974); 8 Weekly Compilation of Presidential Documents 64 (1972).

11. A. Cairncross, *Control of Long Term Capital Movements* (1973).

12. See S. Robbins, R. Stobaugh, and D. Schydlowski, *Money in the Multinational Enterprise: A Study of Financial Policy* 63-71 (1973).

13. S. Rubin, "Of Cuba and Our Foreign Subsidiaries," letter to the editor, New York Times, Mar. 13, 1974, editorial page.

14. G. Reuber et al., *Private Foreign Investment in Development* (1973).

15. Organization of American States, "Behavior of Transnational Enterprises Operating in the Region and Need for a Code of Conduct to be Observed by Such Enterprises," CP/Res. 154, at 167-75 (July 10, 1975).

16. H. Kissinger, speech to the American Bar Association, Montreal, Canada, August 11, 1975; September 1975 Address to the UN General Assembly.

17. For an excellent summary of international activities in the area see S. Rubin, "Reflections Concerning the United Nations Commission on Transnational Corporations," mimeographed paper (July 1975).

18. A. Buchan, *Can International Relations Be Professed?* (1973).

19. R. Cooper, "The Future of the Dollar," 9 Foreign Policy 18 at 3, 5-17 (Winter 1972-3).

20. L. Model, "The Politics of Private Foreign Investment," 45 For. Affairs 639 (1967).

21. C. Kaiser, "International Relations as a Threat to the Democratic Process," 25 Int'l Organization 706 (1971).

CHAPTER

13

CONCLUSION

I began by taking up the suggestion of some that, in effect, "there ought to be a law" for multinational corporations. What do I conclude? that "there ought not to be a law," or at least that "there will not be a law"? I believe it remains impossible to frame or enact a "law," that is an explicit treaty, establishing an effective international investment organization at this time.

At the time of writing, there are many distractions, even in regard to international areas that are already regulated. The petrodollar problem, while abating, is still with us. The developing countries want to discuss the use of their resources and a new economic order. Floating rates may or may not have lost their shine, but international affairs are too distracted to permit a proper reform of the IMF. The new Multilateral Trade Negotiations in the GATT are just beginning. Threats of inflation and/or recession continue.

People are not paying that much attention, but if they were, an international investment organization would not be perceived by enough relevant people and interests, either in the United States or elsewhere, to be a lesser risk or a positive good.

The United Nations, the OECD, and the OAS will continue their work and to undertake studies. They may develop "codes of conduct." They can educate us further about multinational corporations. Are the multinationals the boon that David Rockefeller suggests: "the most important instruments in the unprecedented expansion that has taken place in world trade."[1]? Or are they the bane that Bella Abzug suggests: "Our multinational corporations go out and exploit . . . foreign women by paying them low wages. Then the goods [wearing apparel] are brought back to our own country and sold more cheaply than our own women could make them for, and so our own women are exploited too."[2]

They might at some point study the responses of countries like Canada or of the Andean group or the EEC, or they can study some of the U.S. congressional response to possible foreign direct investment, not yet formed into multinational corporations, by the Arabs.

They can consider the program of a possible international investment organization in the field of tax, antitrust, capital movement, or labor. They might focus on possible action by nation-states rather than by the multinational corporations themselves. Attention can be given to information gathering by the United Nations Center on Transnational Corporations and other agencies, otherwise, if it is remembered that information must serve a purpose and that attention must therefore be given to the purpose the information is intended to serve.

For the time being I do not believe that we will have more than these studies, plus a variety of initiatives in existing international organizations--including possible "codes of conduct" of various kinds--none of which will lead in the foreseeable future to a strong and effective international investment organization. Have I set up a straw man, only to knock him down? I do not think so. My guess is that if we continue with our present international economic system, and I believe we largely will, that the straw man may some day become a real organization.

NOTES

1. Address at the Manchester, England, stock exchange. New York Times (City Edition) April 23, 1975, at 55, col. 3.

2. Speech at the International Women's Year Tribute, Mexico City. New York Times (City Edition) July 2, 1975, at 31, col. 1.

APPENDIXES

APPENDIX A

THE PROBABLE RESPONSE OF VARIOUS COUNTRIES TO PROPOSALS FOR AN INTERNATIONAL INVESTMENT ORGANIZATION

The following are small sketches of the position of various countries with respect to an open or free trade world economy as opposed to a closed world economy, that is, national autarchy, and more specifically to the process of international investment and multinational corporations. Their probable response to proposals for an international investment organization of the sort outlined in Chapters 9 and 10 are also sketched. The discussion, especially of their response, is speculative and impressionistic and derives from the position of each country with respect to an open economy and other evidence. It also makes assumptions about the operation of a possible series of developments whereby pressures on the open economic policies of a country might lead to its support for an international investment organization. It is difficult to envision the circumstances in which the series of developments described in the text would simultaneously occur in all relevant countries. It also suggests that, to a degree, the country would be prepared to follow the leadership of the United States in the direction of an international investment organization.

The sketch of each country brings in many economic, political, and historical factors, not all of which are directed to the prospects for an international investment organization. This is the only feasible approach, since there is no single litmus test, such as the reaction of a country to the recent oil price and petrodollar crisis that can detect the attitude of a country toward a possible multinational investment organization. The factors cited for each of the countries or groups are not always the same.

Additional national data is set out in Appendix B. More data will become available with respect to OECD members, should the OECD adopt the code of conduct for multinational corporations and other measures that it is now considering.

The countries and groups of countries discussed are the United Kingdom, France, Germany, other member countries of the European Economic Community, the European Economic Community itself, other European countries, Japan, Canada, Australia, Latin America as a group, and the developing countries as a group. I have not singled out the oil exporting countries. I do not discuss the

Communist Bloc countries, despite the fact that a number of them are capital importers with investments laws and joint ventures with foreign investors and that some of their state enterprises have become outward foreign investors.

I have given the most information about the United Kingdom, since this has been the most readily available to me. The discussion of the United Kingdom could serve as a model for more detailed discussions of other countries.

UNITED KINGDOM

The United Kingdom would likely be in general sympathy with an international investment organization, given the development of the events previously suggested.

Openness

The general history of the foreign economic policy of the United Kingdom, as well as its domestic policies, suggests that it remains sympathetic to an open world economy in spite of developments in the 1970s. The continued prosperity of the City bears on this. In the nineteenth century the United Kingdom became the principal exponent of free trade and of domestic laissez faire liberalism; despite changes and pressures, the customary traditions die hard.

Britain, along with the United States, was one of the principal sponsors of the Bretton Woods system, and the name of John Maynard Keynes will always be associated with Bretton Woods. However, it is interesting to note that Keynes may have influenced the use of capital controls by Britain between the wars.[1]

In the debate preceding Bretton Woods, Keynes argued for exchange controls: there is no country that can, in future, safely allow the flight of funds for political reasons, to evade domestic taxation, or in anticipation of the owner turning refugee. Equally, there is no country that can safely receive fugitive funds, which cannot safely be used for fixed investment and might turn it into a surplus country against its will and contrary to the real facts.[2]

Despite its present and prior socialist governments, the United Kingdom has never had a truly *dirigiste* economic approach. There have been national planning efforts such as those associated with The National Economic Development Institute (Neddy). The Labor government has established a National Enterprise Board, as well as a body (British National Oil Corporation) to deal with North Sea oil. There have been similar initiatives in the past. Its monopolies and related policies have occasionally permitted and promoted mergers, rather than the opposite, to help against foreign competitors.

I would guess that prosperity tends to push a country toward openness. The United Kingdom has sadly declined since the war: its entry into the European Economic Community in 1973 has been seen by many as an attempt to create markets and to reverse this trend. Prime Minister Heath became somewhat Gaullist at the time of the oil crisis, possibly more than the socialists have been; moreover, the British seem to be as "nationalist" as any country when it concerns their North Sea oil.

The United Kingdom is enormously dependent on foreign trade and international exchange, and the City remains a hub of international finance, earning valuable foreign exchange through its "invisible" services.

The Process of International Investment and Multinational Corporations

British policy with respect to inward and outward foreign direct investment has been open in general. Restraints have been placed on outward investment because of balance of payments constraints, but these have been placed, much as the U.S. foreign direct investment controls were, on the flow of capital and have not been directed toward the establishment of British enterprise and multinational corporations abroad. For a similar reason, inward foreign investment has been generally welcomed because of the general policy of openness and because of technological and balance-of-payments benefits. There has been very little nationalism with respect to inward foreign investment.[3]

From the early nineteenth century, Britain was almost always the principal capital exporter in the world. In 1974 the gross outward foreign direct investment of Britain was $3.3 billion and the gross inward foreign direct investment was $1.6 billion, leaving a net of $1.7 billion outward foreign direct investment.[4] In 1971 stock of U.S. foreign direct investment stood at $86 billion, and that of the United Kingdom at $24 billion, spread among the United States, Europe, the Commonwealth, and elsewhere. In third position was France with a stock of $9.5 billion. Existing stocks of foreign direct investment abroad create hostages to a somewhat open policy.[5]

The United Kingdom is home base of the largest number of multinational corporations after the United States; this is somewhat inconsistent with the generalization about the allocation of foreign direct investment.[6] Of the top 12 multinational corporations by total volume of sales, three, British Petroleum, the Royal Dutch/ Shell Group, and Unilever, are wholly or partly British.[7] There is substantial British foreign direct investment in real estate and other fields. The stock in 1970 of inward foreign direct investment in the United Kingdom stood at about $7.1 billion.[8] The investment is considerable in many sectors; the roughly 75 percent of the automobile industry that is owned by American companies is exceptional.

The United Kingdom acts as host to numerous multinational corporations. Because foreign direct investment is deemed to assist the balance of payments, the Bank of England, which has authority to restrict inward foreign direct investment, has exercised its power leniently.[9] This situation continues despite the establishment of the National Enterprise Board and the policies designed to obtain a larger tax share of North Sea oil.

Position toward an International Investment Organization

It is difficult to estimate the extent of pressures in the United Kingdom of a protectionist variety that might trigger development of opinion in favor of establishment of an international investment organization, notwithstanding a Labour government and various union difficulties.

The United Kingdom voted, along with the United States, against the 1974 UN Charter of Economic Rights and Duties (the charter represented something of an assault on the open order) and takes an open position with respect to the Law of the Sea (that is, toward freedom of the seas and commerce). The United Kingdom is the principal home of the international law tradition to which the United States subscribes.

The current Labour government is possibly even more pro-American than the last Conservative government, and it is likely to follow the lead of the United States. It remains wary of the Soviet Union and does not view the European Economic Community as a possible political leader. There is much U.S. investment in the United Kingdom and vice versa: each country is the principal foreign direct investor in the other. Britain has called for U.S. leadership with respect to oil and energy matters.

FRANCE

France, in spite of its idiosyncratic foreign policy positions, might in fact follow the lead of the United States for an international investment organization if the situation favoring one were operative in France at the same time it was operative in the United States.

Openness

The history of France is quite different from that of the United Kingdom. France has always pursued a nationalist approach, as typified by the policies of Charles De Gaulle. It has been suggested that at one time France sought to use the EEC as a means of limiting the role of the United States and the penetration of U.S. multinational companies in Europe.[10] It was a Frenchman, J. J. Servan-Schreiber,[11] who sounded the alarm about the invasion of Europe by U.S. companies. Moreover, the French have a dirigiste approach to national economic management, and government, industry, and unions regularly discuss their economic plans. Notwithstanding its history and approach, the general move of France toward greater prosperity suggests that it would ultimately be prepared to subscribe to an international investment organization of the variety suggested in Chapters 9 and 10. This is no more than a hunch, and certainly such a hunch seems to be belied by the position that France has taken with respect to many international economic matters.

The Process of International Investment and Multinational Corporations

France is the home of a number of multinational corporations and has a good deal of outward foreign direct investment. There is considerable French investment in the United States; in this sense, the United States holds some French "hostages." At the end of 1974 the stock of French foreign direct investment in the United States was $726 million.[12]

The position with respect to inward foreign direct investment is somewhat ambiguous, although France has become more receptive to such investment. The 1974 stock of U.S. foreign direct investment in France was $4.9 billion.[13] Although a great deal is said in France about domestic control of the key sectors, the position associated with the name of Servan-Schreiber, France has permitted important inward investments. For instance, Minneapolis-Honeywell was permitted to take over Machines Bull. On the other hand, Fiat was not allowed to acquire Citroen. Arab investment has been welcomed in portfolio form and in banks. The government has exercised a general control and review over licenses, takeovers, and all foreign direct investment since 1967, including foreign direct investment from other countries within the EEC, despite the possibility that this violates the Treaty of Rome.[14]

Position Toward International Investment Organization

French nationalism has been evident in a number of votes in the United Nations, for example with respect to the payment of dues, and in the position of France with respect to nuclear testing in the Pacific. It has quite consistently dissociated itself from U.S. leadership, whether in NATO, in the International Energy Agency, or in commodity producer-consumer talks.

In spite of the above, France voted against the Charter of Economic Rights and Duties, and I think that France may be sympathetic to an international investment organization, given a development of events that would be conducive to it.

GERMANY

Germany, which is, along with Japan and the United States, the most prosperous of the Western industrialized countries, would, along with these countries and the United Kingdom, be a principal proponent of openness and, if need be, of an international investment organization.

Openness

Germany does not have a history like that of the United Kingdom with respect to economic liberalism, free trade, and international finance; nor is it such a home base for multinational corporations. It was not a sponsor of Bretton Woods. However, its so-called Economic Miracle based on principles of economic liberalism, its remarkable prosperity since World War II, and its dependence increasingly on foreign resources all suggest a deep attachment to an open world economy. This attachment seems to be common to all the major parties: the Social Democratic Party (SPD), the Free Democrats, and the Christian Democratic Union (CDU).

The Germans now follow a fairly vigorous antitrust or anti-cartel policy, probably inspired by the example of the United States.

Their banks have an important position in the ownership of industry, and the labor unions press for greater worker participation or codetermination, the latter move having recently led to a protest by U.S. companies in Germany.

The Process of International Investment and Multinational Corporations

Given its active economy, the overseas direct investment of Germany has probably been less than might be expected. Germany has relied enormously on exports for its foreign exchange earnings. The German reluctance to invest may be explained in part by the expropriation of its investments in the United States and elsewhere during, and as a result of, World Wars I and II. It has relied on "guest workers" coming from Turkey and elsewhere. It is likely that German employment of migratory labor has reached its peak and that in the future there will be more German investment in such places as Turkey. Moreover, Germany begins to see a need to invest abroad in order to obtain access to foreign resources.

Inward investment has been substantial, and Germany has been open to such inward investment from the United States as well as elsewhere. It has also welcomed investment from Iran and Arab countries, although the latter triggered a debate. It has been suggested that Germany has welcomed U.S. investment in order to secure the commitment of the United States to its political independence, presumably as opposed to the Soviets.[15] Foreign investment does not dominate any particular sector except possibly that of petrochemicals.[16] Its oil industry is largely foreign, although it has promoted the development of a German company, Veba.

The German government has the authority to review foreign investments, but has exercised this authority very liberally, as was seen at the time of the Kuwaiti attempt to take over Daimler-Benz. Germany has imposed capital controls on inward short-term capital movements in order to avoid their inflationary pressure. The left wing of the SPD has exacted a promise from Chancellor Helmut Schmidt to consider the subject of multinational companies.

Position Toward International Investment Organization

Since World War II Germany has subscribed to general norms of international law. Germany seems prepared to follow the U.S. lead in international economic matters, as it did at the time of the 1974 energy conference in Washington. Moreover, Schmidt has been to the United States more than once to urge it to exercise international economic leadership, for example to reflate in order to stimulate the German economy.

OTHER MEMBER COUNTRIES OF THE EUROPEAN ECONOMIC COMMUNITY

Italy would probably support an international investment organization. Although it excludes foreigners from certain sectors and discourages "nonproductive" investment, that is, takeovers,[17] and sometimes bargains with prospective foreign investors,[18] it has sought to attract foreign investment to develop itself. Italy has become extremely dependent on foreign capital since the increase in oil prices.

Belgium would probably also be sympathetic to an international investment organization. At the national and regional levels Belgium has sought to attract foreign investment by various incentives. U.S. and other foreign direct investment in Belgium represents the largest percentage of new investment in any European country. Belgium occasionally bargains with foreign investors for favorable arrangements[19] and from time to time reviews takeover bids. Belgium is itself the source and home of foreign direct investment and multinational corporations in Europe, Zaire (the former Belgian Congo), and other places.

The Netherlands would certainly be sympathetic to an international investment organization. After the United States and the United Kingdom, it is the largest home of multinational companies. It has also promoted inward foreign direct investment to promote development. Moreover, as a small country dependent on trade, which is not limited to the EEC, and foreign natural resources, the Netherlands is committed to an open economic system.

Like Belgium, Denmark has relied on inward foreign investment to promote its development.[20]

THE EUROPEAN ECONOMIC COMMUNITY

On balance I believe that the EEC, both the commission and the council, which is little more than the sum of its members, would be sympathetic to an international investment organization of the kind outlined in Chapters 9 and 10, given developments of the sort we have assumed.

Openness

It is not clear what the exact status and strength of the EEC is, or whether it is a power base that is independent of its member countries or little more than an elaborate OECD, with a large bureaucracy, that is subject to the normal principles of the confederal maximum. To the extent that the EEC is an independent force, it is reasonably clear that it is a force for openness in the European setting. It is seen as such by many. It is also seen as a capitalist force, especially by socialists in its member countries. The basic thrust of the EEC has been to create one common market and economic community that overrides the markets and economies of its individual members.

It seems likely that in opening up the economies of individual members it will be difficult to stop at the borders of the community. As Italy or France is opened up to the EEC it tends also to be opened up to Japanese, U.S., and other companies and to trade. The French have sought to use the EEC to stop this, but probably not successfully. Thus if member governments are persuaded to eliminate their preference for local procurement, this will create opportunities for foreign companies, including noncommunity companies. The attempt to harmonize tax, company, and other laws works in the same direction. Even without such harmonization, U.S. companies and their local subsidiaries have been able to establish Europe-wide operations more rapidly than European companies, and U.S. company mergers with local companies have exceeded inter-European mergers. Mergers within member countries, such as between two French companies, of course exceed both. The experiences of trans-European mergers such as Dunlop-Pierelli, have not been uniformly happy. The rights of free establishment and free access to services in the Treaty of Rome have been applied to the local subsidiaries of foreign, including U.S., companies. Various actual and prospective developments with respect to competition and merger policy, to multinational companies as such, and to the proposed European Company law do not seem as if they will be necessarily inward-looking in their operations.

The Process of International Investment and Multinational Corporations

The various proposals with respect to multinational corporations, especially the resolution of November 7, 1973, speak of nondiscrimination and a nonrestrictive approach to foreign, including U.S., companies, and there is no reason to disbelieve this. However, these developments have moved slowly.

Position Toward an International Investment Organization

In its resolution of November 7, 1973, the EEC Commission suggested that regulation of multinational companies might take place at an international level and that there should be cooperation with international bodies such as the OECD. Although the model of an international investment organization proposed in Chapters 9 and 10 would subordinate a body such as the EEC to that organization, I think the EEC would still welcome that sort of organization, given the developments suggested.

Europe has been weakened in its collective economic position by the events associated with the oil crisis, the petrodollar problem, recession, and inflation.

It is reasonably clear that the EEC, collectively, would be disposed to follow a U.S. lead on a multinational organization.

OTHER EUROPEAN COUNTRIES

Switzerland probably would be in favor of an international investment organization. It is certainly open to international trade, business, investment, and financial flows. The receptiveness of its banking system is well known. It is the home of its own multinational companies. In addition to outward foreign direct investment, Switzerland has entertained inward investment. It has restrictions with respect to the ownership of land by foreigners and the need for Swiss directors and personnel, as well as certain requirements with respect to share ownership.[21] It has also, like Germany, sought on occasion to control the inward movement of short-term capital in order to avoid its inflationary effect. Despite its neutrality in various settings, I think Switzerland would be in favor of an international investment organization, given the emergence of the situation I have suggested.

Sweden, too, would be sympathetic. Notwithstanding socialist governments, it has a substantial private sector and liberal approach to the domestic economy. There are some restrictions on inward foreign direct investment with respect to the ownership of land and forests. Sweden is, however, the base of outward foreign direct investment and some multinational companies. It has followed a neutralist political policy with respect to international economic politics. Within the OECD it has pushed for social controls over multinational companies.

Norway would follow a similar policy, although its oil finds may make it somewhat nationalistic with respect to that particular commodity.

JAPAN

With Germany and the United States, Japan would probably be as much in favor of such an organization as any country.

Openness

The dependence of Japan on foreign markets and resources, the need for access to which has induced considerable Japanese foreign direct investment, is well known and indeed has been underlined by the recent oil crisis. Unlike the United Kingdom, Japan has no EEC within which to merge itself.

The Process of International Investment and Multinational Corporations

The foreign direct investments of Japan have continued to increase both in Southeast Asia, with respect to resources, and in the United States, where it has large export markets. Its balance-of-payments problems have required it to moderate its outward foreign investment from time to time. Unlike Germany it has exported investment instead of importing workers, for example to Korea. European, and to some extent U.S.,[22] resistance to Japanese investments is something that Japan will want to overcome.

The Japanese have been reluctant to have inward foreign direct investment, although increasingly it is opening up to at least new investments if not to takeovers, although both of these remain subject to the administrative guidance of the government.[23]

Position Toward International Investment Organization

The above information, and close ties between Japan and the United States, suggest that Japan would be very sympathetic to an international investment organization if the United States were.

CANADA

I have referred to Canada at various places in the text. Canada would probably be in favor of an international investment organization under some circumstances.

Openness

The position of Canada is unique because of its close proximity to the United States, the largest economic market in the world, and because of the similar institutions of the two countries, despite the inevitable nationalist sensitivities of Canada. The Canadian problem is illustrated by the history of the U.S. interest equalization tax, of the U.S. foreign direct investment controls, and of the U.S. Federal Reserve guidelines on lending, from all of which Canada sought exemptions because of its dependence on U.S. capital. At the same time Canada has established its Foreign Investment Review Agency to screen U.S. and other foreign direct investments.

When confronted by consequences of the overwhelming control of the Canadian automobile industry by U.S. companies, Canada sought a free market with the United States in the U.S. Canadian Automotive Products Agreement. Basically its economic policy is liberal, although it has become concerned about the export of its resources to the United States and elsewhere. At the same time it remains enormously dependent on the U.S. market.

The Process of International Investment and Multinational Corporations

Canada is the home of some multinational corporations of its own.[24] Although it has not subscribed to the OECD Code of Liberalization of Capital Movements or Code of Liberalization of Current Invisible Transactions, Canada has been extremely liberal toward inward investment and has provided incentives at the federal and provincial levels. The Foreign Investment Review Agency (FIRA) has been established, but inward investment continues because of the basic position of Canada as an importer of capital and technology, given the high standard of living and consumer tastes of its citizens.

Position with Respect to International Investment Organization

One might ask the same question of Canada as of the United States: might an international investment organization really solve its problems? In some circumstances Canada might find such an organization helpful.

Canada subscribes to the traditional international law point of view and is sympathetic to rule of law approaches. The value of an international investment organization, or at least a U.S.-Canadian conference on the matter, has been suggested.[25]

AUSTRALIA; SOUTH AFRICA

The position of Australia is similar to that of Canada, although the United States is not so dominant in relation to it, there being substantial British, Japanese, and other foreign investment. Australia has relied for its development on inward investment and immigration.[26] It has permitted Japanese investment, with respect to its natural resources, probably for political and economic reasons, to establish some Asian solidarity. Like Canada, Australia has sought exemption from the U.S. interest equalization tax and the foreign direct investment controls. It has talked of screening inward investment. For balance-of-payments reasons it continues to permit inward investment.

The position of South Africa would probably be similar to that of Australia: Both are likely to favor an international investment organization, given the appropriate situation.

LATIN AMERICA

It is difficult to generalize the situation of the Latin American countries. As a group, and in this sort of policy making they might tend to act as a group, they would probably be rather hostile to an international investment organization, at least if it were proposed by the United States along the lines outlined in Chapters 9 and 10.

To some extent the Latin American countries represent an aspect of the position of the developing countries. Like other developing countries, they are not entirely hostile to an open world economy and would certainly wish to share in its benefits. At the same time they feel a certain inferiority or "dependencia."

The Latin American countries have resorted to national or regional controls and measures such as the Andean Pact, although these are basically intended to increase their bargaining position with multinational companies rather than merely to exclude them. Eventually certain countries, such as Brazil, Mexico, and Venezuela, may become the homes of outward foreign investment and multinational companies of their own. For example Pemex, the Mexican state oil company, is already providing technical assistance and technology to Venezuela.

To some extent the public international law position of the Latins hinders them from subscribing to an international investment organization. Many have not signed investment bilateral treaties or treaties of friendship, commerce, and navigation with the United States. They espouse the Calvo doctrine and ask foreign investors to eschew the diplomatic protection of their governments. They have been almost uniformly hostile to the International Center for the Settlement of Investment Disputes, with its possible reference to international law. To some extent this merely reflects a fear of U.S. and other foreign domination. Thus Latins might believe that an international investment organization that was sponsored by the

United States would not only be dominated by the United States but would in fact excessively legitimize the multinational companies and the present world economic balance.[27] They would therefore be reluctant to follow a U.S. lead, although at the same time they must inevitably negotiate economic matters with the United States.

OTHER DEVELOPING COUNTRIES

Generalizing about the situation of so large and diverse a group as the developing countries is almost impossible, but at the same time the positions of these countries with respect to international public measures may be more predictable than their positions with respect to the negotiation of individual investment arrangements, of which developing countries of course conclude many. The group includes the Arabs, the Iranians, other oil producing countries, and the Latins. Before long, many of the developing countries will become sources of outward foreign direct investment of their own; these would include Iran, Nigeria, Korea, Singapore, Taiwan, Hong Kong, and Malaysia.

The developing countries remain ambivalent with respect to inward investment. In Chapter 1 I noted the suggestion that "the only thing worse than having multinational companies is not having them." Basically the developing countries wish to negotiate more effectively with multinational corporations and gain more of the benefits of foreign direct investment. This is not inconsistent with a belief in an open system, but one over which they have more control. Developing countries frequently negotiate treaties to attract foreign direct investment, such as the 1975 Egyptian-Swiss Treaty. As a group they have leaned heavily on the UN Charter of Economic Rights and Duties, which, for example, has only an indirect, if that, reference to international law, with respect to the need to compensate for expropriation. Although they do not actually push for an open global economy, at the same time it is not clear what alternate model they do subscribe to. They have positions similar to the infant industry protection position. It is not inconceivable that against certain domestic pressures many civil servants and other members of developing country elites might support an international investment organization as a bulwark of moderation, if they believed that their countries would have a large and legitimate role in such an organization.

NOTES

1. A. Cairncross, op. cit., at 10-11.

2. Ibid., at 83, citing the "Keynes Plan" in J. Horsefield, 3 The International Monetary Fund, 1945-1965: Twenty Years of International Monetary Cooperation par. 30 (1969).

3. See, for example, W. Reddaway et al., Effects of U.K. Direct Investment Overseas: Final Report (1968); J. Dunning, The Role of American Investment in the British Economy (1969); M. Steuer et al., The Impact of Foreign Direct Investment on the United Kingdom (1973).

4. U.K. Balance of Payments, 1964-74, Central Statistical Office, at 23, Table 20. Figures are rounded to a 1975 rate of \$2.10 = 1 Pound Sterling.

5. United Nations Department of Economic and Social Affairs, Multinational Corporations in World Development 151 (1974).

6. L. Brown, World Without Borders 212 (1972).

7. Fortune 163 (Aug. 1975).

8. M. Hedges, Multinational Corporations and National Government (1974).

9. See J. Dunning, op. cit.; M. Steuer, op. cit.; Canadian Government, Foreign Direct Investment in Canada (1972) also known as the Gray Report.

10. E. Stein, Harmonization of European Company Laws, National Reform and Transnational Coordination 75 (1971).

11. O. Sonkel, Big Business and "Dependencia": A Latin American View, 50 For. Affairs 517 (1972). J. J. Servan-Schreiber, Le Defi Americain (1967).

12. U.S. Department of Commerce, Survey of Current Business (Oct. 1975).

13. Ibid.

14. Gray Report, op. cit., at 334; J. J. Boddewyn, "EEC Policies toward U.S. Investors," Moorgate and Wall St. Rev. 44, 62 (1973).

15. Gray Report, op. cit., at 330.

16. Ibid., at 329.

17. Ibid., at 333.

18. Ibid., at 330.

19. Ibid.

20. Ibid.

21. Ibid., at 334.

22. See, for example, the Culver-Inouye Act, "Foreign Investment Study Act of 1974," Pub. L. No. 93-479, 88 Stat. 1450 (1974).

23. Gray Report, op. cit., at 331.

24. Ibid., at 443.

25. Ibid., at 392.

26. Ibid.

27. See C. Vaitzos, in International Control of Investment (Wallace, ed., 1974). R. Prebisch, in ibid., at 168.

APPENDIX B

MISCELLANEOUS TABLES

TABLE B.1

Membership in the General Agreement on Tariffs and Trade
and Participants in the Multilateral Trade Negotiations
(as of December 31, 1974)

A. GATT Membership

1. Contracting Parties (83)

Argentina	Greece	Norway
Australia	Guyana	Pakistan
Austria	Haiti	Peru
Bangladesh	Hungary	Poland
Barbados	Iceland	Portugal
Belgium	India	Rhodesia
Brazil	Indonesia	Romania
Burma	Ireland	Rwanda
Burundi	Israel	Senegal
Cameroon	Italy	Sierra Leone
Canada	Ivory Coast	Singapore
Central African Republic	Jamaica	South Africa
Chad	Japan	Spain
Chile	Kenya	Sri Lanka
Congo	Korea	Sweden
Cuba	Kuwait	Switzerland
Cyprus	Luxembourg	Tanzania
Czechoslovakia	Madagascar	Togo
Dahomey	Malawi	Trinidad and Tobago
Denmark	Malaysia	Turkey
Dominican Republic	Malta	Uganda
Egypt	Mauritania	United Kingdom
Finland	Mauritius	United States
France	Netherlands	Upper Volta
Gabon	New Zealand	Uruguay
Gambia	Nicaragua	Yugoslavia
Germany, Federal Republic of	Niger	Zaire
Ghana	Nigeria	

2. Acceded Provisionally (2)

Philippines
Tunisia

3. Countries to the territories of which the GATT has been applied and that now, as independent states, maintain a de facto application of the GATT pending final decisions about their future commercial policy (17)

Algeria	Grenada	Swaziland
Bahamas	Khmer Republic	Tonga
Bahrein	Lesotho	United Arab Emirates
Botswana	Maldives	Yemen
Equatorial Guinea	Mali	Zambia
Fiji	Qatar	

(continued)

B. Countries Participating in the Membership of Trade Negotiations Committee (MTN) (90)

Algeria[a]
Argentina
Australia
Austria
Bangladesh
Belgium
Bolivia[a]
Botswana[a]
Brazil
Bulgaria[a]
Burma
Canada
Chile
Colombia[a]
Congo
Costa Rica[a]
Cuba
Czechoslovakia
Dahomey
Denmark
Dominican Republic
Ecuador[a]
Egypt
El Salvador[a]
Ethiopia[a]
Finland
France
Gabon
Germany, Federal Republic of
Ghana
Greece
Guatemala[a]
Haiti
Honduras[a]
Hungary
Iceland
India
Indonesia
Iran[a]
Iraq[a]
Ireland
Israel
Italy
Ivory Coast
Jamaica
Japan
Kenya
Korea
Luxembourg
Madagascar
Malawi
Malaysia
Mauritius
Mexico[a]
Netherlands
New Zealand
Nicaragua
Nigeria
Norway
Pakistan
Panama[a]
Peru
Philippines[b]
Poland
Portugal
Romania
Senegal
Singapore
South Africa
Spain
Sri Lanka
Sudan[a]
Swaziland[a]
Sweden
Switzerland
Tanzania
Thailand[a]
Togo
Trinidad and Tobago
Tunisia[b]
Turkey
Uganda
United Kingdom
United States
Uruguay
Venezuela[a]
Viet Nam[a]
Yugoslavia
Zaire
Zambia[a]

European Communities

[a]Not contracting parties to GATT.

[b]Acceded provisionally to GATT.

Source: Nineteenth Annual Report of the President of the U.S. on the Trade Agreements Program (1974).

TABLE B.2

International Monetary Fund Members

Article VIII	Article XIV	
Argentina	Afghanistan	Mali
Australia	Algeria	Malta
Austria	Bangladesh	Mauritania
Bahamas	Barbados	Mauritius
Bahrain	Botswana	Morocco
Belgium-Luxembourg	Brazil	Nepal
Bolivia	Burma	New Zealand
Canada	Burundi	Niger
Costa Rica	Cameroon	Nigeria
Denmark	Central African Republic	Pakistan
Dominican Republic	Chad	Paraguay
Ecuador	Chile	Philippines
El Salvador	China, Republic of	Portugal
Fiji	Colombia	Romania
France	Congo, People's	Rwanda
Germany, Federal	Republic of	Senegal
Republic of	Cyprus	Sierra Leone
Guatemala	Dahomey	Somalia
Guyana	Egypt	Spain
Haiti	Equatorial Guinea	Sri Lanka
Honduras	Ethiopia	Sudan
Hong Kong	Finland	Swaziland
Ireland	Gabon	Syrian Arab Republic
Italy	The Gambia	Tanzania
Jamaica	Ghana	Thailand
Japan	Greece	Togo
Kuwait	Guinea	Trinidad and Tobago
Malaysia	Iceland	Tunisia
Mexico	India	Turkey
Netherlands	Indonesia	Uganda
Netherlands Antilles	Iran	Upper Volta
Nicaragua	Iraq	Uruguay
Norway	Israel	Venezuela
Oman	Ivory Coast	Viet Nam
Panama	Jordan	Western Samoa
Peru	Kenya	Yemen Arab Republic
Qatar	Khmer Republic	Yemen, Peoples
Saudi Arabia	Korea	Democratic Republic
Singapore	Laos	Yugoslavia
South Africa	Lebanon	Zaire
Surinam	Lesotho	Zambia
Sweden	Liberia	
United Arab Emirates	Libyan Arab Republic	
United Kingdom	Malagasy Republic	
United States	Malawi	

Source: International Monetary Fund, 26th Annual Report on Exchange Restriction (1975).

TABLE B.3

Membership in the Organization for Economic Cooperation and Development

Australia	Japan
Austria	Luxembourg
Belgium	Netherlands
Canada	New Zealand
Denmark	Norway
Finland	Portugal
France	Spain
Germany, Federal Republic of	Sweden
Greece	Switzerland
Iceland	Turkey
Ireland	United Kingdom
Italy	United States

Source: OECD, Activities of OECD in 1974, Report by the Secretary General, 91, Annex iv (1975).

TABLE B.4

Summary of Guarantee Schemes

DAC Countries[2] (Name of Executive agency or department)	Types of Risks Insured a) expropriation risks b) war risks c) transfer risks	Geographic Coverage a) worldwide b) developing countries only c) countries having signed bilateral agreement only	Type of Investment Covered[3] a) equity b) loans and advances c) licenses and royalties d) other	Legal Eligibility Requirements a) development effect b) link with national export c) global ceiling
AUSTRALIA Export Payments Insurance Corp. (EPIC)	a) b) c)	a)	a) b) c)	b) c) $122 million
BELGIUM Office National du Ducroire	a) b) c) and catastrophic risks in some cases	a) c)	a) b)	a) b) c) $18.8 million
CANADA Export Development Corp. (EDC)	a) b) c)	b)	a) b) c)	a) and b) c) $150 million
DENMARK Danish International Development Agency (DANIDA)	a) b) c)	b)	a) b) c)	a) b) c) $70 million
FRANCE Caisse Centrale de Cooperation Economique	a) b) c) for capital only	b) but presently applicable to 14 countries only c) for countries other than the above	a) only, in principle b) exceptionally long-term loans from shareholders	a) b)
GERMANY Deutsche Revisions-- und--Treuhand AG and Interministerial Board	a) b) c)	b) c) in principle (39 countries)	a) b) c)	a)
JAPAN[5] Ministry of International Trade and Industry (MITI)	a) b) c) and credit risks in some cases	a)	a) b) d)	a)
NETHERLANDS Netherlands Credit Insurance Company	a) b) c)	b) c) in principle	a) b) c)	a) b)
NORWAY Institute for Export Credits Guarantees	a) b) c)	a)	a) or a) and b) together	a) c) $90 million (covering both export credits and investments)
SWEDEN Swedish Export Credits Guarantee Board (EKN)	a) b) c)	b) eleven countries only	a) b)	a) c) $80 million
SWITZERLAND	a) b) c) in addition insolvability or refusal to pay by local public entities	b) in principle	a) b) c)	a) b) in some cases c) $130 million
UNITED KINGDOM[2] Export Credit Guarantee Department (ECGD)	a) b) c)	a)	a) b) c)	c) $650 million
UNITED STATES[6] Overseas Private Investment Corporation (OPIC)	a) b) c)	b) c) (to date some 92 countries)	a) b) c) d)	a) c) 1970-74 authority for $7.5 billion new insurance

(continued)

TABLE B.4 (continued)

DAC Countries[2] (Name of Executive agency or department)	Coverage of Principal and Earnings[4] a) initial investment b) reinvested earnings c) remitted earnings (% of original investment)	Coverage in Case of Loss: Basis for Evaluation	Coverage in Case of Loss: Loss Payable
AUSTRALIA Export Payments Insurance Corp. (EPIC)	a) 100% b) 100% c)	financial statements	up to 90%
BELGIUM Office National du Ducroire	a) b) c)	phasing out on a case to case basis	up to 90%
CANADA Export Development Corp. (EDC)	a) 100% b) 50% c) 150% (total cover (limit: 200%	phasing out on a case to case basis	up to 85%
DENMARK Danish International Development Agency (DANIDA)	a) 100% b) c) 8% p.a. for up to 3 years	financial statements	up to 85% or 90%
FRANCE Caisse Centrale de Cooperation Economique	a) only	schedule of amortization: 20% of the original nominal amount per year over the last 5 years of coverage	75% normally up to 90% in some cases
GERMANY Deutsche Revisions--und--Treuhand AG and Interministerial Board	a) 100% b) 50% c) 8% p.a. for up to 3 years	"going concern" value not exceeding capital brought in	up to 95%
JAPAN[5] Ministry of International Trade and Industry (MITI)	a) 100% b) 100% c) 10% p.a. and up to 100% over the contract life	financial statements	up to 90% up to 80% for credit risks
NETHERLANDS Netherlands Credit Insurance Company	a) 100% b) 50% c) 8% p.a.	limited amortization during last 5 years of coverage	up to 90%
NORWAY Institute for Export Credits Guarantees	a) 100% b) c) 7% p.a. up to three years	fixed schedule of amortization--starts normally after three years	up to 90%
SWEDEN Swedish Export Credits Guarantee Board (EKN)	a) 100% b) c) 8% p.a. of maximum coverage not exceeding 24% of initial amount invested	phasing out on a case by case basis	up to 80-90%
SWITZERLAND	a) 100 % b) c) up to 24% of principal	for equity, in principle regular amortization (around 5% per year)	up to 70%
UNITED KINGDOM[2] Export Credit Guarantee Department (ECGD)	a) 100% b) 100% c) 200% (total cover (limit: 200%	financial statements	up to 90%
UNITED STATES[6] Overseas Private Investment Corporation (OPIC)	a) 100% b) 100% c) 200% (total cover (limit: 200%	financial statements phasing out for large and sensitive projects	up to 100% 50% for large and sensitive projects

Annual Premium Rates (percent of current amounts except where otherwise shown)	Duration of Coverage	Date of Effective Establishment	Total Guarantee Outstanding (in U.S. dollars)	Current Volume of New Guarantee Extended
0.75% on current amount (0.25% per risk) plus half the above on stand-by amount	normally = minimum 5 years; maximum 15 years	1966	year-end 1971: $49 m.	1971 = $25.8 m.
	up to 15 years	February 1971		
0.30% for each of the three risks, plus 1/8 of 1% on stand-by amount	up to 15 years	1969	year-end 1971: $3.6 m.	1971 = $3.6 m.
0.5% for the three risks together	up to 15 years	1966	year-end 1971: $11.7 m.	1971: $4.5 m.
8% per year	up to 15 years	January 1971		
0.5% of current amount for the three risks together	normally = up to 15 years exceptionally = up to 20 years	1960	year-end 1971: $341 m.	1971: $78.1 m.
0.55% for the three risks together and 0.70% when credit risks are added	normally up to 15 years	capital 1956 profits 1957 merger 1970	year-end 1971: $171 m.	1971: $103 m.
0.8% for the three risks together	up to 15 years following completion of the investment	1969	year-end 1971: $17 m.	1971: $13 m.
0.5% of maximum amount for the three risks together	up to 20 years	1964/5	year-end 1971: $16.6 m.	
0.7% for the three together	normally up to 15 years exceptionally up to 20 years	1968		
Normal rates: Principal: 1.25% profits: 4% of expected profits	15 years in principle	1970	March 31, 1972: $11 m.	
1% for the three risks together plus 1/2% on stand-by amount	up to 15 years	1972		
a) 0.30% (convertibility) b) 0.60% (expropriation) c) 0.60% (war) plus 0.25% on stand-by amount	equity = maximum 20 years[7] loan = duration of the loan up to 20 years	1948	June 30, 1972 maximum liability $9.9 billion current liability $5.4 billion	12 months to June 30, 1972 $635 million (maximum liability)

NOTES TO TABLE B.4

[1]Direct investment here includes minority equity participation and also "portfolio participation" to the extent they reflect a substantial interest in the project, as in the management or the profits of the company or through purchase of output. Provisions of individual schemes may in some cases not correspond exactly to the common classification adopted in the table. Financial amounts are expressed in U.S. dollar equicalent at the IMF exchange rates as of the end of 1971.

[2]By August 1972 three Member countries had no comprehensive schemes (Austria, Italy, and Portugal). Portugal has a guarantee scheme for loans to firms in the provinces made by Portuguese or foreign investors. As regards Austria, there is a scheme that relates only to a limited category of investments connected with export operations.

[3]The coverage can apply to equity and loan participations and to fees and royalties. The investment can be made in various forms such as cash, machinery, goods, know-how, and services. d) above covers specific situations such as production-sharing agreements.

[4]This column shows the coverage of principal and earnings for equity investments only. As regards loan investments, schemes usually cover outstanding principal and interest completely, or interest up to 100 percent of principal (United Kingdom).

[5]The table takes into account the revisions made on the Japanese scheme as of January 1972 and following the merger in April-May 1970 of the two existing schemes for capital and profits respectively.

[6]The table gives a presentation of the United States Political Risk Investment Insurance Program only. The Loan Guaranty Program has not been inserted in the table.

[7]Except expropriation for large or sensitive projects, for which the duration of coverage is limited to 12 years.

Source: OECD, Investment in Developing Countries (Paris, France, 1972), at 12-13.

TABLE B.5

Overseas Private Investment Corporation: List of Countries

	Insurance			Finance				Insurance			Finance		
AFGHANISTAN	+	+	+	x	+	+	MALAGASY						
ANTIGUA	+	+	+	+	+	+	REPUBLIC	+	+	+	+	+	+
Argentina	o	x	x	x	+	+	MALAWI	+	+	+	+	+	+
Bangladesh	+	+	+	+	+	+	MALAYSIA	+	+	+	+	+	+
Barbados	+	+	+	+	+	+	Mali	+	+	+	+	+	+
BELIZE							Malta	+	+	+	+	+	+
(BR. HONDURAS)	+	+	+	+	+	+	MAURITANIA	+	+	+	+	+	+
Bolivia	+	+	+	+	+	+	MAURITIUS	+	+	+	+	+	+
BOTSWANA	+	+	+	+	+	+	MOROCCO	+	+	+	+	+	+
Brazil	+	+	+	+	+	+	NEPAL	+	+	+	+	+	+
BURUNDI	+	+	+	+	+	+	Nicaragua	+	+	+	+	+	+
CAMEROON	+	+	+	+	+	+	NIGER	+	+	+	+	+	+
CENTRAL AFRICAN							NIGERIA	+	+	+	+	+	+
REPUBLIC	+	+	+	+	+	+	PAKISTAN	+	+	+	+	+	+
CHAD	+	+	+	+	+	+	Panama	+	+	+	x	+	+
Chile	o	o	o	o	o	o	Paraguay	+	+	+	+	+	+
CHINA, REPUBLIC							Peru	x	x	x	x	x	x
(TAIWAN)	+	+	+	+	+	+	Philippines	+	+	+	+	+	+
Colombia	o	o	o	o	+	+	ROMANIA	+	+	+	+	+	+
CONGO							Rwanda	+	+	+	+	+	+
(BRAZZAVILLE)	x	x	x	x	x	x	ST. CHRISTOPHER						
Costa Rica	+	+	+	+	+	+	(ST. KITT'S)						
CYPRUS	x	x	x	x	x	x	NEVIS ANGUILLA	+	+	+	+	+	+
DAHOMEY	+	+	+	+	+	+	ST. LUCIA	+	+	+	+	+	+
DOMINICA	+	+	+	+	+	+	ST. VINCENT	+	+	+	+	+	+
Dominican Republic	+	+	+	+	+	+	Saudi Arabia*	+	+	+	x	x	+
Ecuador	o	o	o	o	+	+	SENEGAL	+	+	+	+	+	+
EGYPT	+	+	+	+	+	+	SIERRA LEONE	+	+	+	+	+	+
El Salvador	+	+	x	x	+	+	SINGAPORE	+	+	+	+	+	+
ETHIOPIA	+	+	+	+	+	+	SOMALI REPUBLIC	x	x	x	x	x	x
GABON	+	+	+	+	+	+	SRI LANKA						
GAMBIA	+	+	+	+	+	+	(CEYLON)	+	+	+	+	+	+
GHANA	+	+	+	+	+	+	SUDAN	o	o	o	o	o	o
GREECE	+	+	+	+	+	+	SWAZILAND	+	+	+	+	+	+
Grenada	+	+	+	+	+	+	Tanzania (excl.						
Guatemala	+	+	x	x	+	+	Zanzibar)	+	+	+	+	+	+
GUINEA	+	+	+	+	+	+	Thailand	+	+	+	+	+	+
GUYANA	+	+	+	+	+	+	TOGO	+	+	+	+	+	+
Haiti	+	+	+	+	+	+	TRINIDAD-TOBAGO	+	+	+	+	+	+
Honduras	+	+	+	+	+	+	TUNISIA	+	+	+	+	+	+
India	+	+	+	+	+	+	Turkey	+	+	+	+	+	+
INDONESIA	+	+	+	+	+	+	UGANDA	x	x	x	x	x	x
Iran	+	+	+	+	+	+	UPPER VOLTA	+	+	+	+	+	+
Israel	+	+	+	+	+	+	Uruguay	x	x	x	x	+	+
IVORY COAST	+	+	+	+	+	+	Venezuela	o	o	o	o	+	+
JAMAICA	+	+	+	+	+	+	Viet Nam	x	x	x	x	x	x
JORDAN	+	+	+	+	+	+	Western Samoa	+	+	+	+	+	+
KENYA	+	+	+	+	+	+	Yemen (Sanaa)	+	+	+	+	+	+
KOREA	+	+	+	+	+	+	YUGOSLAVIA	+	+	+	+	+	+
Laos	x	x	x	x	x	x	ZAIRE	+	+	+	+	+	+
LESOTHO	+	+	+	+	+	+	ZAMBIA	+	+	+	+	+	+
LIBERIA	+	+	+	+	+	+							

Note: Countries in CAPITAL LETTERS are members of the World Bank International Center for the Settlement of Investment Disputes. Some OPIC programs are also available for a number of the less developed dependencies of France, the Netherlands, Portugal, and the United Kingdom.

+ Program available
x Program not currently available
o Program under review, but letters of registration being issued
* Limited program

Source: OPIC Country List, Office of Information, OPIC, Washington, D.C.

TABLE B. 6

U.S. Treaties of Friendship, Commerce, and Navigation
(as of January 1, 1975)

	Investment Guarantee	Treaty		Investment	Treaty
Afghanistan	x		Latvia		x
Argentina	x	x	Lesotho	x	
Austria	x	x	Liberia	x	x
Bahamas			Lithuania		x[b]
Barbados	x		Luxembourg	x	x
Belgium	x	x	Malagasy Republic	x	x
Bolivia	x	x	Malawi	x	
Botswana	x		Malaysia	x	
Brazil	x		Mali	x	
Brunesi		x	Malta	x	
Burundi	x		Mauritania	x	
Cameroon	x		Mauritius	x	
Canada[a]		x	Morocco	x	
Central African Republic	x		Nepal	x	x
Chad	x		Netherlands	x	x
Chile	x	x	Nicaragua	x	x
China (Taiwan)	x	x	Niger	x	
Colombia	x	x	Nigeria	x	
Congo (Brazzaville)	x		Norway	x	x
Costa Rica	x	x	Oman		x
Cuba	x		Pakistan	x	x
Cyprus	x		Panama	x	
Dahomey	x		Paraguay	x	x
Denmark	x	x	Peru	x	
Dominican Republic	x		Philippines	x	
Ecuador	x	x	Poland		
Egypt	x		Portugal	x	
El Salvador	x		Romania	x	
Estonia		x	Rwanda	x	

Ethiopia	x	x	Saudi Arabia		x[c]
Finland	x	x	Senegal	x	
France	x	x	Sierra Leone	x	
Gabon	x		Singapore	x	
Gambia	x		Somali Republic	x	
Germany, Federal Republic of		x	Sri Lanka	x	
Ghana	x		Sudan	x	
Greece	x	x	Swaziland	x	
Grenada	x		Sweden		
Guatemala	x	x	Switzerland		x
Guinea	x		Syria		
Guyana	x		Tanzania	x	
Haiti	x		Thailand	x	x
Honduras	x	x	Togo	x	x
India	x		Tonga		x
Indonesia	x		Trinidad/Tobago	x	
Iran	x	x	Tunisia	x	
Iraq		x	Turkey	x	x
Ireland	x	x	Uganda	x	
Israel	x	x	United Kingdom[d]		x
Italy	x	x	Upper Volta	x	
Ivory Coast	x		Venezuela	x	
Jamaica	x		South Vietnam	x	x
Japan	x	x	Western Samoa	x	
Jordan	x		Yemen (Sanaa)	x	x
Kenya	x		Yugoslavia	x	x[e]
Korea	x	x	Zaire	x	
Laos	x		Zambia	x	

[a]Based on Treaty of Amity with the United Kingdom.

[b]Not full FCN Treaty; Most Favored Nation (MFN) Treaty only.

[c]Provisional.

[d]The United Kingdom concluded investment guarantee agreements with the United States on behalf of Antigua; Belize; Dominica; St. Christopher, Nevis and Anguilla; St. Lucia and St. Vincent

[e]Treaty of Commerce only.

Source: Treaty Affairs Staff; Office of The Legal Advisor, Dept. of State, Treaties in Force (1975).

TABLE B.7

International Centre for Settlement of Investment Disputes: Signatories (as of June 30, 1974)

Afghanistan (1968)
Austria (1971)
Belgium (1970)
Botswana (1970)
Burundi (1969)
Cameroon (1967)
Central African Republic (1966)
Chad (1966)
China (1969)
Congo (Brazzaville) (1966)
Cyprus (1966)
Dahomey (1966)
Denmark (1968)
Egypt (1972)
Ethiopia (1965)*
Finland (1969)
France (1967)
Gabon (1966)
Germany (1969)
Ghana (1966)
Greece (1969)
Guinea (1968)
Guyana (1969)
Iceland (1966)
Indonesia (1968)
Ireland (1966)*
Italy (1971)
Ivory Coast (1966)
Jamaica (1966)
Japan (1967)
Jordan (1972)
Kenya (1967)
Korea (1967)
Lesotho (1969)
Liberia (1970)
Luxembourg (1970)
Malagasy Republic (1966)
Malawi (1966)
Malaysia (1966)
Mauritania (1966)
Mauritius (1969)
Morocco (1967)
Nepal (1969)
Netherlands (1966)
New Zealand (1970)*
Niger (1966)
Nigeria (1966)
Norway (1967)
Pakistan (1966)
Senegal (1967)
Sierra Leone (1966)
Singapore (1968)
Somalia (1968)
Sri Lanka (1967)
Sudan (1973)
Swaziland (1971)
Sweden (1967)
Switzerland (1968)
Togo (1967)
Trinidad/Tobago (1967)
Tunisia (1966)
Uganda (1966)
United Kingdom (1967)
United States (1966)
Upper Volta (1966)
Yugoslavia (1967)
Zaire (1970)
Zambia (1970)

*Signed only: not entered into force.

Source: International Center for Settlement of Investment Disputes, Eighth Annual Report 1973/74, Annex 1 (1974).

APPENDIX C

OECD CODE OF LIBERALIZATION OF CAPITAL MOVEMENTS

(including Annex A and a summary of
reservations and derogations)

Part I

UNDERTAKINGS WITH REGARD TO CAPITAL MOVEMENTS

Article 1

GENERAL UNDERTAKINGS

a. Members shall progressively abolish between one another, in accordance with the provisions of Article 2, restrictions on movements of capital to the extent necessary for effective economic co-operation. Measures designed to eliminate such restrictions are hereinafter called "measures of liberalisation".

b. Members shall, in particular, endeavour:
 i) to treat all non-resident-owned assets in the same way irrespective of the date of their formation, and
 ii) to permit the liquidation of all non-resident-owned assets and the transfer of such assets or of their liquidation proceeds.

c. Members should use their best offices to ensure that the measures of liberalisation are applied within their overseas territories.

d. Members shall endeavour to extend the measures of liberalisation to all members of the International Monetary Fund.

e. Members shall endeavour to avoid introducing any new exchange restrictions on the movements of capital or the use of non-resident-owned funds and shall endeavour to avoid making existing regulations more restrictive.

Article 2

MEASURES OF LIBERALISATION

a. Subject to the provisions of paragraph (b)(iv), Members shall grant any authorisation required for the conclusion or execution of transactions and for transfers specified in an item set out in List A or List B of Annex A to this Code.

b. A Member may lodge reservations relating to the obligations resulting from paragraph (a) when:

i) an item is added to List A of Annex A to this Code;
ii) obligations relating to an item in that List are extended;
iii) obligations relating to any such item begin to apply to that Member; or
iv) at any time, in respect of an item in List B.

Reservations shall be set out in Annex B to the Code.

c. Whenever the liquidation proceeds of non-resident-owned assets may be transferred, the right of transfer shall include any appreciation of the original assets.

d. Whenever existing regulations or international agreements permit loans between residents of different Members otherwise than by issuing marketable domestic securities or by using, in the country in which the borrower resides, funds the transfer of which is restricted, the repayment obligation may be expressed or guaranteed in the currency of either of the two Members concerned.

Article 3

PUBLIC ORDER AND SECURITY

The provisions of this Code shall not prevent a Member from taking action which it considers necessary for:

i) the maintenance of public order or the protection of public health, morals and safety;
ii) the protection of its essential security interests;
iii) the fulfilment of its obligations relating to international peace and security.

Article 4

OBLIGATIONS IN EXISTING MULTILATERAL INTERNATIONAL AGREEMENTS

Nothing in this Code shall be regarded as altering the obligations undertaken by a Member as a Signatory of the Articles of Agreement of the International Monetary Fund or other existing multilateral international agreements.

Article 5

CONTROLS AND FORMALITIES

a. The measures of liberalisation provided for in this Code shall not limit the powers of Members to verify the authenticity of transactions or transfers nor to take any measures required to prevent evasion of their laws or regulations.

b. Members shall simplify as much as possible all formalities connected with the authorisation or verification of transactions or transfers and shall co-operate, if necessary, to attain such simplification.

Article 6

EXECUTION OF TRANSFERS

A Member shall be deemed to have complied with its obligations as regards transfers whenever a transfer may be made:

i) between persons entitled, by the exchange regulations of the State from which and of the State to which the transfer is to be made, respectively, to make and/or to receive the said transfer;

ii) in accordance with international agreements in force at the time the transfer is to be made; and

iii) in accordance with the monetary arrangements in force between the State from which and the State to which the transfer is to be made.

Article 7

CLAUSES OF DEROGATION

a. If its economic and financial situation justifies such a course, a Member need not take the whole of the measures of liberalisation provided for in Article 2 (a).

b. If any measures of liberalisation taken or maintained in accordance with the provisions of Article 2 (a) result in serious economic and financial disturbance in the Member State concerned, that Member may withdraw those measures.

c. If the overall balance of payments of a Member develops adversely at a rate and in circumstances, including the state of its monetary reserves, which it considers serious, that Member may temporarily suspend the application of measures of liberalisation taken or maintained in accordance with the provisions of Article 2 (a).

d. However, a Member invoking paragraph (c) shall endeavour to ensure that its measures of liberalisation:

i) cover, twelve months after it has invoked that paragraph, to a reasonable extent, having regard to the need for advancing towards the objective defined in sub-paragraph (ii), transactions and transfers which the Member must authorise in accordance with Article 2 (a) and the authorisation of which it has suspended, since it invoked paragraph (c); and

ii) comply, eighteen months after it has invoked that paragraph, with its obligations under Article 2 (a).

e. Any Member invoking the provisions of this Article shall do so in such a way as to avoid unnecessary damage which bears especially on the financial or economic interests of another Member and, in particular, shall avoid any discrimination between other Members.

Article 8

RIGHT TO BENEFIT FROM MEASURES OF LIBERALISATION

Any Member lodging a reservation under Article 2 (b) or invoking the provisions of Article 7 shall, nevertheless, benefit from the measures of liberalisation taken by other Members, provided it has complied with the procedure laid down in Article 12 or Article 13 as the case may be.

Article 9

NON-DISCRIMINATION

A Member shall not discriminate as between other Members in authorising the conclusion and execution of transactions and transfers which are listed in Annex A and which are subject to any degree of liberalisation.

Article 10

EXCEPTIONS TO THE PRINCIPLE OF NON-DISCRIMINATION SPECIAL CUSTOMS OR MONETARY SYSTEMS

Members forming part of a special customs or monetary system may apply to one another, in addition to measures of liberalisation taken in accordance with the provisions of Article 2 (a), other measures of liberalisation without extending them to other Members. Members forming part of such a system shall inform the Organisation of its membership and those of its provisions which have a bearing on this Code.

Part II

PROCEDURE

Article 11

NOTIFICATION AND INFORMATION FROM MEMBERS

a. Members shall notify the Organisation, within the periods which the latter may determine, of the measures of liberalisation which they have taken and of any other measures which have a bearing on this Code, as well as of any modifications of such measures.

b. Members shall notify the Organisation forthwith of any cases in which they have by virtue of remark (ii) against Section I of List A of Annex A to this Code imposed restrictions on specific transactions or transfers relating to direct investments and shall state their reasons for doing so.

c. Members shall submit to the Organisation, at intervals determined by the Organisation, but of no more than eighteen months, information concerning:

i) any channels, other than official channels, through which transfers are made, and any rates of exchange applying to such transfers, if they are different from the official rates of exchange;

ii) any security money markets and any premiums or discounts in relation to official rates of exchange prevailing therein.

d. The Organisation shall consider the notifications submitted to it in accordance with the provisions of paragraphs (a), (b) and (c) with a view to determining whether each Member is complying with its obligations under this Code.

Article 12

NOTIFICATION AND EXAMINATION OF RESERVATIONS LODGED UNDER ARTICLE 2 (b)

a. Each Member lodging a reservation in respect of an item specified in List B of Annex A to the Code shall forthwith notify the Organisation of its reasons therefor.

b. Each Member shall notify the Organisation, within a period to be determined by the Organisation, whether it desires to maintain any reservation lodged by it in respect of an item specified in List A or List B of Annex A to this Code, and if so, state its reasons therefor.

c. The Organisation shall examine each reservation lodged by a Member in respect of an item specified in:

i) List A at intervals of not more than eighteen months;

ii) List B within six months of notification, and at intervals of not more than eighteen months thereafter;

unless the Council decides otherwise.

d. The examinations provided for in paragraph (c) shall be directed to making suitable proposals designed to assist Members to withdraw their reservations.

Article 13

NOTIFICATION AND EXAMINATION OF DEROGATIONS MADE UNDER ARTICLE 7

a. Any Member invoking the provisions of Article 7 shall notify the Organisation forthwith of its action, together with its reasons therefor.

b. The Organisation shall consider the notifications and reasons submitted to it in accordance with the provisions of paragraph (a) with a view to determining whether the Member concerned is justified in invoking the provisions of Article 7 and, in particular, whether it is complying with the provisions of paragraph (e) of that Article.

c. If the action taken by a Member in accordance with the provisions of Article 7 is not disapproved by the Organisation, that action shall be reconsidered by the Organisation every six months or, subject to the provisions of Article 15 on any other date which the latter may deem appropriate.

d. If, however, in the opinion of a Member other than the one which has invoked Article 7, the circumstances justifying the action taken by the latter in accordance with the provisions of that Article have changed, that other Member may at any time refer to the Organisation for reconsideration of the case at issue.

e. If the action taken by a Member in accordance with the provisions of paragraph (a), (b) or (c) of Article 7 has not been disapproved by the Organisation, then, if that Member subsequently invokes paragraph (a), (b) or (c) of Article 7 of the Code of Liberation of Current Invisible Operations, or, having invoked one paragraph of Article 7 of this Code, invokes another paragraph of that Article, its case shall be reconsidered by the Organisation after six months have elapsed since the date of the previous consideration, or on any other date which the latter may deem appropriate. If another Member claims that the Member in question is failing to carry out its obligations under paragraph (e) of Article 7 of this Code or paragraph (e) of Article 7 of the Code of Liberalisation of Current Invisible Operations, the Organisation shall consider the case without delay.

f. i) If the Organisation, following its consideration in accordance with paragraph (b), determines that a Member is not justified in invoking the provisions of Article 7 or is not complying with the provisions of that Article, it shall remain in consultation with the Member concerned, with a view to restoring compliance with the Code.

ii) If, after a reasonable period of time, that Member continues to invoke the provisions of Article 7, the Organisation shall reconsider the matter. If the Organisation is then unable to determine that the Member concerned is justified in invoking the provisions of Article 7 or is complying with the provisions of that Article, the situation of that Member shall be examined by a special Ministerial Group, unless the Organisation decides on some other exceptional procedure.

Article 14

EXAMINATION OF DEROGATIONS MADE IN ACCORDANCE WITH ARTICLE 7 MEMBERS IN PROCESS OF ECONOMIC DEVELOPMENT

a. In examining the case of any Member which it considers to be in the process of economic development and which has invoked the provisions of Article 7 the Organisation shall have special regard to the effect that the economic development of the Member has upon its ability to carry out its obligations under paragraph (a) of Articles 1 and 2.

b. In order to reconcile the obligations of the Member concerned under paragraph (a) of Article 2 with the requirements of its economic development, the Organisation may grant that Member a special dispensation from those obligations.

Article 15

SPECIAL REPORT AND EXAMINATION CONCERNING DEROGATIONS MADE UNDER ARTICLE 7

a. A Member invoking the provisions of paragraph (c) of Article 7 shall report to the Organisation, within ten months after such invocation, on the measures of liberalisation it has restored or proposes to restore in order to attain the objective determined in sub-paragraph (d) (i) of Article 7. The Member shall, if it continues to invoke these provisions, report to the Organisation again on the same subject--but with reference to the objective determined in sub-paragraph (d) (ii) of Article 7--within sixteen months after such invocation.

b. If the Member considers that it will not be able to attain the objective, it shall indicate its reasons in its report and, in addition, shall state:

i) what internal measures it has taken to restore its economic equilibrium and what results have already been attained, and

ii) what further internal measures it proposes to take and what additional period it considers it will need in order to attain the objective determined in sub-paragraph (d) (i) or (d) (ii) of Article 7.

c. In cases referred to in paragraph (b), the Organisation shall consider within a period of twelve months, and, if required, of eighteen months from the date on which the Member invoked the provisions of paragraph (c) of Article 7, whether the situation of that Member appears to justify its failure to attain the objective determined in sub-paragraph (d) (i) or (d) (ii) of Article 7 and whether the measures taken or envisaged and the period considered by it as necessary for attaining the objective determined, appear acceptable in the light of the objectives of the Organisation in the commercial and financial fields.

d. If a Member invokes the provisions of both paragraph (c) of Article 7 of this Code and paragraph (c) of Article of the Code of Liberalisation of Current Invisible Operations the periods of twelve and eighteen months referred to in paragraph (c) shall run from the date of the earlier invocation.

e. If following any of the examinations provided for in paragraph (c) the Organisation is unable to approve the arguments advanced by the Member concerned in accordance with the provisions of paragraph (b) the situation of that Member shall be examined by a special Ministerial Group, unless the Organisation decides on some other exceptional procedure.

Article 16

REFERENCE TO THE ORGANISATION
INTERNAL ARRANGEMENTS

a. If a Member considers that the measures of liberalisation taken or maintained by another Member, in accordance with Article 2 (a), are frustrated by internal arrangements likely to restrict the possibility of effecting transactions or transfers, and if it considers itself prejudiced by such arrangements, for instance because of their discriminatory effect, it may refer to the Organisation.

b. If, following the consideration of a matter referred to it under paragraph (a) the Organisation determines that internal arrangements introduced or maintained by the Member concerned have the effect of frustrating its measures of liberalisation, the Organisation may make suitable suggestions with regard to the removal or modification of such arrangements.

Article 17

REFERENCE TO THE ORGANISATION RETENTION,
INTRODUCTION OR RE-INTRODUCTION
OF RESTRICTIONS

a. If a Member considers that another Member which has not invoked the provisions or Article 7 has retained, introduced or re-introduced restrictions on capital movements or the use of non-resident-owned funds contrary to the provisions of Articles 1, 2, 9, or 10, and if it considers itself to be prejudiced thereby, it may refer to the Organisation.

b. The fact that the case is under consideration by the Organisation shall not preclude the Member which has referred to the Organisation from entering into bilateral conversations on the matter with the other Member concerned.

Part III

TERMS OF REFERENCE

Article 18

COMMITTEE FOR INVISIBLE TRANSACTIONS
GENERAL TASKS

a. The Committee for Invisible Transactions shall consider all questions concerning the interpretation or implementation of the provisions of this Code or other Acts of the Council relating to the liberalisation of capital movements and the use of non-resident-owned funds and shall report its conclusions thereon to the Council as appropriate.

b. The Committee for Invisible Transactions shall submit to the Council any appropriate proposals in connection with its tasks as defined in paragraph (a) and, in particular, with the extension of measures of liberalisation as provided in Article 1 of this Code.

Article 19

COMMITTEE FOR INVISIBLE TRANSACTIONS SPECIAL TASKS

a. The Committee for Invisible Transactions shall:

i) determine the periods within which the information provided for in paragraphs (a) and (c) of Article 11 and the reasons provided for in paragraph (b) of Article 12 should be notified to the Organisation by the Members concerned;

ii) subject to paragraph (c) of This Article, consider, in conformity with paragraphs (c) and (d) of Article 12, each reservation notified to the Organisation in accordance with paragraphs (a) and (b) of that Article and make, where appropriate, suitable proposals designed to assist Members to withdraw their reservations;

iii) determine, in accordance with the provisions of Article 12, the date on which any reservation should be re-examined, if the reservation has not been withdrawn in the meantime;

iv) consider, in accordance with the provisions of paragraph (d) of Article 11, the notifications submitted to the Organisation;

v) consider reports and references submitted to the Organisation in accordance with the provisions of Article 13 or paragraphs (a) and (b) of Article 15 where a Member has invoked the provisions of Article 7, or submitted in accordance with the provisions of Article 16 or Article 17;

vi) determine the date on which the case of a Member which has invoked Article 7 should be reconsidered in accordance with the provisions of paragraph (c), paragraph (e) or paragraph (f) (ii) of Article 13;

vii) transmit to the United States Government, with any comments it considers appropriate, notifications received from Members in accordance with paragraph 2 (a) of the Decision in Annex C to the Code; and

viii) consider information received from the United States Government in accordance with paragraph 2 (b) of the Decision in Annex C to the Code.

b. When examining the reservations notified in accordance with paragraph (b) of Article 12, the Committee may, at its discretion, consider together either all reservations made by the same Member or all reservations made in respect of the same item specified in Annex A to this Code.

c. The Committee shall, however, not consider any reservations notified to the Organisation in accordance with paragraph (b) of Article 12 by a Member which, at the time of the examination in respect of the item subject to that reservation, is invoking the provisions of Article 7 or is enjoying a dispensation in accordance with paragraph (b) of Article 14.

d. In the cases provided for in sub-paragraphs (ii), (iv), (v) and (viii) of paragraph (a), the Committee shall report to the Council, except in cases of notification under Article 11 (b) on which the Committee shall report only if it considers this appropriate.

e. The Committee shall, whenever it considers it necessary:

i) consult other Committees of the Organisation on any questions relating to the liberalisation of capital movements; and, in particular,

ii) request other Committees of the Organisation to give their views on any questions relating to the balance of payments and the state of the monetary reserves of a Member.

Article 20

PAYMENTS COMMITTEE

Before they are considered by the Council, the Payments Committee shall:

i) review the reports and proposals by the Committee for Invisible Transactions made in accordance with the provisions of this Code; and

ii) forward to the Council any comments thereon which it considers necessary.

Part IV

MISCELLANEOUS

Article 21

DEFINITIONS

In this Code:

i) "Blocked funds" shall mean funds owned by residents of other Member States in accordance with the laws and regulations of the Member where the funds are held and blocked for balance of payments reasons;

ii) "Collective investment securities" shall mean the share certificates, registry entries or other evidence of investor interest in an institution for collective investment which, irrespective of legal form, is organised for the purpose of managing investments in securities or in other assets, applies the principle of risk-spreading, issues its own securities to the public on demand either continuously or at frequent intervals and is required on the request of the holder to redeem such securities, directly or indirectly, within a specified period and at their net asset value;

iii) "Domestic securities" shall mean securities issued or to be issued by a resident;

iv) "Financial institutions" shall mean banks, savings banks, bodies which specialise in the granting of credits, insurance companies, building societies, investment companies, and other establishments of a similar nature;

v) "Foreign securities" shall mean securities issued or to be issued by a non-resident;

vi) "Member" shall mean a Member of the Organisation which adheres to this Code;

vii) "Official channels" shall mean foreign exchange markets in which an officially established rate or officially established rates apply and in which spot transactions take place at rates which are free to fluctuate within the official margins;

viii) "Recognised security market" shall mean a stock exchange or security market in a Member country, (including an over-the-counter market organised by a recognised association of security dealers),

-- which is officially recognised in the country where it operates,
-- on which the public can buy and sell securities, and
-- on which dealings take place in accordance with fixed rules;

ix) Security dealing on a "spot basis" shall mean dealing with payment and delivery to be made immediately the transaction is concluded or on the next periodic settlement date of the stock exchange where the transaction takes place;

x) "Securities quoted on a recognised security market" shall mean securities which have been granted an official quotation or are officially listed on such market or for which dealing prices on such a market are published not less frequently than once a week;

xi) "Unit of account" shall mean the unit of account as defined in Article 24 of the European Monetary Agreement of 5th August, 1955".

Article 22

TITLE OF DECISION

This Decision, referred to in the present text as the "Code", shall be known as the "Code of Liberalisation of Capital Movements".

Article 23

WITHDRAWAL

Any Member may withdraw from the Code by transmitting a notice in writing to the Secretary-General of the Organisation. The withdrawal shall become effective twelve months from the date on which such notice is received.

Annex A

LIBERALISATION LISTS OF CAPITAL MOVEMENTS

List A

I. DIRECT INVESTMENT

Investment for the purpose of establishing lasting economic relations with an undertaking such as, in particular, investments which give the possibility of exercising an effective influence on the management thereof:

A. In the country concerned by non-residents by means of:
   1. creation or extension of a wholly-owned enterprise, subsidiary or branch, acquisition of full ownership of an existing enterprise;
   2. participation in a new or existing enterprise;
   3. a long-term loan (five years and longer).

B. Abroad by residents by means of:

1. creation or extension of a wholly-owned enterprise, subsidiary or branch, acquisition of full ownership of an existing enterprise;
2. participation in a new or existing enterprise;
3. a long-term loan (five years and longer).

Remark: Transactions and transfers under A and B shall be free unless:

i) an investment is of a purely financial character designed only to gain for the investor indirect access to the money or financial market of another country; or
ii) in view of the amount involved or of other factors a specific transaction or transfer would have an exceptionally detrimental effect on the interests of the Member concerned.

B. Operations abroad by residents:

1. Purchase of collective investment securities.
2. Sale of collective investment securities.

Remarks: Transfers of sales proceeds under A2 shall be free subject, in the case of investments by means of blocked funds, to the remark against Section XV/B1.

Members shall have the power:

a) with regard to transactions and transfers under A and B to lay down that:
   i) such transactions and transfers must be carried out through authorised resident agents;
   ii) in connection with such transactions and transfers residents may hold funds and securities only through the intermediary of such agents; and
   iii) purchases and sales may be contracted only on a spot basis;
b) with regard to transactions and transfers under A2, to take measures for the protection of investors, including the regulations of promotional activities, provided such measures do not discriminate against institutions for collective investment organised under the laws of any other Member country;
c) with regard to transactions and transfers under B1, to regulate on their territory any promotional activities of foreign institutions for collective investment.

VI. OPERATIONS IN REAL ESTATE[1]

A. Operations in the country concerned by non-residents:
   1. (See List B).
   2. Sale.

B. Operations abroad by residents:
   1. (See List B).
   2. Sale.

VIII. CREDITS DIRECTLY LINKED WITH INTERNATIONAL COMMERCIAL TRANSACTIONS OR WITH THE RENDERING OF INTERNATIONAL SERVICES

i) In cases where a resident participates in the underlying commercial or service transaction.

A. Credits granted by non-residents to residents on:
   1. Short-term (less than one year);
   2. Medium-term (from one to five years).

B. Credits granted by residents to non-residents on:
   1. Short-term (less than one year);
   2. Medium-term (from one to five years).

Remark: Transactions and transfers under A and B shall be free provided they are in conformity with normal commercial practice.

XI. PERSONAL CAPITAL MOVEMENTS

A. Family loans.

B. Gifts and endowments.

C. Dowries.

D. Inheritances and legacies.

Remark: Transfers under D shall be free provided that the deceased was resident and the beneficiary non-resident at the time of the deceased's death.

E. Settlement of debts in their country of origin by immigrants.

F. Emigrants' assets.

---

[1]Other than operations falling under Section I or II of the General List.

Remark: Transfers under F shall be free upon emigration irrespective of the nationality of the emigrant.

G. (See List B).

H. Savings of non-resident workers.

XII. LIFE ASSURANCE

Capital transfers arising under life assurance contracts:[1]

A. Transfers of capital and annuities certain due to resident beneficiaries from non-resident insurers.

B. Transfers of capital and annuities certain due to non-resident beneficiaries from resident insurers.

Remark: Transfers under A and B shall be free also in the case of contracts under which the persons from whom premiums are due or the beneficiaries to whom disbursements are due were residents of the same country as the insurer at the time of the conclusion of the contract but have changed their residence since.

XIII. SURETIES AND GUARANTEES

A. By non-residents in favour of residents.

B. By residents in favour of non-residents.

Remark: Transactions and transfers under A and B shall be free if they are directly related to international trade, international current invisible operations or international capital movement operations in which a resident participates and which do not require authorisation or have been authorised by the Member State concerned.

XIV. PHYSICAL MOVEMENT OF CAPITAL ASSETS

A. Securities and other documents of title to capital assets:
1. Import.
2. Export.

---

[1]Transfers of premiums and pensions and annuities, other than annuities certain, in connection with life assurance contracts are governed by the Code of Liberalisation of Current Invisible Operations (Item D/3). Transfers of whatever kind or size under other than life assurance contracts are always considered to be of a current nature and are consequently governed by the Current Invisibles Code.

Remark: In the case of residents the obligation to permit an export applies only to the export of foreign securities and then only on a temporary basis for administrative purposes.

XV. DISPOSAL OF NON-RESIDENT-OWNED BLOCKED FUNDS

A. Transfer of blocked funds.

Remarks: Transfers of blocked funds by their owners shall be free in cases of hardship.
Annual transfer of blocked funds by their owners within general limits or percentages of the total holdings to be determined by the Member States concerned shall be free. Such limits or percentages shall be uniform for all cases.

B. Use of blocked funds in the country concerned:
1. For operations of a capital nature.

Remark: The use of blocked funds for capital payments for account of the holder shall be free to the extent that the transaction does not require authorisation or is authorised for transferable funds by the Member States where the blocked funds are held. The general terms and conditions on which blocked funds may be so used shall be the same as those applying to transferable funds except that the Member State concerned shall have the right to re-impose the original status on such funds in case of liquidation within three years of any investment for which they have been used.

2. For current operations.

Remark: The use of blocked funds for current expenses for account of the holder for any non-commercial purpose shall be free.

C. Cession of blocked funds between non-residents.

List B

III. ADMISSION OF SECURITIES TO CAPITAL MARKETS[1]

A. Admission of domestic securities on a foreign capital market:
1. Issue through placing or public sale of:
   a) shares or other securities of a participating nature;
   b) bonds.

2. (See List A).

---

[1]Other than operations falling under Section V of the General List.

B. Admission of foreign securities on the domestic capital market:
   1. Issue through placing or public sale of:
      a) shares or other securities of a participating nature;
      b) bonds.
   2. (See List A).

IV. BUYING AND SELLING OF SECURITIES[1]

A. Operations in the country concerned by non-residents:
   1. (See List A).
   2. (See List A).
   3. Purchase of securities not quoted on a recognised security market:
      a) shares or other securities of a participating nature;
      b) bonds.
   4. Sale of securities not quoted on a recognised security market:
      a) share or other securities of a participating nature;
      b) bonds.

B. Operations abroad by residents:
   1. (See List A).
   2. (See List A).
   3. Purchase of securities not quoted on a recognised security market:
      a) shares or other securities of a participating nature;
      b) bonds.
   4. Sale of securities not quoted on a recognised security market:
      a) shares or other securities of a participating nature;
      b) bonds.

Remarks: Transfers and sales proceeds under A4 shall be free subject, in case of investments by means of blocked funds, to the remark against Section XV/B1.

Members shall have the power to lay down with regard to transactions and transfers under A and B that:

i) such transactions and transfers must be carried out through authorised resident agents;

ii) in connection with such transactions and transfers residents may hold funds and securities only through the intermediary of such agents; and

iii) purchases and sales may be contracted only on a spot basis.

---

[1]Other than operations falling under Section I, II, III or V of the General List.

VI. OPERATIONS IN REAL ESTATE[1]

A. Operations in the country concerned by non-residents:
   1. Building or purchase.
   2. (See List A).

B. Operations abroad by residents:
   1. Building or purchase.
   2. (See List A).

VIII. CREDITS DIRECTLY LINKED WITH INTERNATIONAL COMMERCIAL TRANSACTIONS OR WITH THE RENDERING OF INTERNATIONAL SERVICES

ii) In cases where no resident participates in the underlying commercial or service transaction.

A. --

B. Credits granted by residents to non-residents on:
   1. short-term (less than one year);
   2. medium-term (from one to five years).

   Remark: Transactions and transfers shall be free provided:
   i) they are in conformity with normal commercial practice; and
   ii) the credits are granted by a financial institution.

IX. FINANCIAL CREDITS AND LOANS[2]

A. Credits and loans granted by non-residents to residents on:
   1. --
   2. Medium-term (from one to five years);
      a) The debtor being a financial institution.
      b) --
   3. Long-term (five years and longer):
      a) The debtor being a financial institution.
      b) --

B. Credits and loans granted by residents to non-residents on:
   1. --
   2. Medium-term (from one to five years):
      a) The creditor being a financial institution.
      b) --

---

[1]Other than operations falling under Section I, or II of the General List.

[2]Other than credits and loans falling under Sections I, II, VIII and XI in List A, or Section VIII in List B.

3. Long-term (five years and longer):
   a) The creditor being a financial institution.
   b) --

XI. PERSONAL CAPITAL MOVEMENTS

A to F. (See List A).

G. Gaming.

Remark: Transfers under G shall be free only in respect of winnings; the provision does not cover the stakes wagered.

H. (See List A).

FIGURE C.1

Present Reservations in the OECD Code of Liberalization of Capital Movements

● Full Reservation
0 Limited Reservation

	Australia	Austria	Belgium	Denmark	Finland	France	Germany	Ireland	Italy	Japan	Luxembourg	Netherlands	New Zealand	Norway	Portugal	Spain	Sweden	Switzerland	United Kingdom	United States
Inward direct investment	●	0		0	0			0		0			●	0	0	0	0			0
Outward direct investment	●				●				0	0			●	●	0	●				
Introduction of domestic securities on a recognized foreign security exchange															0					
Introduction of foreign securities on a recognized domestic security exchange	●		●	●	●	●			●			0	●	●	●	●	●	0		
Purchase in the country concerned by non-residents of listed securities		0		0						0			0	0	0	0	0			
Sale in the country concerned by non-residents of listed securities	0			0	0			0		0			0	0	0	0	0		0	
Purchase abroad by residents of listed securities	0			0	0			0	0	0		0	●	0	0	0	0		0	
Sale abroad by residents of listed securities				0				0	0					0			0		0	
Purchase in the country concerned by non-residents of collective investment securities				0						0			0		0		0			
Sale in the country concerned by non-residents of collective investment securities	0	0	●	0	0	●		0	●				0	0	0	0	0		0	
Purchase abroad by residents of collective investment securities	0	0	0	0	0			0	●				●	0	0	●	0		0	
Sale abroad by residents of collective investment securities				0				0						0			0		0	
Sale of real estate by non-residents																0				
Inward commercial credits (in cases where a resident participates in the underlying commercial or service transaction)					0				0	0				0						
Outward commercial credits (in cases where a resident participates in the commercial or service transaction)	0				0			0	0	0					0				0	
Personal capital movements		0			0			0	0						0				0	
Life assurance															0					
Sureties and guarantees by residents in favour of non-residents	0				●									●	0					
Use of blocked funds for operations of a capital nature																0				

Source: The above table is based on the table appearing in OECD's Code of Liberalization of Capital Movements, reprinted from the OECD Observer, 4 (December 1971), and updated to reflect new information appearing in Organization for Economic Cooperation and Development, Code of Liberalization of Capital Movements (reprinted, August 1973), at 39-109, which also contains the specific provisions of the reservations. As of June, 1974, Canada did not adhere to the obligations of the Code, and Greece, Iceland, and Turkey had obtained a general exemption to the Code under a derogation clause. Thus, they are not included in the above table. The above table does not include the reservations from List B dealing with the issue of securities, operations in unlisted securities, credits and loans not connected with trade in goods or services, etc., on which reservations may be lodged or reintroduced.

APPENDIX D

OECD CODE OF LIBERALIZATION OF CURRENT INVISIBLE OPERATIONS

(including a summary of reservations and derogations)

Part I

UNDERTAKINGS WITH REGARD TO CURRENT INVISIBLE OPERATIONS

Article 1

GENERAL UNDERTAKINGS

a. Members shall eliminate between one another, in accordance with the provisions of Article 2, restrictions on current invisible transactions and transfers, hereinafter called "current invisible operations". Measures designed for this purpose are hereinafter called "measures of liberalisation".

b. Where Members are not bound, by virtue of the provisions of this Code, to grant authorisations in respect of current invisible operations, they shall deal with applications in as liberal a manner as possible.

c. Members shall use their best offices to ensure that the measures of liberalisation are applied within their overseas territories.

d. Members shall endeavour to extend the measures of liberalisation to all members of the International Monetary Fund.

e. "Member" shall mean a Member of the Organisation which adheres to this Code.

Article 2

MEASURES OF LIBERALISATION

a. Members shall grant any authorisation required for a current invisible operation specified in an item set out in Annex A to this Code.

b. A Member may lodge reservations relating to the obligations resulting from paragraph (a) when:

i) an item is added to Annex A to this Code;
ii) obligations relating to an item in that Annex are extended; or
iii) obligations relating to any such item begin to apply to that Member.

Reservations shall be set out in Annex B to this Code.

Article 3

PUBLIC ORDER AND SECURITY

The provisions of this Code shall not prevent a Member from taking action which it considers necessary for:

i) the maintenance of public order or the protection of public health, morals and safety;
ii) the protection of its essential security interests; or
iii) the fulfilment of its obligations relating to international peace and security.

Article 4

OBLIGATIONS IN EXISTING MULTILATERAL INTERNATIONAL AGREEMENTS

Nothing in this Code shall be regarded as altering the obligations undertaken by a Member as a Signatory of the Articles of Agreement of the International Monetary Fund or other existing multilateral international agreements.

Article 5

CONTROLS AND FORMALITIES

a. The measures of liberalisation provided for in this Code shall not limit the powers of Members to verify the authenticity of current invisible operations nor to take any measures required to prevent evasion of their laws or regulations.

b. Members shall simplify as much as possible all formalities connected with the authorisation or verification of current invisible operations and shall co-operate, if necessary, to attain such simplification.

Article 6

EXECUTION OF TRANSFERS

a. A Member shall be deemed to have complied with its obligations as regards transfers whenever a transfer may be made:

i) between persons entitled, by the exchange regulations of the State from which and of the State to which the transfer is to be made, respectively, to make and/or to receive the said transfer;

ii) in accordance with international agreements in force at the time the transfer is to be made; and

iii) in accordance with the monetary arrangements in force between the State from which and the State to which the transfer is to be made.

b. The provisions of paragraph (a) do not preclude Members from demanding payment of maritime freights in the currency of a third State, provided that such a demand is in conformity with established maritime practice.

Article 7

CLAUSES OF DEROGATION

a. If its economic and financial situation justifies such a course, a Member need not take the whole of the measures of liberalisation provided for in Article 2 (a).

b. If any measures of liberalisation taken or maintained in accordance with the provisions of Article 2 (a) result in serious economic disturbance in the Member State concerned, that Member may withdraw those measures.

c. If the overall balance of payments of a Member develops adversely at a rate and in circumstances, including the state of its monetary reserves, which it considers serious that Member may temporarily suspend the application of measures of liberalisation taken or maintained in accordance with the provisions of Article 2 (a).

d. However, a Member invoking paragraph (c) shall endeavour to ensure that its measures of liberalisation:

i) cover, twelve months after it has invoked that paragraph, to a reasonable extent, having regard to the need for advancing towards the objective defined in sub-paragraph (ii), current invisible operations which the Member must authorise in accordance with Article 2 (a) and the authorisation of which it has suspended since it invoked paragraph (c), and, in particular current invisible operations relating to tourism if, in whole or in part, their authorisation has been suspended; and

ii) comply, eighteen months after it has invoked that paragraph, with its obligations under Article 2 (a).

e. Any Member invoking the provisions of this Article shall do so in such a way as to avoid unnecessary damage which bears especially on the commercial or economic interests of another Member and, in particular, shall avoid any discrimination between other Members.

Article 8

RIGHT TO BENEFIT FROM MEASURES OF LIBERALISATION

Any Member lodging a reservation under Article 2 (b) or invoking the provisions of Article 7 shall, nevertheless, benefit from the measures of liberalisation taken by other Members provided it has complied with the procedure laid down in Article 12 or Article 13 as the case may be.

Article 9

NON-DISCRIMINATION

A Member shall not discriminate as between other Members in authorising current invisible operations which are listed in Annex A and which are subject to any degree of liberalisation.

Article 10

EXCEPTIONS TO THE PRINCIPLE OF NON-DISCRIMINATION SPECIAL CUSTOMS OR MONETARY SYSTEMS

Members forming part of a special customs or monetary system may apply to one another in addition to measures of liberalisation taken in accordance with the provisions of Article 2 (a) other measures of liberalisation without extending them to other Members. Members forming part of such a system shall inform the Organisation of its membership and those of its provisions which have a bearing on this Code.

Part II

PROCEDURE

Article 11

NOTIFICATIONS AND INFORMATION FROM MEMBERS

a. Members shall notify the Organisation, within the periods which the latter may determine, of the measures of liberalisation which they have taken and of any other measures which have a bearing on this Code, as well as of any modification of such measures.

b. The Organisation shall consider the notifications submitted to it in accordance with the provisions of paragraph (a) with a view to determining whether each Member is complying with its obligations under this Code.

Article 12

NOTIFICATION AND EXAMINATION OF RESERVATIONS LODGED UNDER ARTICLE 2 b

a. Each Member shall notify the Organisation within a period to be determined by the Organisation, whether it desires to maintain any reservation lodged by it in respect of an item specified in Annex A to this Code, and, if so, state its reasons therefor.

b. The Organisation shall examine each reservation lodged by a Member in respect of an item specified in Annex A to this Code at intervals of not more than 18 months, unless the Council decides otherwise.

c. The examination provided for in paragraph (b) shall be directed to making suitable proposals designed to assist Members to withdraw their reservations.

Article 13

NOTIFICATION AND EXAMINATION OF DEROGATIONS MADE UNDER ARTICLE 7

a. Any Member invoking the provisions of Article 7 shall notify the Organisation forthwith of its action, together with its reasons therefor.

b. The Organisation shall consider the notifications and reasons submitted to it in accordance with the provisions of paragraph (a) with a view to determining whether the Member concerned is justified in invoking the provisions of Article 7 and, in particular, whether it is complying with the provisions of paragraph (e) of that Article.

c. If the action taken by a Member in accordance with the provisions of Article 7 is not disapproved by the Organisation, that action shall be reconsidered by the Organisation every six months or, subject to the provisions of Article 15, on any other date which the latter may deem appropriate.

d. If, however, in the opinion of a Member other than the one which has invoked Article 7, the circumstances justifying the action taken by the latter in accordance with the provisions of that Article have changed, that other Member may at any time refer to the Organisation for reconsideration of the case at issue.

e. If the action taken by a Member in accordance with the provisions of paragraphs (a), (b) or (c) of Article 7 has not been disapproved by the Organisation, then, if that Member subsequently invokes paragraphs (a), (b) or (c) of Article 7 of the Code of Liberalisation of Capital Movements, or, having invoked one paragraph of Article 7 of this Code, invokes another paragraph of that Article, its case shall be reconsidered by the Organisation after six months have elapsed since the date of the previous consideration, or on any other date which the latter may deem appropriate. If another Member claims that the Member in question is failing to carry out its obligations under paragraph (e) of Article 7 of this Code or paragraph (e) of Article 7 of the Code of Liberalisation of Capital Movements, the Organisation shall consider the case without delay.

f. i) If the Organisation, following its consideration in accordance with paragraph (b), determines that a Member is not justified in invoking the provisions of Article 7 or is not complying with the provisions of that Article, it shall remain in consultation with the Member concerned, with a view to restoring compliance with the Code.

ii) If, after a reasonable period of time, that Member continues to invoke the provisions of Article 7, the Organisation shall reconsider the matter. If the Organisation is then unable to determine that the Member concerned is justified in invoking the provisions of Article 7 or is complying with the provisions of that Article, the situation of that Member shall be examined by a special Ministerial Group, unless the Organisation decides on some other exceptional procedure.

Article 14

EXAMINATION OF DEROGATIONS MADE IN ACCORDANCE WITH ARTICLE 7 MEMBERS IN PROCESS OF ECONOMIC DEVELOPMENT

a. In examining the case of a Member which it considers to be in process of economic development and which has invoked the provisions of Article 7, the Organisation shall have special regard to the effect that the economic development of that Member has upon its ability to carry out its obligations under paragraph (a) of Articles 1 and 2.

b. In order to reconcile the obligations of the Member concerned under paragraph (a) of Article 2 with the requirements of its economic development, the Organisation may grant that Member a special dispensation from those obligations.

Article 15

SPECIAL REPORT AND EXAMINATION CONCERNING DEROGATIONS MADE UNDER ARTICLE 7

a. A Member invoking the provisions of paragraph (c) of Article 7 shall report to the Organisation, within ten months after such invocation, on the measures of liberalisation it has restored or proposes to restore in order to attain the objective determined in sub-paragraph (d)(i) of Article 7. The Member shall, if it continues to invoke these provisions, report to the Organisation again on the same subject--but with reference to the objective determined in sub-paragraph (d) (ii) of Article 7--within sixteen months after such invocation.

b. If the Member considers that it will not be able to attain the objective, it shall indicate its reasons in its report and, in addition, shall state:

i) what internal measures it has taken to restore its economic equilibrium and what results have already been attained; and
ii) what further internal measures it proposes to take and what additional period it considers it will need in order to attain the objectives determined in sub-paragraphs (d) (i) or (d) (ii) of Article 7.

c. In cases referred to in paragraph (b), the Organisation shall consider within a period of twelve months, and, if required, of eighteen months from the date on which the Member invoked the provisions of paragraph (c) of Article 7, whether the situation of that Member appears to justify its failure to attain the objective determined in sub-paragraph (d) (i) or (d) (ii) of Article 7, and whether the measures taken or envisaged and the period considered by it as necessary for attaining the objective determined, appear acceptable in the light of the objectives of the Organisation in the commercial and financial fields.

d. If a Member invokes the provisions of both paragraph (c) of Article 7 of this Code and paragraph (c) of Article 7 of the Code of Liberalisation of Capital Movements, the periods of twelve and eighteen months referred to in paragraph (c) shall run from the date of the earlier invocation.

e. If, following any of the examinations provided in paragraph (c), the Organisation is unable to approve the arguments advanced by the Member concerned in accordance with the provisions of paragraph (b), the situation of that Member shall be examined by a special Ministerial Group, unless the Organisation decides on some other exceptional procedure.

Article 16

REFERENCE TO THE ORGANISATION INTERNAL ARRANGEMENTS

a. If a Member considers that the measures of liberalisation taken or maintained by another Member in accordance with Article 2(a) are frustrated by internal arrangements likely to restrict the possibility of effecting current invisible operations, and if it considers itself to be prejudiced thereby, it may refer to the Organisation.

b. If, following the consideration of a matter referred to it under paragraph (a), the Organisation determines that internal arrangements introduced or maintained by the Member concerned have the effect of frustrating its measures of liberalisation, the Organisation may make suitable suggestions with regard to the removal or modification of such arrangements.

Article 17

REFERENCE TO THE ORGANISATION RETENTION, INTRODUCTION OR RE-INTRODUCTION OF RESTRICTIONS

a. If a Member considers that another Member which has not invoked the provisions of Article 7 has retained, introduced or re-introduced restrictions on current invisible operations, contrary to the provisions of Article 1, paragraph (a) of Article 2, or Article 9, and if it considers itself to be prejudiced thereby, it may refer to the Organisation.

b. The fact that the case is under consideration by the Organisation shall not preclude the Member which has referred to the Organisation from entering into bilateral conversations on the matter with the other Member concerned.

Part III

TERMS OF REFERENCE

Article 18

COMMITTEE FOR INVISIBLE TRANSACTIONS

a. The Committee for Invisible Transactions shall consist of twelve members chosen by reason of the knowledge they have of problems relating to invisible transactions and of the personal standing which they enjoy within the Organisation or in their respective countries. They shall be appointed by the Council from persons nominated by the Member States, and the Council shall ensure that, by rotation, persons of the nationalities of the various Member States wishing to take part in the work of the Committee are appointed to it. Unless the Council decides otherwise, the terms of office of members of the Committee shall be one year; they may be re-appointed.

b. Each Member of the Committee shall designate an alternate. Alternates may attend meetings of the Committee and shall exercise the functions of members if the latter are unable to attend.

c. The Council shall designate each year from among the members of the Committee a Chairman and a Vice-Chairman.

d. A delegate of any Member State, a national of which is not serving on the Committee, may attend its meetings as an observer.

e. The Chairman or the Vice-Chairman of the Payments Committee may also attend the meetings of the Committee with the right to participate in discussion. The Committee may invite other persons to attend its meetings.

f. The proposals of the Committee shall be adopted by a majority represented by not less than seven of its members. A member who is in disagreement with the majority may request that his views should be recorded in the report of the Committee.

g. The Committee shall adopt its own rules of procedure.

Article 19

COMMITTEE FOR INVISIBLE TRANSACTIONS GENERAL TASKS

The Committee for Invisible Transactions shall consider all questions concerning the interpretation or implementation of the provisions of this Code or other acts of the Council relating to the liberalisation of current invisible operations and shall report its conclusions thereon to the Council as appropriate.

Article 20

COMMITTEE FOR INVISIBLE TRANSACTIONS SPECIAL TASKS

a. The Committee for Invisible Transactions shall:

i) determine the periods within which the information provided for in paragraph (a) of Article 11 and the reasons provided for in paragraph (a) of Article 12 should be notified to the Organisation by the Members concerned;

ii) subject to paragraph (c) of this Article, consider, in conformity with paragraphs (b) and (c) of Article 12, each reservation notified to the Organisation in accordance with paragraph (a) of that Article and make, where appropriate, suitable proposals designed to assist Members to withdraw their reservations;

iii) determine, in accordance with the provisions of Article 12, the date on which any reservations should be re-examined, if the reservation has not been withdrawn in the meantime;

iv) consider, in accordance with the provisions of paragraph (b) of Article 11, the notifications submitted to the Organisation;

v) consider reports and references submitted to the Organisation in accordance with the provisions of Article 13 or paragraphs (a) and (b) of Article 15 where a Member has invoked the provisions of Article 7, or submitted in accordance with the provisions of Article 16 or Article 17;

vi) determine the date on which the case of a Member which has invoked Article 7 should be reconsidered in accordance with the provisions of paragraph (c), paragraph (e) or paragraph (f) (ii) of Article 13;

vii) transmit to the United States Government, with any comments it considers appropriate, notifications received from Members in accordance with paragraph 2 (a) of the Decision in Annex C to the Code; and

viii) consider information received from the United States Government in accordance with paragraph 2 (b) of the Decision in Annex C to the Code.

b. When examining the reservations notified in accordance with the provisions of paragraph (a) of Article 12 the Committee may, as it deems fit, consider together either all reservations made by the same Member or all reservations made in respect of the same item specified in Annex A to this Code.

c. The Committee shall, however, not consider any reservations notified to the Organisation in accordance with the provisions of paragraph (a) of Article 12 by a Member which, at the time of the examination in respect of the item subject to that reservation, is invoking the provisions of Article 7 or is enjoying a dispensation in accordance with paragraph (b) of Article 14.

d. In the cases provided for in sub-paragraphs (ii), (iv) and (viii) of paragraph (a) the Committee shall report to the Council.

e. The Committee shall, whenever it considers it necessary:

i) consult other Committees of the Organisation on any questions relating to the liberalisation of current invisible operations; and, in particular,

ii) request other Committees of the Organisation to give their views on any questions relating to the balance of payments and the state of the monetary reserves of a Member.

Article 21

PAYMENTS COMMITTEE

Before they are considered by the Council, the Payments Committee shall:

i) review the reports and proposals by the Committee for Invisible Transactions made in accordance with the provisions of this Code; and

ii) forward to the Council any comments thereon which it considers necessary.

Part IV

MISCELLANEOUS

Article 22

TITLE OF DECISION

This Decision, referred to in the present text as the "Code", shall be known as the "Code of Liberalisation of Current Invisible Operations".

Article 23

WITHDRAWAL

Any Member may withdraw from the Code by transmitting a notice in writing to the Secretary-General of the Organisation. The withdrawal shall become effective twelve months from the date on which such notice is received.

FIGURE D.1

Present Reservations to the OECD Code of Liberalization of Current Invisible Operations

● Full Reservation 0 Limited Reservation	Australia	Austria	Belgium	Canada	Denmark	Finland	France	Germany	Iceland	Ireland	Italy	Japan	Luxembourg	Netherlands	Norway	Portugal	Spain	Sweden	Switzerland	United Kingdom	United States
Processing, finishing, processing of work under contract and other services of the same nature											0										
Technical assistance												0									
Author's royalties. Assignment and licensing of patent rights, designs, trade marks and inventions												0									
Maritime freights				0			0														0
Inland waterway freights, including chartering				0		0	0	0						0	0	0	0	0	0	0	0
Road transport: passengers and freight including chartering		0	0	0	0	0	0	0		0	0		0	0							0
Repair of ships									●												
Insurance relating to goods in international trade		●					●			●	●					●					
Life assurance	●	0	0		●	0	●	0	●	●	0	●	0	0	●	0	●		●	●	
All other insurance		●		0		0	●	0	●	●	●	●	0	0	0	●	●		●		
Transactions and transfers in connection with reinsurance and retrocession							0			0	0	0									
Insurance business operations abroad	●		●		0	0	●		●	●		●	0	●	0	0	●	0	0		
Importation, distribution and use of printed films and other recordings	0	0				0		0			0					●	0		0		0
Tourism									0												
Subscription to newspapers, periodicals, books, musical publications and records. Newspapers, periodicals, books, musical publications and records			0																		

Source: Organization for Economic Cooperation and Development, Code of Liberalization of Current Invisible Operations (reprinted, March 1973). The above table notes countries having full or partial reservations to subjects covered in Annex A and the annexes thereto, as of March 1973. The liberalization obligations did not apply to Greece and Turkey at that time, and the Government of New Zealand did not become a member of the OECD until May 29, 1973. Thus they are not included in the above table. For the specific provisions of the annexes and reservations, see ibid., at 25-78.

ABOUT THE AUTHOR

DON WALLACE, JR. is a graduate of Yale and Harvard. He is Professor of Law at Georgetown University and Director of the Institute for International and Foreign Trade Law. He also serves as codirector of the Institute's Investment Negotiation Center.

He practiced law in New York from 1957 to 1962, worked as Deputy Assistant General Counsel for the Agency for International Development, and spent a year in Turkey as a Fulbright scholar. He spent the 1973-74 academic year on sabbatical leave as a Senior Fellow at St. Anthony's College, Oxford, and will be an Eisenhower Exchange Fellow this spring, studying the policy of the EEC toward multinational companies.

He is vice-chairman of the international law section of the American Bar Association, chairman of the Committee on Transnational Corporations of the American Branch of the International Law Association, a member of the international investment panel of the U.S. Chamber of Commerce and a member of the research council of the Center for Strategic and International Studies of Georgetown University.

He is the author, editor, or coeditor of numerous articles and books, including *Introduction to Turkish Law*, *Legal Environment for Foreign Direct Investment in the United States*, *International Control of Investment: The Dusseldorf Conference on Multinational Corporations*, the second edition of *A Lawyer's Guide to International Business Transactions* (forthcoming), and *The Future of International Economic Organizations* (forthcoming).

RELATED TITLES
Published by
Praeger Special Studies

ECONOMIC ANALYSIS AND THE MULTINATIONAL ENTERPRISE*
edited by John H. Dunning

FOREIGN DISINVESTMENTS BY U.S. MULTINATIONAL CORPORATIONS: With Eight Case Studies
Roger L. Torneden

INTERNATIONAL LABOR AND THE MULTINATIONAL ENTERPRISE
edited by Duane Kujawa

INTERNATIONAL CONTROL OF INVESTMENTS: The Dusseldorf Conference on Multinational Corporations
Don Wallace, Jr., assisted by Helga Ruof-Koch

MANAGING MULTINATIONAL CORPORATIONS†
Arvind V. Phatak

MULTINATIONAL CORPORATIONS AND GOVERNMENT: Business-Government Relations in an International Context
edited by Patrick M. Boarman and Hans Schollhammer

THE NATION-STATE AND TRANSNATIONAL CORPORATIONS IN CONFLICT: With Special Reference to Latin America
edited by Jon P. Gunnemann

*For sale in the U.S. and Philippines only.
†Also available in paperback as a PSS Student Edition.